BEGIN

HIS LIFE, WORDS AND DEEDS

BEGIN

HIS LIFE, WORDS AND DEEDS

Zvi Harry Hurwitz

gefen
publishing house בית הוצאה לאור
JERUSALEM ◆ NEW YORK

The first book, *Menachem Begin* was published by The Jewish Herald (PTY) Ltd., Johannesburg, South Africa, December 1977; the second version, *Menachem Begin: A Portrait* was published by B'nai B'rith Books, Washington, DC, 1994; this third version is published in Jerusalem, Israel, 2003/2004.

First Printed in the United States of America by
BookCrafters, Fredericksburg, Virginia, 1994

Typesetting: Raphaël Freeman, Jerusalem Typesetting
Cover Design: Studio Paz, Jerusalem
Photo Editing: Ronen Goldberg

3   5   7   9   8   6   4   2

Gefen Publishing House
6 Hatzvi Street, Jerusalem 94386, Israel
972-2-538-0247
orders@gefenpublishing.com

Gefen Books
12 New Street, Hewlett, NY 11557, USA
516-295-2805
orders@gefenpublishing.com

www.israelbooks.com

Printed in Israel   *Send for our free catalogue*

ISBN 965-229-324-5

Library of Congress Cataloging-in-Publication Data
Hurwitz, Harry Zvi, 1924–
Begin: a portrait / Harry Zvi Hurwitz
p. cm.
Includes index.
ISBN 0 910250 27 8 (cloth): ISBN 0 910250 28 6 (pbk.)
1. Begin, Menachem, 1913–1992   2. Prime ministers – Israel – Biography.
3. Revisionist Zionists – Israel – Biography.   4. Israel – Politics and government.
DS126.6.B33H86   1994 956.9405'4'092-dc20 [B]9489

To our dear grandchildren

Sharon Rinat
Nirit Merav
&
Ilan Matan

who represent the future for which
Menachem Begin strove all his life.

CONTENTS

INTRODUCTION

MY FIRST BOOK on Menachem Begin was published six months after the May 1977 election victory that brought him to the premiership of Israel after a tenacious, 30-year uphill struggle in the Opposition. At the time it was, to the best of my knowledge, the first book about the new Israeli leader, certainly the first in English. My purpose in writing it was to introduce the reader to one of the most outstanding men of our time.

It gave me a great deal of satisfaction that the book was widely read, especially by the younger generation in the English-speaking countries, and even in Israel; it thrilled me to see a student on a park bench in Jerusalem engrossed in my book, to find it in libraries and on many bookshelves. It was quoted fairly extensively in later books on Begin and in essays and articles. I was interviewed at length by researchers and producers of television and radio programs in various countries. The book, entitled simply *Menachem Begin*, was translated and published in Finland, and translated into Russian (but not yet published); an updated version has been published in Chinese by the Yunnan University in Kunming, China.

I stated in the introduction to *Menachem Begin* that it was not intended to be the definitive biography of Menachem Begin: "That task awaits the future researcher and historian." A number of subsequent books, written mainly by people who did not know the man personally, can likewise not be regarded as definitive. *Menachem Begin* was simply my own story of the man, based on my personal knowledge of him through our long and close association.

Published in November 1977, the book ended with the visit of President Anwar Sadat to Jerusalem, an event that inaugurated a new phase in the history of Israel and the Middle East. Almost six more years were to pass from then until Begin's resignation in August 1983, and another nine years until his death in March 1992. This second book, longer and more elaborate than its predecessor, was completed a year after his death.

The intervening years between the two books only added to Begin's stature as the leader of Israel and of the Jewish people. He achieved universal recognition and distinction when he was awarded the Nobel Prize for Peace (an event I had predicted in my first book) for his exceptional role in concluding a peace agreement with Egypt. The plans and proposals that Menachem Begin set out in that agreement serve even today as the basis for the elaborate peace process that began in Madrid in October 1991 and still engages Israel, her immediate neighbors and the Palestinian Arabs.

I was privileged to be more closely associated with Menachem Begin during his premiership and the years of his seclusion and retirement than I had been before, when we lived continents apart. At his request, my wife Freda and I emigrated from South Africa to Israel in 1978 so that I could join his personal staff, first as adviser on external information and later as adviser on Diaspora Jewry. During the three years between these two assignments, I served at the Israeli embassy in Washington as Minister of Information, in which capacity I was in direct and regular contact with the Prime Minister in Jerusalem.

There is profound regret that Menachem Begin did not write his intended five-volume autobiography, to be entitled *The Generation of Destruction and Redemption*. As the title indicates, the volumes were to span the most momentous era in Jewish history, from its darkest years – the Holocaust – to the rebirth and revival of our free nation in Eretz Israel. Menachem Begin shaped a major part of that saga. What a story he had to tell! But it was not to be. He took his story and his innermost feelings with him to the grave.

I have therefore attempted, as much as possible, to enable him to speak through these pages, in which I quote extensively from his addresses in the Knesset, his statements, announcements, interviews and my own notes. At least thus we can recall some of his thoughts and observations, some of his vision and his aspirations. Some of this material is reproduced from the important volumes *Israel's Foreign Relations (Selected Documents)*, published by the Ministry of Foreign Affairs and compiled and edited by Meron Medzini, to whom I am indebted.

I would like to record my profound appreciation to my good friend, Dr. Michael Neiditch, founder of B'nai B'rith Books, who had the foresight to suggest that I re-write my earlier book, update it and bring the remarkable Begin story to its end.

My first book was dedicated to my dear wife, Freda, who shared so many of my experiences, and to my son and daughter-in-law, Hillel Ze'ev and Jennifer.

In 1997, they and their three children came on aliyah and settled in Ra'anana where Hillel is a respected physician and Jennifer, a popular teacher. Our eldest granddaughter, Sharon Rinat, was married in July 2003 to Jay Wohlgelernter, a young doctor from Toronto. They now live in Jerusalem.

In the years since the publication of my first book, the world has literally been transformed. Mighty empires have declined and disintegrated. Brutal dictators have been crushed. Freedom has swept over the globe like a tidal wave and, as described above, our own lives have changed dramatically.

For the first time "in 2000 years" this branch of the Hurwitz family is living together in the Land of Israel, where our new generation is shaping their future. Therefore, the original dedicatees in the first edition of the book will understand if I dedicate this new version to our grandchildren: Sharon Rinat and Jay, Nirit Merav and Ilan Matan, who represent the beautiful future for which Menachem Begin strove all his life and who will, with the help of the Almighty, enjoy its bounty.

This new edition of my book is especially dear to me because it is published in Israel to coincide with the opening of the Menachem Begin Heritage Center in Jerusalem, which I had the privilege of initiating and founding, thereby converting a dream into a reality.

Zvi Harry Hurwitz
Jerusalem, 2004

Chapter 1

THE WHEEL OF HISTORY

"How do you feel being here as the Prime Minister of Israel?" I asked Menachem Begin, several days after he had moved into the official residence at 3 Balfour Street, Jerusalem.

"Very good," he replied. "As if we have always been here."

"We are not strangers to the privilege of serving our people," he continued. "We have served our people all our lives. This particular responsibility is, of course, great. We have to care for the welfare and future of our people, our children and grandchildren. But there is no national position, including the premiership, that can compare with what we accomplished in the War of Independence.

"This is an interesting job. It becomes more interesting every day," he said smilingly, and he went on to relate that, in the first months of the existence of Israel, one of the Cabinet Ministers used to say: "Every day we become sovereigner and sovereigner."

"So it is with us," he continued. "Every day it becomes more interesting. We have to make important decisions – including military decisions."

It struck me that Begin was conducting the affairs of state as though he had groomed himself for years for this challenging period in his life. His every action was suffused with meaning; his first pronouncements seemed as if they had been phrased in his mind years before. Begin knew all along what he would say to the leaders of the West and the East at their initial encounters, how he would address himself to the citizens of Israel and to world Jewry, and what his priorities would be in international affairs and the many internal problems besetting Israel. He had long known what he would say to Arab rulers if they should ever come face to face; he knew what he would say the first time he paid an official visit to London, where he would meet the Prime Minister and other leaders of Great Britain (whose government had put a price on his head 30 years earlier, when he led the relentless War of Jewish Liberation as commander of the Irgun).

As he showed us into the large reception rooms of the Prime Minister's official residence, he said jokingly: "You see this one room? It is bigger than the whole of 1 Rosenbaum Street" (the tiny apartment in which he had lived, with his wife Aliza and their three children, for all the 29 years of statehood). Before Begin, the residence had been occupied by Moshe Sharett and Abba Eban (as Foreign Ministers) and by Golda Meir and Yitzhak Rabin (as Prime Ministers). "Do you know who was here in the forties?" he asked. "General Barker!" – the General Officer Commanding of the British forces in Palestine at a peak period in the struggle, who issued the notorious anti-Semitic order banning fraternization with the Jewish community.

"I am determined that they should be punished and made aware of our feelings of contempt and disgust at their behavior," Barker said at the time in his written instructions to the 100,000 British troops under his command. "I understand that these measures will create difficulties for the troops, but I am certain that if my reasons are explained to them, they will understand their duty *and* will punish the Jews in the manner this race dislikes most by hitting them in the pocket, which will demonstrate our disgust for them."

"And where is Barker now?" someone asked. Begin shrugged his shoulders. "If he is still alive, he must be a very old man."

"The first time I ever came to this house was in 1948, after the British left the country, when we used it as a hospital for wounded Irgun boys. They were lying here, in this room, in rows awaiting medical attention," he said, as a far-away look appeared in his eyes. The wheel of history had turned full circle.

The once-powerful Barker left the stage, and Menachem Begin, the Jewish freedom fighter on whose head the British placed a price, was now the elected Prime Minister of the sovereign State of Israel, loved in Jerusalem, honored in Washington, Bucharest, London, Paris and other world capitals, and respected – or feared – in Cairo, Damascus and Amman.

Israel's new Prime Minister was not some obscure political mediocrity suddenly rocketed into prominence after a surprise election upset in his country. For the 33 years before he ascended to the premiership, Menachem Begin occupied a dominant place in his nation's affairs, decisively and profoundly influencing Jewish and world history.

It is said that some men are born great, and make history; others, made by history, have greatness thrust upon them. Menachem Begin was an outstanding example of the former. When the events of our times are chronicled by objective historians, he will emerge as one of the greatest Jews of this era – the Bar Kochba of the twentieth century. (Bar Kochba was the valiant political and military leader of the Jews in their war against the Romans 132–135.)

He was molded by the two main events affecting Jews in this century: the Holocaust, in which 6,000,000 Jews were massacred, and the Jewish War of Liberation that paved the way for the renewal of Jewish statehood. Begin saw a direct link between these two events; at the 13th Herut National Convention, in the first days of 1977, he revealed his ardent desire to write a major work entitled *The Generation of Destruction and Redemption*.

He always regarded himself as a survivor of the Holocaust in which his parents and others of his family were destroyed. This was brought home to me poignantly when I met him in Jerusalem a few days after the Knesset majority had given him its vote of confidence. The whole country was still talking about his masterful acceptance speech, which was recorded and televised live. "If I did not break down when I mentioned my mother and father," he said to me, "it was only because the Almighty was guiding me. Chasya and Ze'ev. Wiped out. Disappeared without trace."

This experience reinforced his frequent and resolute statements such as: "Never again will Jews be attacked without being able to defend themselves and hitting back." And it heightened his resolve to make the State of Israel invulnerable and invincible by, among other things, building a military deterrent powerful enough to persuade its enemies to abandon the hopeless path of war and come to terms, at last, with the inevitability of Israel's existence in their midst.

To the causes of peace and security for his nation he devoted his rare qualities of leadership and his many talents: his brilliant oratory that could move masses and persuade the most pragmatic; his inspiring and prolific writings that educated a generation in Israel and abroad; his incisive political mind that could cut through the haze of confusion, doubt and misunderstanding; his encyclopedic knowledge and phenomenal memory; his optimism, his confidence and, above all, his selfless dedication.

Jerusalem, 1994

Chapter 2
PRISONER IN RUSSIA

Menachem begin was born in 1913 in Brest-Litovsk, Poland, on Shabbat Nahamu ("the Sabbath of Comfort" – hence the name Menachem). His parents were Ze'ev-Dov and Chasya Begin. He was raised and educated at the Mizrachi Hebrew School and the Polish Gymnasium (high school).

As a child, he showed unusual intellectual capacity; as a schoolboy, he gave private tuition in Latin to help pay for his later studies. He often quoted Latin phrases extensively. He entered the Warsaw University in 1931 and received his law degree in 1935.

For a short while, he was a member of the Hashomer Hatzair youth movement, but left when it changed its ideology to identify with revolutionary Socialism. At that time he saw and heard Vladimir (Ze'ev) Jabotinsky. That encounter was to change his life and profoundly affect the destiny of the Jewish People. Begin found in Jabotinsky those things that he, like thousands of other young Jews, had been seeking: faith, vision, pride, courage, action. At the age of 16, Begin joined Jabotinsky's Betar youth movement, which soon recognized his qualities and sincerity and elected him to positions of leadership – at first as head of the Organization Department of Betar for Poland, and later as head of the movement in Czechoslovakia. In 1937 he returned to Poland, where he was imprisoned for leading a demonstration in front of the British Legation in Warsaw protesting British mandatory policy in Palestine. He also organized groups of Betar members who went to Eretz Israel as "illegal immigrants" and, in 1938, became the head of the tens of thousands of members in the movement in Poland. His oratorical prowess was evident when he was 12, and as a young man he was in demand as a speaker at conferences and rallies.

As clouds of war enveloped Europe, the Betar leaders stepped up their efforts to educate youth – as Begin later revealed – "to toil for the rebuilding of the Jewish State, to be ready to fight for it, suffer for it and, if needs be, die for it."

Begin was in Warsaw at the outbreak of the war, but by the time the Germans entered the Polish capital he had succeeded in escaping to Vilna in neighboring Lithuania, soon to be occupied by the Russians.

Ironically, he was arrested by the Communists as a British agent. When the secret police came to remove him, he insisted on shining his shoes before taking leave of his young wife, whom he had married only months earlier.

"The Special Advisory Commission to the People's Commissariat for Internal Affairs finds Menachem Wolfovitch Begin to be a dangerous element in society and decrees that he be imprisoned in a correctional labor-camp for a period of eight years." This fateful pronouncement was made on 1 April 1941, after Begin had suffered many days and nights of solitary confinement and interrogation, in which the Communists solemnly and earnestly accused him of being "one of the important helpers, practically an agent, of Great Britain."

He would later write in his book *The Revolt* that, during the endless nights of interrogation, he took part in wide-ranging debates with his interrogators on the Russian Revolution, Britain and Zionism, Herzl and Jabotinsky, on Weizmann's meetings with Mussolini, on the Russian commune and the Jewish kibbutz, on

Zionist youth movements, on Marx and Engels, Bukharin and Stalin, on capitalism, socialism and communism, on the mystery of life and death, on theism and science, on the Spanish Civil War and the French Popular Front, on idealistic theory and materialistic philosophy. "At times," he said, "it was much more of a free discussion than an interrogation."

This must have been one of the rare instances when, in the stifling atmosphere of hopelessness and despair, a prisoner of the Soviets stood up to his captors and interrogators, turned the tables on them and lectured them about faith and the meaning of life in free society. More recently, the brave dissidents in the Soviet Union – including the Zionist activists – have had the advantage of world opinion championing their cause, holding a watching brief for them, supporting them and appealing on their behalf. But in those days, a Soviet prisoner was alone, isolated, hopeless, and in danger of simply disappearing from the face of the earth.

In subsequent writings, Begin revealed that the Soviets told him that "Zionism in all its forms is a farce and a deception, a puppet show. It is not true that you aim to set up a Jewish State in Palestine, or that you intend to bring millions of Jews there. Both these aims are utterly impracticable, and the Zionist leaders are perfectly well aware of it. This talk of a State conceals the true purpose of Zionism – which is to divert the Jewish youth from the ranks of the revolution in Europe and put them at the disposal of British imperialism in the Middle East. This is the kernel of Zionism. All the rest is an artificial shell, deliberately made to deceive. As for you, Menachem Wolfovitch, either you know the truth and are one of the deliberate deceivers serving Great Britain and the international bourgeoisie, or you are one of the dupes hoping to divert the masses from their duty of fighting here against exploitation. In either case your guilt is great indeed."

All Begin's efforts to counter such theorizing were to no avail. His stony interrogators were oblivious of and unreceptive to the story of the age-old connection between the Jew and Eretz Israel, the references to the Land, and to the prayers and the hopes of his people.

When asked why he had not joined the Popular Communist Front to help bring about the world revolution that would solve all problems – including the Jewish problem – Begin replied: "Imagine, Citizen Judge, that you are walking in the street and see a house on fire. What do you do? Obviously you call the fire brigade. But if you suddenly hear the cry of a woman, or of a child coming from the house, do you wait for the firemen? Surely not. You rush in and try to save them. That's our situation. Assuming, for a moment, that the Revolution is the final solution for the homeless Jewish people – though the Birobidjan experiment shows that even the Soviet Union realizes that we Jews need a territory of our own – can't you see that we are like men and women trapped in a burning house? You know what militant anti-Semitism has done to us. Not only are our houses burning; our families are in flames. Could we – can we wait till the fire brigade arrives? And what if they're late? No, our people must be saved now. We have been trying to get them out of the flames, into our Homeland. Is that such a bad thing?"

So strong was the faith of Menachem Begin and his Zionist companions that, as they were driven to a prison camp, somebody whispered: "This is the beginning of the journey to Eretz Israel."

The correctional labor camp to which Menachem Begin was sentenced for eight years was deep in Siberia, on the banks of the Pechora River – cut off from civilization, from any contact with family or friends where the danger was ever-present of transfer to another, perhaps worse, camp.

Transfers were carried out by land and water, irrespective of weather conditions, in a region where winter lasts nine months and the days and nights are white. Hundreds of prisoners were crowded into freight boats to travel huge distances to their camp, where they labored under excruciating conditions on the northern railway, enduring long queues for food and basic necessities.

On one such boat, en route to the Arctic Sea, an order arrived to release all Polish citizens aboard. By that time, Germany had invaded the Soviet Union, which then joined the Allies in the war against the Axis. General Sikorski of the Free Polish Government signed a pact with Stalin to enable all Polish citizens to join his forces.

On foot, in goods trains and in crowded passenger trains, the newly freed Poles proceeded south to join the army of General Anders, which was moving deliberately toward the Middle East and the outskirts of Eretz Israel. There, in May 1942 – barely a year after he had been sentenced to eight years of correctional labor – Menachem Begin was reunited with his wife, who had been spirited out of Poland by close friends in the Betar leadership.

His friends urged him to desert the Anders Army, but he refused to do any such dishonorable thing and waited until, as a result of negotiations, he was discharged and permitted to enter Eretz Israel, then under British mandatory rule.

The full account of Begin's imprisonment by the Russians is told in his book *White Nights* (MacDonald Press, London, 1957). After its appearance, we saw further evidence of the lasting effects of that dreadful experience on Begin's philosophy and actions.

The Soviets did not realize it at the time, but by imprisoning Begin and subjecting him to interrogation, solitary confinement and slave labor, they rendered the Jewish people an incomparable service, for their conduct gave added impetus to his resolve to fight for the creation of a Jewish State in Eretz Israel, so that Jews would never again have to endure such hardships. Begin's experience with the Soviets impressed itself indelibly on his mind, and later influenced his efforts to initiate, intensify and maintain the struggle for Soviet Jewry's right to be repatriated to Eretz Israel. He was not the only Jewish leader to concern himself with this problem but, while others espoused the cause with varying degrees of enthusiasm, for Begin it remained an issue of life and death. Without respite, he championed the cause of the "Prisoners of Zion" then in Soviet concentration camps, gave backing to Zionist activists, and encouraged Diaspora Jews to take the bold step of seeking aliyah (emigrating to Israel).

Begin's attitude toward the Soviet Union's relationship with Israel was also influenced by the Soviets' treatment of his brothers and sisters behind the Iron Curtain. It was inconceivable to him that Soviet diplomats should one day attend receptions in Jerusalem while Jews still languished in concentration camps in the Soviet Union because of *their* desire to emigrate to Jerusalem.

NB: A new, revised edition (in Hebrew) of *White Nights* was published in Israel. It contained documents and photographs that were in the file of the NKVD interrogators of Menachem Begin. Their record of the interrogation describes the dialogue between Menachem Begin and the Soviet Secret Police. The file was obtained by an Israeli journalist who gave it to Benny Begin. He enlisted the help of Natan Sharansky. They both learned, to their great satisfaction, that every word that Menachem Begin had written from memory in his book was inscribed in the NKVD record. The revised Hebrew version of *White Nights* was prepared by Benny Begin and published by the Menachem Begin Heritage Center.

Chapter 3

COMMANDER IN CHIEF

THE IRGUN ZVAI LEUMI (National Military Organization) was created by Ze'ev Jabotinsky to protect Jewish life and property and combat Arab terrorism in Palestine in the 1930s. Later it played an active role in the Aliyah Beth (illegal immigration) of Jews from Europe, bringing it into conflict with the British mandatory authorities.

At the time, the British government was restricting the entry of Jews into Palestine by issuing a limited number of immigration certificates. To circumvent this policy, Jabotinsky called on Jewish youth to make their free immigration into the country the "national sport." Scores of ships of all shapes and sizes attempted to evade the British fleet in the Mediterranean; some succeeded in unloading their valuable human cargo. Lord Josiah Wedgewood, a fearless champion of the Jewish cause, later said of this "sport": "I think all the illegal immigrants in Palestine owe Jabotinsky and the Revisionists their lives and present liberties. Others would not have dared to conduct 'illegal immigration' had they not led the way."

Before long, it became apparent to Jabotinsky and his lieutenants that the Irgun would have to be in the vanguard of a war of liberation against the British – who, in their view, were flagrantly violating the trust placed in them as the Mandatory for Palestine.

11

In preparation, some Irgun officers and soldiers were sent from Eretz Israel to Europe (mainly Poland) for specialized training and arms-gathering missions. There were even thoughts of an armada to invade Palestine, and it was rumored that Jabotinsky himself would lead some 10,000 Irgun and Betar men to take the country by storm – not at all a far-fetched idea – for, at that time, the British had only several thousand troops and police there.

The outbreak of World War II trapped European Jewry; the death of Jabotinsky in 1940 and of David Raziel (Commander of the Irgun Zvai Leumi) one year later put an end to these plans and the hopes they had engendered.

The Irgun was divided over its future course of action, with the majority feeling that Britain was, after all, taking the brunt of the battle against the Jews' mortal enemy and that, accordingly, a truce should be called until the German evil was stamped out. Men of the Irgun volunteered for service in the Palestine forces. The active Jewish struggle for Liberation came to a halt – temporarily, at any rate. A small group, headed by Abraham Stern, objected to the abandoning of the struggle against the British, and split away to form the Fighters for the Freedom of Israel (Lechi).

As the tide of war turned and evidence of the enormous catastrophe of European Jewry was revealed, Britain's callousness in continuing to prevent the entry into Palestine of those Jews who could save themselves shocked the Yishuv (the Jewish community of Palestine). Irgun leaders, who had been inactive, felt that the time had come to end the truce. However, much of the momentum of the struggle had gone. The Organization was dormant; the few hundred members had scattered and were already occupied with other matters. A fresh start was needed, under new, dynamic leadership. Inspiration had to be found and generated anew.

The timing of Menachem Begin's arrival in Eretz Israel was providential: his reputation as a brilliant young leader, orator and writer had preceded him; his burning faith in his people's cause was known; his strong will and fearlessness were already recognized. Not surprisingly, he was at once offered the command of the Irgun by Ya'acov Meridor, who was holding the fort since the death of his friend, David Raziel. With the readiness for service that has characterized his whole life, Begin accepted.

And so, at the age of 29, Menachem Begin became the commander in chief of the Irgun Zvai Leumi. He immediately started preparing for the battle for Jewish Statehood against mighty Britain, the superpower of the 1940s.

It is ironic that the man whom the Russian Communists had imprisoned as "an agent of British imperialism" was to lead the first major anti-colonialist struggle. The story of the Irgun is now part of Jewish History. But in 1942 and 1943, it was regarded as sheer lunacy to challenge Great Britain, to pit a few motley fighters armed with pistols against powerful, experienced and highly trained troops. When the Irgun's intentions first became known, they were derided or simply dismissed as irresponsible and simple-minded.

Begin recognized that major psychological hurdles would have to be overcome in the Jewish community, and even among the small, weakened, depleted forces available to him. With patience and deliberation he set about changing the prevailing mentality. In retrospect, this might be regarded as his most outstanding contribution to the struggle for Jewish statehood and peoplehood. From the depths of the Underground he embarked on a difficult program of re-education. His first stirring message: As long as the British Mandatory barred the gates of Eretz Israel to suffering Jews desperately needing to emigrate from Europe, Britain would remain the enemy of the Jewish people.

History – especially the history of ancient Israel – is filled with examples of the battles of the few against the many, the weak against the strong. We can succeed, he told his comrades. We shall triumph. Later he would cite the examples of Garibaldi and his small band of patriots in Italy, of the Boers in their guerrilla war against the British in South Africa, of the American rebels against British authority, and of the various South American freedom fighters.

Others have cited these examples before. Begin, with his literary flair and deep faith, succeeded in giving the sentiments glorious overtones. The spirit of ancient Israel came alive in the proclamations that he penned in a new language of pride, resoluteness and confidence in victory.

In the Irgun's first proclamation, he wrote:

> Four years have passed since the world war began, and all the hopes that beat in your hearts then have evaporated without a trace. We have not been accorded international status. No Jewish Army has been set up. The gates of the country have not been opened. The British regime has sealed its shameful betrayal of the Jewish people and there is no moral basis for its presence in Eretz Israel.
>
> We shall fearlessly draw conclusions. There is no longer any armistice between the Jewish People and the British Administration in Eretz Israel, which hands our brothers over to Hitler. Our People is at war with this regime – war to the end.
>
> This is our demand: Immediate transfer of power in Eretz Israel to a provisional Hebrew government.
>
> We will fight, every Jew in the Homeland will fight. The God of Israel, the Lord of Hosts, will aid us. There will be no retreat. Freedom – or death.
>
> The fighting youth will not flinch from tribulation and sacrifice, from blood and suffering. They will not lay down their arms until they have renewed our days as of old, until they have ensured for our People a Homeland, freedom, honor, bread and justice. And if you will give them your aid, you will see in our days the Return to Zion and the restoration of Israel.

Knowing that his small band of dedicated men and women could not match the British forces in conventional combat, Begin took a different course, which he later described as follows:

> History and our observations persuaded us that if we could suc-
> ceed in destroying the Government's prestige in Eretz Israel, the
> removal of its rule would follow automatically. Thenceforward,
> we gave no peace to the weak spot. Throughout all the years
> of our uprising, we hit at the British Government's prestige,
> deliberately, tirelessly and unceasingly.

In these few lines, Begin summed up four and one-half years of struggle; nearly 1600 days and nights of non-stop war of "the few against the many." In hundreds of operations, the Irgun struck blow after blow at the Administration's military camps, police fortresses, military trains and prisons.

On Begin's express orders, civilians were not to be attacked and, to avoid unnecessary casualties, warnings were issued – often to the detriment of the Irgun themselves, who were deprived of the element of surprise. Clear examples of this policy were seen in the Irgun's attack on the King David Hotel (headquarters of the British) and the operation against Dir Yassin in 1948, which has since been distorted by hostile propagandists.

As the months turned into years, so the Irgun actions became more daring and assumed larger dimensions. With remarkable ingenuity and improvisation, Irgun units penetrated the heart of the British military fortresses and often left with desperately needed arms.

At the height of the struggle, Moshe Dayan – then a young officer in the Haganah (the semi-legal defense organization oper-ating under orders of the Jewish Agency, which was vehemently opposed to the Irgun's "dissident" activities) – said to Begin: "You have already accomplished an historic act. You have proved that it was possible to attack the British."

The Irgun leader and his High Command planned the various operations in the greatest detail. Begin had to be satisfied that the men he was sending into action had a reasonable prospect of escape after carrying out their assignments, and that every possible precaution would be taken to avoid civilian casualties.

Of course, war carries its own risks and, though the number of casualties among the Jewish freedom fighters was remarkably low for such a protracted and intensive struggle, they nevertheless paid a heavy price. But nothing could any longer deter them – not the threat of imprisonment, not exile and banishment to concentration camps in Africa, not flogging, not hanging.

The Irgun's spectacular successes won the respect of a large part of the Yishuv, stunned the British, and threw the Jewish Agency into disarray. As the officially recognized leadership of the Jewish community and of the Zionist movement, the Jewish Agency continued to believe in the possibility of achieving its Zionist aspirations by cooperation with the British.

At one point, when they felt that they were losing their grip on the Jewish community in Palestine, the Jewish Agency and the leftist elements that supported them decided on open and active cooperation with the British in eradicating the "dissident Irgun cancer," as they called it.

This presented Begin with one of the gravest decisions of his career. Pursuant to their offer to collaborate with the British in an open fight against the Irgun, the Agency proclaimed an "open season" on the Irgun, calling men of the Haganah and Palmach (the Haganah's shock troops) to join the hunt for the Irgun fighters. Some were captured, others tortured, and many, many hundreds (Richard Crossman, the British politician and journalist put the number at 1,200) were handed over to the British authorities.

The situation was explosive. One word from Begin and fratricidal war would have broken out. But, ever mindful of the ultimate goal, and remembering the tragic end of the early Jewish Commonwealths, he refused to be drawn into this brothers' conflict, and moved heaven and earth to prevent civil war.

When the Agency finally gave up on the hope of British fair play, they called off the "season" and ordered the Haganah and Palmach to enter, with the Irgun and Lechi (the Stern Group), into a United Resistance movement that lasted about nine months. By that time, Menachem Begin was well on his way to becoming a legendary figure. Within a relatively short time, he had succeeded in instilling new pride into a fighting generation, and renewed belief in the possibility of victory. His declarations, political analyses and stirring messages to his soldiers, distributed as wall newspapers, posters and handbills, made a profound impression upon the Yishuv and sent ripples beyond the borders of the country.

The hallmark of his writings was his absolute adherence to truth. Nothing was withheld. If an operation succeeded, it was reported accordingly, and the success was claimed. If it failed, it was likewise faithfully reported, and the failure or mishap admitted.

Chapter 4

VICTORY

THE IRGUN'S ACTIONS echoed and reverberated throughout the world, especially in London. After the British Labour Party's election victory in 1945, its promises to the Jewish People were quickly forgotten, and the anti-Zionist policy of the Colonial Office became, if anything, more repressive.

The battle in Palestine was now literally between Begin and Ernest Bevin, Britain's Foreign Secretary, the chief and rather crude exponent of the anti-Zionist policy who, for example, warned Jews still languishing in D.P. camps against "pushing to the head of the queue."

The redoubtable Winston Churchill was in the opposition. As police stations were attacked, air bases bombed, the Administration headquarters razed, British officers flogged in retaliation for the flogging of Jewish soldiers, he rose in the Commons to ask "how much longer will this squalid war go on?"

And when the Irgun struck its master blow – the mass break at Acre Fortress – the "Fall of the Bastille," as Begin later described it – Churchill insisted that, if Britain was unable to govern in Palestine, it should return the Mandate to the United Nations. Shouting angrily and thumping a dispatch box in front of him, he demanded:

"Is there no means of accelerating the appeal to the United Nations, or are we just to drift on, month after month, with these horrible outrages and counter-measures, which are necessary but, nevertheless, objectionable – necessary but painful?"

Ever concerned with the prestige of the British Empire, Churchill returned to the subject again a week later, after the Irgun had flogged two British officers and ripples of laughter were heard around the globe. "In this small Palestine…we are to pour out all our treasure and keep 100,000 men marching around in most vexatious and painful circumstances, when we have no real interest in the matter," he declared.

Britain did eventually refer the matter to the United Nations which, on 29 November 1947, voted by a two-thirds majority for a resolution giving international recognition to the Jewish people's right to independent existence, and endorsing the creation of a Jewish State in partitioned Eretz Israel. The Zionist striving and the Irgun's struggle had borne their first fruit.

Six months were yet to pass before independence. In that period, the Irgun maintained its pressure, lest the British change their minds, and in April 1948 undertook one of its biggest operations: the liberation of Jaffa which, according to the UN Partition Plan, was to have remained in Arab hands.

At the height of the outpouring of joy on Israel's declaration of independence on Saturday, 15 May 1948, Menachem Begin – who had lived in the Underground for almost five years, with a minimum of outside contact and at times in disguise – addressed his people over the secret radio station of the Irgun Zvai Leumi. Every radio in the country must have been tuned in. The nation listened to the voice of the commander in chief of the Irgun Zvai Leumi, a man whom they had neither previously heard or seen, but who had profoundly and dramatically changed their individual and national life.

After many years of Underground warfare, years of persecution and moral and physical suffering, the rebels against the oppressor stand before you with a blessing of thanks on their lips and a prayer in their hearts.

The blessing is the age-old blessing with which our fathers and our forefathers have always greeted Holy Days. It was with this blessing that they used to taste any fruit for the first time in the season. Today is truly a holiday, a Holy Day, and a new fruit is visible before our eyes.

The Hebrew Revolt of 1944–1948 has been blessed with success – the first Hebrew revolt since the Hasmonean insurrection that has ended in victory. The rule of oppression in our country has been beaten, uprooted; it has crumbled and been dispersed. The State of Israel has arisen in bloody battle. The highway for the mass return to Zion has been cast up.

The foundation has been laid – but only the foundation – for true independence. One phase of the battle for freedom, for the return of the whole People of Israel to its Homeland, for the restoration of the whole Land of Israel to its God-covenanted owners has ended. But only one phase…

The State of Israel has arisen. And it has arisen 'Only Thus': Through blood, through fire, with an outstretched hand and a mighty arm, with suffering and with sacrifices.

It could not have been otherwise. And yet, even before our State is able to set up its normal national institutions, it is compelled to fight – or to continue to fight – satanic enemies and bloodthirsty mercenaries, on land, in the air and on the sea. In these circumstances, the warning sounded by the philosopher-president Thomas Masaryk to the Czechoslovak nation when it attained its freedom after three hundred years of slavery, has a special significance for us.

In 1918 when Masaryk stepped out onto the Wilson railway station in Prague, he warned his cheering countrymen: 'It is difficult to set up a State; it is even more difficult to keep it going.'

In truth, it has been difficult for us to set up our State. Tens of generations and millions of wanderers, from one land of massacre to another, were needed; it was necessary that there be exile, burning at the stake and torture in the dungeons; we had to suffer agonizing disillusionments; we needed the warnings – though they often went unheeded – of prophets and of seers; we needed the sweat and toil of generations of pioneers and builders; we had to have an uprising of rebels to crush the enemy; we had to have the gallows, the banishments beyond the seas, the prisons and the cages in the deserts – all this was necessary that we might reach the present stage where 600,000 Jews are in the Homeland, where the direct rule of oppression has been driven out and Hebrew Independence declared in part, at least, of the country, the whole of which is ours.

It has been difficult to create our State. But it will be still more difficult to keep it going. We are surrounded by enemies who long for our destruction. And that same oppressor, who has been defeated by us directly, is trying indirectly to make us surrender with the aid of mercenaries from the south, the north and the east. Our one-day-old State is set up in the midst of the flames of battle.

The first pillar of our State must, therefore, be victory. Total victory, in the war that is raging all over the country. For this victory, without which we shall have neither freedom nor life, we need arms, weapons of all sorts, in order to strike the enemies, in order to disperse the invaders, in order to free the entire length and breadth of the country, from its destroyers.

But in addition to these arms, each and every one of us has need of another weapon, a spiritual weapon, the weapon of unflinching endurance in the face of attack from the air; in the face of grievous casualties; in the face of local disasters and temporary defeats; unflinching resistance to threats and cajolers. If, in the coming days and weeks, we can put on the armor of an undying nation in resurrection, we shall in the meantime receive the blessed arms with which to drive off the enemy and bring freedom and peace to our nation and country.

But, even after emerging victorious from this campaign – and victorious we shall be – we shall still have to exert superhuman efforts in order to remain independent, in order to free our country.

First of all, it will be necessary to increase and strengthen the fighting arm of Israel, without which there can be no freedom and no survival for our Homeland.

It would be necessary to convert the Declaration of Independence into reality, he said. Israel would require a wise foreign policy based on reciprocity with the nations of the world.

There must be no self-denigration. There must be no surrender, no favoritism. There must be reciprocity. Enmity for enmity. Aid for aid. Friendship must be repaid with friendship. We must foster friendship and understanding between us and every nation, great or small, strong or weak, near or far, which recognizes our independence, which aids our national regeneration and which is interested, even as we are, in international justice and peace among nations.

Begin then turned to internal affairs of the Jewish State, and made an impassioned appeal for ships to bring immigrants into the country:

For heaven's sake, let us have ships for our immigrants, let us not hear talk of absorptive capacity, or a limitation of immigration. Speed is of the essence! Our people cannot wait. Bring them in their hundreds of thousands. We can brook no delay.

We are now in the midst of a war for survival and our tomorrow, and theirs, depends on the quickest concentration of our nation's exiles.

If there will not be sufficient houses for them, we shall find tents, and if there are not tents – no matter – there is the firmament above, the blue skies of our Homeland.

And within our Homeland, Justice must be the supreme ruler, the ruler over all rulers. There must be no tyranny. The ministers and officials must be the servants of the nation, not their masters. There must be no exploitation. There must be no man within our country – be he citizen or foreigner – compelled to go hungry, to want a roof over his head, or to lack elementary education.

"Remember, Ye were strangers in the land of Egypt" – this supreme rule must continually light our way in our relations with the strangers within our gates. "Righteousness, righteousness, shalt thou pursue!" Righteousness must be the guiding principle in our relations among ourselves.

Announcing that the Irgun Zvai Leumi was leaving the Underground within the boundaries of the Hebrew Independent State, the commander in chief said:

We went Underground, we arose in the Underground under the rule of oppression in order to strike at oppression and to overthrow it. Now, for the time being we have Hebrew rule in part of our Homeland. And as in this part there will be Hebrew Law – and that is the only rightful law in this country – there is no need for the Hebrew Underground. In the State of Israel, we shall be soldiers and builders. And we shall respect its Government, for it is our Government.

The State of Israel has arisen, but we must remember that our country is not yet liberated. The battle continues, and you see now the words of your Irgun fighters were not vain words;

it is Hebrew arms which decide the boundaries of the Hebrew State. So it is now in this battle; so it will be in the future.

Then followed a statement that remained the cornerstone of his policy to the end of his political life:

> Our God-given country is a unity. The attempt to dissect it is not only a crime, but a blasphemy and an abortion. Whoever does not recognize our natural right to our entire Homeland, does not recognize our right to any part of it. And we shall never forego this natural right. We shall continue to foster the aspirations of full independence. The soldiers of Israel will yet unfurl our flag over the Tower of David and our ploughshares will yet cleave the fields of Gilead.
>
> Citizens of the Hebrew State, soldiers of Israel, we are in the midst of battle. Difficult days lie ahead of us…we cannot buy peace from our enemies with appeasement. There is only one kind of peace that can be bought – the peace of the grave-yard, the peace of Treblinka. Be brave of spirit, and ready for more trials. We shall withstand them. The Lord of Hosts will help us; he will sustain the bravery of the Hebrew youth, the bravery of he Hebrew mothers who, like Hannah, offer their sons on the altar of God.

Addressing himself to his fighting brothers, the soldiers of the Underground forces, sons of the Fighting Family, as he put it, the commander in chief said:

> Your eyes witness that those who sow with blood reap with liberty. You were alone and persecuted, rejected, despised, and numbered with the transgressors.
>
> But you fought on with deep faith and did not retreat; you were tortured but you did not submit; you were cast into

prison, but your spirit was not crushed; you were banished from your Homeland, but you were not broken; you were sent to the gallows, and you went forth with a song. You have written a glorious page in history. And there are many more that you will write. Not with ink but with blood and sweat. Not with pen; but with the sword and the ploughshare.

You will forget the injustices that were done, and you will not demand a reward. Our only reward is the privilege of seeing our nation being liberated and fighting – all fighting as one man – for its liberty, and our final reward will be – if we return alive from the battlefield – to be privileged to wander in cities of our Homeland, in its mountains and valleys; and there to see Jewish children at play, with no one to disturb them, and above their tiny heads – more dear to us than anything – will circle an aircraft – and it will be a Jewish aircraft; and approaching them a soldier, a Hebrew soldier; and from afar the roar of a train, a Jewish train. O brethren, can there be greater happiness than this?…

As we march forward, soldiers of the Lord of Hosts, we shall be escorted by the spirit of our ancient warriors, the conquerors of Canaan and the rebels of Judah. We shall be accompanied by the spirit of those who revived our nation: Theodore Herzl, Max Nordau, Joseph Trumpeldor and the father of resurrected Hebrew heroism, Ze'ev Jabotinsky.

We shall be accompanied by the spirit of David Raziel, the greatest of the Hebrew commanders of our day; and by Dov Gruner, one of the greatest Hebrew soldiers. We shall be accompanied into battle by the spirit of the heroes of the gallows, by conquerors of death, and we shall be accompanied by the spirit of millions of martyrs, our ancestors, tortured and burnt for their faith, our murdered fathers and butchered mothers, our murdered brothers and strangled children. And in this battle we shall break the enemy and bring salvation to

our people, tried in the furnace of persecution, thirsting only
for freedom, for righteousness and for Justice…

With the proclamation of the State of Israel, the Irgun Zvai
Leumi was disbanded; its members entered the ranks of the Israel
Defense Forces. Only in Jerusalem – which was to become an international city, according to the United Nations Partition Plan – did
it retain its separate identity and existence, working in cooperation
with the Haganah and Lechi.

Time and again the Irgun urged and initiated action to free
the Old City, but each time the thrust was frustrated, until the final
truce that left the most sacred shrines of the Jewish People in the
hands of Arab occupiers for 19 more years.

To protect and relieve Jerusalem, the various fighting organizations attacked Arab villages and strongholds on the hills overlooking the main road to the capital city. One such stronghold, Dir
Yassin, in which Iraqi mercenaries were stationed, was assaulted
by the Irgun and Lechi with the knowledge and understanding of
the Haganah. The Irgun's customary advance warning was given
to enable civilians to move out of the range of fire. The loudspeak-
ers blared: "You are being attacked by superior forces…The west
exit of Dir Yassin leading to Ein Karem is open for you! Run immediately."

Later in 1955, Yunes Assad, a prominent inhabitant of Dir
Yassin who survived the battle said that "the Jews never intended
to hurt the population of the village, but were forced to do so after
they met enemy fire from the population."*

It was also largely over the battle for Jerusalem that the tragic
Altalena incident occurred. Once more, but for Begin's patriotism,
the incident could quite easily have sparked a civil war. Long

---

* "Background Notes on Current Affairs," No. 6, published by the Information
Department of the Israel Ministry of Foreign Affairs, 16 March 1969.

before the United Nations' truces came into effect, the Irgun had prepared to send some 1,000 fighting men and large quantities of desperately needed arms (supplied by France) to embattled Israel on a ship bearing Jabotinsky's pen name "Altalena." As the vessel, under the command of Eliyahu Lankin, approached the shores of Israel, a dispute arose over the ownership of the arms and, later, over allocating only a portion to the Irgun forces in Jerusalem, with the bulk going to the new Israel Defense Army.

Suddenly, Ben Gurion, the head of the Provisional Government, turned on the Irgun – whom he accused of planning a putsch – by ordering that the "Altalena" be fired on. Subsequently he praised the "holy gun" that sank the ship with its valuable cargo of arms.

In the raging fire, twelve men who had come to fight for Israel were killed by the guns of their own brothers. It was later revealed that Air Force personnel – volunteers from abroad who were ordered to bomb the ship – refused to do so, saying: "We came here to fight *for* the Jews, not *against* Jews." Some argued that the attack was ordered in the hope of eliminating Begin, who was aboard the blazing vessel, stubbornly refusing to leave it.

After many agonizing hours, when the flames began to spark off explosions in the ammunition caches, Begin was forced to leave the ship. He went straight to the Irgun radio station and broadcast his version of the agreements between the Irgun and the Haganah and the Provisional Government, of the broken undertakings and of the unprovoked attack.

He wept unabashedly as he spoke. Some mocked him for it. But those tears averted a civil war at a crucial moment in Jewish history. Begin later said that "sometimes it is better that one man should pour tears from his heart over an abomination committed in Israel than that many, many should weep over its consequences."

Within weeks of his election as Prime Minister in 1977, Menachem Begin participated in a memorial service for the 16 members of the Irgun who died when the ship was attacked; he used the occasion to reveal that, some years earlier, "one of the leaders of the State who is still an active member of the Labor Party, a figure occupying a central position in our national life, came to me on his own initiative to say that Labor officials had re-investigated the Altalena incident and had come to the conclusion that Ben Gurion had been deliberately misled as to the Irgun's intentions when he ordered the shelling of the ship."

Begin said his informant had refused to elaborate on this, but his assertion endorsed his own charges over the years that "innocent Jewish blood had been spilt." Clearly, it was with good reason that *Veritas vincit* – "Truth will triumph" – was one of Menachem Begin's favorite Latin expressions.

Chapter 5

A MAN OF FAITH

It was at the height of the Irgun uprising – January 1947 – that I first met Menachem Begin. Some of the most dramatic and daring actions had already taken place. The struggle was raging in all its fury.

The King David Hotel – headquarters of the British Administration – had been bombed. Young Irgun men had been flogged, and British officers were likewise punished. Jewish fighters had been executed, others were under sentence of death. In fact, my friends and I arrived at Lydda airport on 31 December 1946 – the very day on which the Irgun whipped two Englishmen in Haifa. Not having heard any news for several days, we were amazed at the many roadblocks, mounted by troops, all along the road from the airport to Tel Aviv. Our taxi driver told us about the floggings, adding jokingly: "You know, an eye for an eye, a tooth for a tooth, a…"

The final stages of the Dov Gruner drama were being played out. Gruner had been wounded in an attack on the Ramat Gan police fortress, was caught, summarily tried and sentenced to death. Refusing to appeal to the British for clemency, it was Gruner who, in a letter smuggled out to Begin, said that if he had the chance to live his life again he would follow the same path. His sister, Helen

Friedman, who lived in the United States, was in Palestine at the time trying desperately to save him by legal action and by her own appeals to the Privy Council – to no avail. Gruner was executed two months later, and became a symbol of the unbending and undaunted Jewish freedom fighter.

The commander in chief of the Irgun was the most wanted man in the country, the British having placed a high price on his head. It was known that, at various stages, to evade detection, he assumed disguises as a rabbi or as a respectable German-Jewish bookkeeper, and thus successfully deceived the British (although he had several very narrow escapes).

This was also the period when the official Jewish leadership and others opposed to the Irgun's activities were maligning the Irgun commander as some sort of terrible ogre; some opponents actively collaborated with the British in their hunt for the Irgun fighters.

Few people other than his immediate family and his comrades of the Irgun High Command had set eyes on him. I did not know quite what to expect.

My clandestine meeting with Menachem Begin had been arranged a number of weeks earlier, when I attended the first post-war World Zionist Congress in Basle, Switzerland, where I met several representatives of the Irgun. On the prearranged day, I was to proceed to a certain corner in Tel Aviv, where I would find a man in a fawn raincoat, holding a briefcase under his arm. I followed the instructions to the letter and, indeed, met the man – who turned out to be Haim Landau, then Chief of Staff of the Irgun, later one of the top leaders of the Herut Party, a Minister in the Government of National Unity in 1969 and one of our closest and dearest personal friends.

Without saying much, he took me on a long walk which, I subsequently discovered, was literally a case of walking around in circles, lest we were followed. At last we approached a building in the neighborhood of the Habimah Theatre and entered the apartment on the ground floor without fuss. No special signals. It was the modest little flat that was to remain the Begin family home and I subsequently visited scores of times, until his move to the Prime Minister's residence in Jerusalem in July 1977. On being ushered into his presence, I was conscious of the privilege to face this pale, balding, thin man of medium height; glasses and thick mustache gave him a stern look – and yet he was quiet-spoken, modest, and relaxed. His warmth and strength of character were captivating.

This was no trigger-happy gunman bent on senseless adventures. There was nothing military about him or his surroundings. Contrary to my expectations, there were, to the best of my knowledge, no armed guards in or around the apartment. In fact, the only people present were Menachem Begin, Haim Landau, and a young woman who, I was later to learn, was his wife Aliza.

That is how it must have been in Bar Kochba's time or in the days of Judas Maccabeus, when the enemy was becoming ever more powerful and arrogant, and some Jews more timid. Only a man of the greatest personal courage could withstand the decadence around him, could find the will to carry on in spite of all. Furthermore, it was in these surroundings that I first realized that this was a man of immense and supreme faith.

Menachem Begin's great faith was derived from his parents, staunch Zionists who believed implicitly in *Shivat Zion*, the Return to Zion; it was derived from his school and from his Jewish studies, which he devoured with the hunger of a starving man.

His father, Ze'ev-Dov Begin, had been the secretary of the Brest-Litovsk Jewish community, and it was later learnt that he went to his death at the hands of the Germans in the Holocaust, leading his fellow-Jews in defiant singing of "Hatikvah" (the Jewish song of Hope which later became the national anthem of the State of Israel).

Mainly, however, his faith came from the man whom he had

heard and seen and to whose teachings and movement he dedicated himself selflessly, as had thousands of others. That man was
Ze'ev Jabotinsky.

The Jewish masses in Europe acclaimed Jabotinsky their "king"
and the political heir to Herzl, founder of modern Zionism. They
honored him as the creator of the Jewish Legion in World War I
and saluted him as the defender of Jerusalem in defiance of British orders. His Betar youth movement and Zionist Revisionist
Organization attracted hundreds of thousands of followers, for
whom Jabotinsky's ideals represented the great hope for Jewish
future and salvation.

Throughout the many examples in the history of nations of a
disciple's devotion to his mentor, rarely can we find anything re-
sembling the attachment of Menachem Begin to the memory, the
teachings and the precepts of Ze'ev Jabotinsky. For him, Jabotinsky
was not some personality from the past, nor was his philosophy
a form of ideological archaeology. Jabotinsky remained for Begin
a pulsating, living reality; his teachings guided the affairs of the
nation every day and influenced every event. Menachem Begin
proudly acknowledged that his life was molded by Jabotinsky,
whom he continually honored as the greatest man he had ever
met.

In October 1971, I heard Begin deliver an impromptu speech
to a group of supporters and friends. He was in a relaxed and
reminiscent mood as he revealed his innermost feelings.

> We have learnt many things from Rosh Betar. But two of
> the most important lessons are:
>> Belief in your ideal and readiness to sacrifice for it.
>> Do not bow to the mighty.

These two lessons were characteristic of Begin's own career and,
especially, his conduct in the six years he served as Israel's Prime

Minister. I often had the impression that Begin communed with the spirit of his great teacher; that he sought his guidance and inspiration and reported to him on the major developments.

On one occasion, at the height of negotiations with the Americans about the Middle East peace process, I advised a senior U.S. official that, if they wanted to understand the mind of Begin, they should read the biography of Jabotinsky. Next day there was a request from the U.S. embassy for a set of the two volumes by Joseph B. Schechtman, *Rebel and Statesman and Fighter and Prophet*.*

Some months after the establishment of Israel, Begin visited the United States, where his first act was to go to the cemetery on Long Island to pay homage at the grave of Ze'ev Jabotinsky.

"Adoni Rosh Betar," he said at the emotional ceremony, "I have come to report that the Revolt of your sons has been triumphant. The Jewish State has arisen *b'dam va'esh* – in blood and fire – as you foretold…"

Jabotinsky died in New York in August 1940, by which time he was completely convinced that the Jewish State would arise within years. In fact, on 27 November 1938, he wrote to a young man in South Africa, saying: "I think, on a very conservative estimate, that in the next ten years the Jewish State of Palestine will not only be proclaimed, but a reality, probably in less than ten." In fact, the United Nations adopted its famous Jewish State resolution on 29 November 1947 – nine years after those prophetic words were written; the independent State of Israel was proclaimed six months later.

---

* Long considered the definitive biography of Jabotinsky, these volumes were originally published in 1956 and 1961. Dr. Michael Neiditch, Director of Programs at B'nai B'rith, published a new edition of the work with a foreword by Mr. Begin (Washington, DC: Eshel Books, 1986, distributed by B'nai B'rith Books). Shmuel Katz's biography which was published in Hebrew by Dvir in 1993, is a carefully researched two-volume work that has been warmly received and acclaimed. The English version of *Lone Wolf* was published in two volumes by Barricade Books in 1996.

This same faith was also expressed in Jabotinsky's will, in which he said merely:

"I want to be buried where I die, and my remains, should I be buried outside Palestine, may *not* be transferred to Palestine unless by order of that country's eventual Jewish Government."

The first Governments of Israel, led by Ben Gurion, chose to ignore this request. "We bring living Jews to Israel, not dead ones," Ben Gurion once stated.

Menachem Begin and his movement, however, strove to correct this injustice and faithfully to preserve the memory of the man who provided so much of the motivation for the great revolution. Efforts and appeals for the fulfillment of Jabotinsky's will were maintained and increased – always in great dignity and with *hadar* (honor, respect). They were supported in Israel by the B'nai B'rith Lodge – the only public body to take a stand on the issue. But it was not until 1964, when Ben Gurion finally retired and Levi Eshkol became Prime Minister, that the Israeli Government made the decision to order the transfer of the remains of Ze'ev Jabotinsky and those of his wife Johanna (who died in 1950) from New York to Jerusalem for re-interment on Mount Herzl. It was a fitting reward for a movement's perseverance; for Menachem Begin, it was a palpable triumph.

The ceremonies in New York, Paris, Lod Airport, Tel Aviv, Ramat Gan and Jerusalem were planned with the tender love of children showing respect for an honored father. Hundreds of thousands of citizens paid homage to the man who had breathed new life into the long-suffering nation. Though much could be said, this was not an occasion for speeches – only a few telling words. When the caskets were lowered from the El Al plane and placed on the soil of Eretz Israel, Menachem Begin spoke:

> On your return, with your helpmeet who accompanied you on your way, in your suffering and liberating activities, not

only your disciples await you. The whole liberated nation, to which you devoted your life until your last moment on earth, awaits you with holy awe, with honor, with thankfulness and great love.

My wife and I were there with our son, Hillel Ze'ev; we could sense that this was one of the most deeply moving experiences in Begin's life. The following day, after unprecedented scenes of national tribute from the citizens of Jerusalem and prior to the final ceremony on Mt. Herzl, Begin passed me a note on which he had written: "He left the country as an exile; he has returned a conquering hero."

Ze'ev Jabotinsky found peace at last in the land for which he had fought with so much tenacity and amongst the people whom he loved. As the events of those three days of national homage demonstrated, he belongs not to the past, but to the present, to posterity. His grave has become a shrine of pilgrimage and inspiration.

And indeed, for Menachem Begin, Jabotinsky "belonged to the present." No one was surprised when, in his first television appearance after the Knesset election results showed that he would be Israel's next Prime Minister, Begin paid gracious tribute to his great mentor and guide, Ze'ev Jabotinsky. He implied, in fact, that the victory of the Likud (Unity) party was Jabotinsky's posthumous triumph, and that he was the privileged and chosen instrument to carry it into effect.

Begin's most specific act of homage to Jabotinsky did not come until some two months later. He deliberately delayed his journey to the United States for his first meeting with President Carter in order to be in Jerusalem on the 37th anniversary of Jabotinsky's death. As had been the custom since 1964, a memorial ceremony was arranged at the graves of Ze'ev and Johanna Jabotinsky. But this time, it took on a different significance. Though still not an official State occasion, it had all the luster and grandeur of such an event.

President Ephraim Katzir, Cabinet Ministers, Knesset members, and other dignitaries were all present in the large assembly that came to pay tribute.

Several days earlier, I was with Prime Minister Begin when he gave his final approval to the program arrangements submitted by his old friend, Joseph Klarman, who was in charge of the proceedings. Ever since 1964, an understanding existed that there would be no speeches at the annual commemoration. The main feature of the program was to be a reading from Jabotinsky's own writings or addresses.

"When you welcome the Speaker of the Knesset, Yitzhak Shamir, please be sure to announce him as a former member of the Lechi High Command," Begin requested. "In my case, please introduce me first as Commander of the Irgun Zvai Leumi and then as Prime Minister," he said.

As expected, the crowd at the 1977 Yahrzeit ceremony was bigger than usual. Only persons with admission cards could enter the small enclosure – and those cards were in great demand and quickly snapped up.

All present naturally expected Menachem Begin to speak on this occasion. He did not. Rabbi L.I. Rabinowitz, writing from Jerusalem in the South African Jewish Herald, described the scene – which was also witnessed by hundreds of thousands of television viewers in the country – as follows:

> Menachem Begin, accompanied by President Katzir and Joseph Klarman, stepped forward to lay their wreaths upon the grave. The other two withdrew and Menachem Begin stood there alone before the resting place of his revered master and teacher.
>
> There he stood in silence, in spiritual communion with him, who had been the inspiration of his life – and the tears welled out of his eyes and ran unrestrainedly down his cheeks.

Who shall deny that the silence was more eloquent than the most inspiring and brilliant of oratorical exercises that the most brilliant orator could express?

The only time Menachem Begin did speak at the graveside of Ze'ev and Johanna Jabotinsky was upon the completion of the centennial year of Jabotinsky's birth in 1981 when, as Prime Minister and head of the movement, he paid homage to his master and teacher, reporting to him that:

> Jerusalem, the city that has become bound together, the eternal capital of Israel and of the Land of Israel, shall not be subjected to any division. It is our liberated and indivisible capital and so it shall remain from generation to generation.
>
> The western part of the Land of Israel is entirely under our control and it shall not be partitioned any more. No part of this land shall be given over to a foreign administration, to foreign sovereignty.
>
> We believe that a day will come when the two parts of the Land of Israel shall establish, peacefully, in agreement and understanding, a covenant of alliance, a free confederation, for the purpose of joint cooperation, and then we shall see the fulfillment of your words:
>
>> "From the abundance in our land shall prosper the Arab, the Christian and the Jew."
>
> We defend the dignity of Jewish people wherever they may be, since that is the basis for safeguarding the existence and future of our nation. We shall remember until the very last day of our lives and shall bequeath to our children after us, that those who arose in this generation to annihilate us, did not carry out their evil designs until they had succeeded in debasing our condemned people and depriving them of their human dignity.

We guard the security of our nation as the pupil of our eyes. Many are those who wait to entrap us. The path of tribulations has not yet come to an end. We shall, however, ensure our national security with all the means at our disposal, with the heroism of our children, for whom you sang from the depths of your loving and believing heart:

"Do not say that there is no more within us
    the blood of our father, the Maccabee,
    for three drops from him
    have been mixed into my blood.

"When the enemy shall break from ambush,
    we shall rise and we shall fight,
    Long live the youth: Long live the sword,
    Long live the Maccabean blood."

We will continue to pursue peace and to act, by virtue of our inalienable right, for its realization; for wars are abhorrent to us, and the vision of eternal peace, conceived by the Prophets of Israel, the Prophets of truth and justice, dwells in our hearts and appears before us always.

We undertake a continuous endeavor in the rejuvenation of the Hebrew language, which today we and our children use fluently. It is beautiful in content, and not merely great in its expression, as you have taught us:

"The most wonderful of all languages, the language of thousands of opposites, hard and strong as steel and at the same time soft and illuminating as gold; poor in words but rich in concepts; cruel in anger and living in ridicule as well as dainty in a mother's song at a time of comfort and conciliation. It is a language whose voice often echoes like that of stones falling steeply from the mountain and often as the rumblings of grass in a spring morning. An unwieldy language, with bear-like claws and widespread wings of birds in flight. The language of the ten commandments, and the song of Moses on the day of his death; the language of censure and the language of the Song of Songs; the language of David's lament and Isaiah's song of comfort; the language forgotten and unforgotten, already buried and yet living eternally."

We will continue to act for the promotion of social justice in the lives of our people so that there be light for Jew and Gentile together. The vision of justice, as we received it from you, Adoni Rosh Betar, is that poverty shall vanish from the face of the earth.

The return to Zion of most of the Jews from the West, the East, the North and the South is our aspiration, and it shall continue to serve as a beacon of light for our guidance.

We observe the ancient traditions of our people, the faith in the God of our fathers, since these are the sources of Israel's eternal existence.

One more message from our lips, Adoni Rosh Betar:

In those difficult days we saw you in your pain and suffering. We heard you calling our people, who did not want to heed: Save yourselves, liquidate the Diaspora before the Diaspora liquidates you. In those days, on the threshold of those awful days, you told us – your disciples, your children: a day will come when our People will call upon you to conduct their affairs, to take responsibility for their future.

That day has come.

To them, to your pupils, our nation in its homeland has again given the trust to bear the responsibility for assuring its liberty, its security, its peace, dignity, welfare and future, in the Land of Israel restored.

Blessed are the pupils, Adoni Rosh Betar, for whom a teacher like you arose and who continues to live in their hearts.

Blessed be the teacher, whose pupils carry aloft his flag, believe in his vision and diligently fulfill his tenets.

Begin's speeches and articles about Jabotinsky are classics. Of the many, one stands out as his finest evaluation of his great teacher and master. Originally entitled "What Did We Learn From Him?" the article has appeared in dozens of languages under different titles. Because of its beauty of language and sensitive evaluation, I reproduce it fully in the next chapter.

Chapter 6

"ZE'EV JABOTINSKY: WHAT DID WE LEARN FROM HIM?"

Menachem Begin, 1965

A VERSATILE BRAIN, applying itself to various fields of creation and excelling in all of them, is a rare phenomenon in human history. Aristotle, Maimonides, Da Vinci – and, above all, the greatest of leaders and lawgivers – Moses; these are the names of the very few who prove the existence of this phenomenon and its extreme rarity. Ze'ev Jabotinsky was such a versatile brain. He was poet, philologist, statesman, sociologist, author, orator and soldier. What has our generation learned from Ze'ev Jabotinsky, and what will future generations learn from him?

Poetry and the era

We can say about the reciprocal relationship between poetry and the era the same as has been said about the relationship between personality and the era. Materialists claim that the era creates man, while idealists believe that man creates the era. The wisdom of life and its experience teach us that there is a reciprocal influence between man and his time.

Here is one of the most striking examples in history: but for the French Revolution and the uprisings, the invasion, the defeats and the re-awakening, the strange sounding Italian name of an artillery officer would have been known only to his closest fellow-officers. On the other hand, however, but for the personal vision of Napoleon Bonaparte, the events of the end of the 18th century and the beginning of the 19th century (between Madrid and Moscow) would not have occurred.

There exists a similar reciprocal influence between poetry and literature in general, and the era. Sometimes, the era produces the poet. Sometimes one creates the other. But the poetry and the literary works of Ze'ev Jabotinsky preceded an era – created an era. He wrote of Jewish might even before it came into being; of revolt before it took place; of a Jewish Army while its weapons were still a dream; of a Jewish State when many of our contemporaries still derided its very mention and of *Hadar* (honor, respect) while the manners – or lack of manners – of the ghetto still prevailed in our people.

Beautification of Hebrew

He used to say: "I absorb a language out of the air." And he would say: "I must work hard in order to learn a language." Is there any contradiction between the two? Yes and no. Ze'ev Jabotinsky was capable of absorbing a new language as out of the air. But while learning its syllables, he worked hard and intensively in the search for its roots in order to master it completely; in order to open up for himself and for his pupils the new world which every new language opens up before those who learn it. In the latter half of his life, however, he devoted his unparalleled philological talents mainly to one task: The improvement and beautification of the Hebrew tongue – in expression and pronunciation. We, his disciples, who were granted the privilege of drinking at his source can testify that Ze'ev Jabotinsky stood in awe before this unique phenomenon – the Hebrew tongue.

He was prepared, at any time, to bow his head in admiration and emotion before the brevity and the depth, the conciseness and the onomatopoeia all contained in Hebrew – the language of the Prophets and of the vision, of the Holy Scriptures, the Psalms and the Song of Songs, the language of life and of renascence – the tongue of the Bible.

True, only the people of Israel could have resuscitated the Hebrew tongue. But it was only the Hebrew language that could have been brought back to life. And a language – so Ze'ev Jabotinsky believed – is like a garden. Just as one tends one's garden, waters it and weeds it, so one has to tend the tongue of one's people – especially eternal, reborn Hebrew. Therefore, Ze'ev Jabotinsky not only entreated us to use Hebrew as our tongue and that of our children, but also exhorted us always to remember that it is no ordinary language we are speaking, but the beautiful tongue of the poets of Israel.

In our homeland, we all speak Hebrew. The language is reborn and rejuvenated. At times we are wont to smile apologetically when hearing our children mingling foreign expressions with the Hebrew mother tongue. But in such cases it is no longer the living language of the past which the proud Hebrew wishes to hear. If in days gone by – in foreign lands or on the soil of our forefathers – the command was *Learn thy language and speak thy tongue*, then in our day, under Israel's free sky, the command is *Honor thy tongue*. Remember that you are using this wonderful language, the tongue of the Bible.

The statesman

Is there such a thing as a statesman? Or is the domain of politics just an open field where anyone can pitch his tent and declare: I am a statesman?

It is, at times, strange to see the lack of understanding of this conception or rather – let us not hesitate to say so – this particular science and wisdom which is called statesmanship.

Why do we recognize the outstanding talents of a man who takes a small instrument into his hands and draws from it sounds so heavenly that they carry us into the lofty realms of beauty whither – according to the primitive thinkers – the soul, which has become detached, returns on hearing or seeing splendor reincarnated? The violinist can do it. You, with the same fingers, with the same instrument, cannot do it.

Why do we recognize the rare gifts of the man who takes a brush into his hands and produces a picture before the beauty of which we bow our heads in admiration: we and the generations that follow us?

Or for what reason do we recognize the particular creative talents of the man who takes a stone, a hammer and a chisel and creates beauty and splendor?

Let us recognize that just as there is the great musician, the painter and the sculptor – and there are but few in the history of mankind – so there is the statesman, who is a statesman by virtue of specific talents which are not bestowed upon many.

But by what do we recognize the statesman? How can he be recognized? In order to answer this question let us ask another one: How does one recognize virtuoso? One does not realize immediately that one is in the presence of talent. Years go by, talent ripens, proof is here, the melody is heard, hearts are conquered, and one day we say – now we know. Here is the Maestro!

He foresaw

So it is also in politics. The statesman is not immediately recognized. But if, one fateful and tragic day, one man gets up and declares: "Britain will open a front in the Middle East" at the very time when most British leaders – and foremost among them Kitchener, the soldier – say the contrary; and after a short time such a front is actually opened in the Middle East – then everyone agrees: the statesman was right, he foresaw events correctly.

If, during World War I, all the officials believed in and demanded neutrality, but one man alone declared: "Accursed and forbidden be neutrality. We must act, we must rise against Turkey for, if her rule over Eretz Israel is not eliminated, then there is no justification for our hopes!" And days go by and years elapse, and all admit – subsequently – that neutrality was vanity, while the alliance was justified. And all knew: the statesman had spoken.

If under the rule of a British High Commissioner of Jewish origin, whom everyone says is the "Ezra of our times," an unanointed prince and bearer of all the hopes of our people – if then one man gets up and says: "Herbert Samuel's rule is the first attempt to liquidate Zionism" – and after but a few years all see that it is thus and not otherwise – again it is recognized that the statesman hath spoken.

And if, in the days when leaders abuse the idea of a Jewish State, oppose it, ban it, repudiate it, fight it – one man stands up and decleares: "A Jewish State is the command of supreme justice, it will arise, in our generation it will come true" – and but a few years elapse, and all asked themselves: "How could we ever have lived without a Jewish State?" – then it also becomes clear to all that the magic fiddle of the stateman has brought forth the melody of faith in national resurrection.

If, in the days when we had no weapons, no army and no strength, and on the forehead of the eternal wanderer was written the terrible word *Hefker* (outcast) – one man stood up and ordered: "Jews – learn to shoot!" and added: "The Jewish Army will come into being. In it there is hope, without it there is no expectation and there will be no survival." And years later all the "pacifists" and all the "anti-militarists" ask themselves in naïve wonderment: "How could we have done it without a Jewish army?," then it is clear that it was the wise statesman, he who foresaw, who had spoken.

Such was Ze'ev Jabotinsky the statesman. And let us remember: the captain proves himself in a storm, the maestro in his music, and the statesman in his analysis, in his prescience.

Laws of justice

As a sociologist, Ze'ev Jabotinsky bequeathed us the laws of true justice. He believed in the equality of man. In one of his letters he stressed that the principle of equality was an obsession with him. But his belief in equality had nothing in common with the vulgarization of equality which contains neither justice nor progress but is, on the contrary, nothing but injustice and regression. He believed in equality through elevation and uplifting. This is justice. This is progress. And he also believed, with all the strength of his heart, that justice and equality – but without freedom – are nothing but empty phrases on the lips of those who shun the light. This was the social creed of Ze'ev Jabotinsky. And he drew it from the rising, eternal springs of the Law of Israel, of the Laws of the Prophets.

And who was proved right? All the –*isms* of our time now lie prostrate before our eyes like broken idols, while the Laws of Justice of Israel's Prophets radiate their eternal splendor.

The orator

Cicero, the greatest of all orators, wrote a small booklet on the art of speech. He explains, perhaps somewhat subjectively, that there is no art like the art of speech. According to him, there are many masters in the arts of sculpture, architecture, literature and poetry. But very few are the real orators of all times.

The truth is that the art of speech cannot be acquired by learning. Every other art, singing music, painting or sculpture, depends in the first place on inborn talent. But in these arts, much if not everything can be acquired through learning. Without learning, the talent will be of no avail. Not so with the art of speech. It is a fact that all the schools of rhetoric, from the dawn of history until this very day, have not produced a single orator worthy of the name. And the few whose names are graven in the annals of mankind taught themselves the art of speech.

And who is an orator? Is it he who has a strong voice, who is quick-spoken, smooth-tongued, producing figures out of his sleeve while from his mouth issue flames which extinguish as they emerge? No.

The orator is he who knows how to combine logic and sentiment, heart and intelligence. It is the speaker from whose heart and brain is spun a thread reaching to the hearts and brains of his audience. And at certain moments, his listeners become one entity, and that orator becomes a part of it. Such an orator was Jabotinsky. Thus did we see him, thus did we hear him. We sat below, he stood over us, and all of a sudden we would feel – each of us individually and all of us together – that we were carried aloft, elevated towards another world which is all faith, brotherhood, love, devotion, hope – a world which is all beauty and goodness. There never was an orator like him; it is doubtful whether there will ever be another.

A fighter

Descartes said: "I think, therefore I am." But there are times when a man can say, "I suffer, therefore I am." And there are other times when a man has to say: "I fight, therefore I am." Ze'ev Jabotinsky proved his existence threefold: he thought, he suffered, he fought.

He was a fighter. He expressed the essence of his fighting spirit by his constant readiness to start anew. In one of his wonderful letters, he recalled what happened to the great inventor Newton. After long years of penetrating and creative thought, Newton put his meditations in writing. The composition was almost finished when the great sage left his room, a lighted candle standing on the table near to his papers. A cat jumped on to the table, upset the candle, and the fruits of a lifetime of labor became a heap of ashes. And then, stressed Jabotinsky – Newton, standing in front of his world gone up in flames, spoke only one sentence: "I shall start anew."

And he started, continued and completed.

A similar story, taken from life, is told of the outstanding thinker and historian, Thomas Carlyle. He wrote his famous work, one of the finest, on history and the philosophy of history: *The French Revolution*. A fire broke out and consumed the manuscript. The work of years was completely destroyed. And what did Thomas Carlyle say? Just as Newton did: "I shall start anew." Subsequently, Carlyle himself declared that his second composition on the French Revolution even surpassed the first one, the one that had been burned.

Thus also did Ze'ev Jabotinsky behave. He never admitted failure, but said: "This is an opening for victory." He never despaired at a withdrawal, this was the beginning of the advance. His spirit never fell at a decline, but he said: "This is a sign of ascent." Such is the soul of a fighter.

The greatness of Jabotinsky the fighter never needed any proof in our eyes. The pygmies, with their abuse, the midgets, with their contempt – we never paid them any attention. We knew his greatness, we thrived in his shadow.

But I think that the greatness of this fighter rose to even greater heights when he fought for his ideal – abstract but real, deep and supreme, eternal and unconquered: Justice. There are times when the striving for justice by mankind in its entirety concentrates on one person alone – be it Dreyfus, Beilis or Stavsky.

Vision of the State

Above all, Ze'ev Jabotinsky was the bearer of the Vision of the State in our generation. After Herzl, there was none but him to carry on high the vision of redemption, even in the face of renegades. This is the truth. There is no need to elaborate.

Therefore we can say: here is the miracle of the standard-bearer, here is the miracle of national rebirth, here is the miracle of the Jewish Army, and here is the miracle of the Return to Zion.

And in all these miracles – those revealed and those hidden – there is a drop of Jabotinsky's lifeblood. Without him, without his vision, without his thinking and his suffering, without his fighting and without his disciples – the State of Israel would not have come into being.

Therefore, our generation, and all the generations to come, owe a debt of gratitude to him who led us and them from slavery to freedom. Is not gratitude a simple and befitting human characteristic? If a man has done his neighbor a favor, does not the latter owe him gratitude? Man cannot always return a favor. But to acknowledge a good deed – is that not a moral duty? And if such is the rule in the relations between man and man, why should it be different between one man and a community – a people? Let us be more explicit. Does not man – every individual, and mankind in its entirety – owe a debt of gratitude to men like Pasteur, Koch or Salk? They benefited mankind. Mankind owes them gratitude.

And if a fighter appears, and gives his entire life to his people, the wealth of his thought, the warmth of his heart, all his talents, his pen of iron and the steel of his character; and toils for them, risks his life, sacrifices himself, helps his people, saves it, and sets it on the path of freedom – do not his compatriots owe him a debt of gratitude?

Gratitude, not reward! A true fighter never asks for a reward. And a reward is never offered. But simple human gratitude, coming from the heart, out of the depth of the soul – why should it be withheld from the man who fought for his people and his country?

Immense love

But there also exists ingratitude. It has various forms – the most terrible of which is hatred towards the benefactor. The great student of the human soul, Dostoyevsky, describes a strange psychological case. One of his heroes declares: "I hate him." His friends ask: "Why? Has he done you wrong?" and receives the following answer: "No, it was I who did him wrong!"

Such ingratitude was the lot of Rosh Betar, Ze'ev Jabotinsky. Thus it was in his lifetime, and thus it is after his death.

But what matters this ingratitude compared with the immense love of tens of hundreds of thousands of our people for him, who paved for them the road to life and freedom!

What love! And what a full life did the Teacher live, who departed from us a quarter of a century ago!

Love. A full life. Now it is clear – only the lover is loved; only the faithful earns faithfulness; only the devoted earns devotion – and after his death, which is eternal life.

NB: This article was translated from the Hebrew by Joe Kuttner of Johannesburg, South Africa, for *"The Jewish Herald."* A leading journalist, he translated many more of Begin's articles and speeches some of which appear in this book. Joe Kuttner has since passed away and these remarks are a tribute to his great talent and ability.

Chapter 7

JABOTINSKY KNEW

How well did jabotinsky know Menachem Begin? Did he see in Begin characteristics that would one day be universally acclaimed?

When Begin joined Jabotinsky's movement, he was one of many thousands in Poland to do so. Jabotinsky traveled the length and breadth of Europe without rest, never in one place for more than a few days or a week.

How much contact could Jabotinsky have had with a young leader of the Betar youth movement? This question intrigued me. When Jabotinsky suffered his fatal heart attack in August 1940, could he have known that he had a brilliant, dynamic successor in the ranks, or did he fear that with him, the movement – already broken by the ravages of the war in Europe – might die too?

After the State of Israel was established, I was once told by our friend, the late Dr. Shimshon Yunitchman, that Jabotinsky had indeed known and recognized Menachem Begin's special qualities, and had singled him out for important leadership when he was still a young man.

According to Yunitchman, one of the leaders of the pre-war Betar in Poland, Begin had come to Jabotinsky's attention at the various national and international conferences of the Betar youth movement, in which he had already established a reputation as an activist, a forceful, logical speaker and something of a rebel.

In an article that he wrote in 1955, Yunitchman described an episode that occurred during one such conference in Cracow in January 1935, when Menachem Begin was not yet 22. It had been a particularly difficult conference; Jabotinsky felt sad and depressed as his young lieutenants questioned his attempts at finding an understanding with Ben Gurion and the Histadrut trade union in Eretz Israel. Jabotinsky confided in Yunitchman that he had hoped the Betar conference "would choose another who would stand at the head of our youth movement."

Yunitchman said in his article that he was "thunderstruck."

"Sir, how could you have entertained such a thought?" he asked. "How could we have chosen another – and in any case, does another leader exist?"

"Rosh Betar answered me quietly, with a smile on his lips," Yunitchman related.

"Yes, of course, there is another – and why didn't you choose him? He is young, the youngest amongst you. He was nurtured and grew up in this land [Poland] and he will continue to grow in stature for the future is his. He is worthy of the command and the command is worthy of him – I mean Begin!"

The Yunitchman revelation fascinated me, but I had not expected to hear confirmation from Menachem Begin himself. It was on one of his visits to South Africa. We were traveling by plane from Johannesburg to Port Elizabeth. He was reading the Bible and paused, looked at me and said with great feeling: "One day, if the Lord spares me, I want to find the time to write a book about Rosh Betar [Jabotinsky], Raziel [who preceded him as Irgun Commander], Yair [Stern – founder of Lechi] and others."

As he reminisced, I asked point blank: "Did Rosh Betar know you and, with his insight, did he realize that you would become Commander of the Irgun and his political successor?"

Menachem Begin actually blushed as he turned to me and answered: "Yes."

Then he told me the remarkable story that during another world Betar Conference Jabotinsky had asked him to accompany him on a ride in a droshke – a horse-drawn cab – and he instructed the driver to take them round and round the city. "We drove right through the night," Begin told me. "He discussed his plans and hopes and revealed some of his innermost feelings to me. And then he honored me by suggesting that I ought to prepare myself for leadership."

By that time Menachem Begin was visibly moved. Suddenly, he looked at me and said: "Now you are one of the few people who knows this story."

I felt that he would have wanted to change the subject, but he added one more thing: "When the war broke out and we were trapped in Europe, he was very worried about me, and tried desperately through the Red Cross to find me and get me out. I learned of this later – after his death."

Chapter 8

UPHILL STRUGGLE

WHEN, as he always put it, the foreign flag was lowered and the blue and white flag was raised to proclaim Israel's sovereignty, Menachem Begin emerged from the Underground to the acclaim of the nation. He had already made his mark and, had he chosen to retire then, his name would have remained fondly remembered in the annals of his people.

But that was only the beginning.

Together with his High Command comrades, he set about forming the Herut (Freedom) Party, which he led from then on right through to its dramatic election victory in 1977.

Menachem Begin's political and parliamentary career is a story of a long and difficult struggle in a society largely dominated by the Labor Party, most of whose members had long opposed the philosophy, policies and leaders of Jabotinsky's Zionist Revisionist movement. There were clearly two schools of thought – worlds apart – and one of them had to prevail. In fact, Labor had been in control of the Zionist Organization and the Yishuv (the Jewish community of Palestine) since the 27th World Zionist Congress in 1931.

At their first public appearances, the Irgun leaders attracted great interest. They were a novelty. For years, the nation had heard of them, but had never seen nor met them. Their public rallies were attended by large, enthusiastic crowds who, at once, acknowledged Menachem Begin as one of the country's most interesting and impressive orators. He became an instant draw.

But in the first Knesset election, Herut won only 14 of the 120 seats, while Labor took 46 and, as the largest party, was called upon to form the Government, choosing as coalition partners the Religious parties and the General Zionists.

Ben Gurion, who headed the provisional Government and the first elected Government, showed disdain for Herut. He remained resentful of the Irgun's defiance of Jewish Agency authority and, probably regretting his own miscalculations – perhaps even ashamed of the sordid "Altalena" affair – later declared his readiness to form a Government in Israel with anyone "except Herut and the Communists."

This vendetta against Jabotinsky's Revisionists became obsessive. Not only did Ben Gurion refuse to carry into effect Jabotinsky's Last Will and Testament but, for years, his Government actively discriminated against the former members of the Irgun and Lechi by refusing to recognize them as fighters for the State, and by denying them the benefits awarded to members of the Haganah. Even the families of the executed, fallen or wounded Underground fighters were denied financial assistance; their sustenance became the obligation of the newly-formed, impoverished Herut party. This "discrimination between blood and blood" caused much anguish to Begin and his friends, who campaigned vigorously against the policy until the injustice was corrected some seven years later.

Herut attacked the Government at all levels and on all issues – foreign policy, military strategy, economic programs, social and educational questions.

Over the years, Menachem Begin consciously strove to enhance the role and status of the "loyal Opposition" in Israel – critical, but always patriotic. State before class, nation above party. By doing this, he made an exceptional contribution to developing and strengthening democracy in Israel; this was later generally acknowledged.

In the second Knesset election, held in August 1951, Herut suffered a severe defeat, being reduced from 14 to 8 Knesset seats. I was in Israel at the time and know that the result affected Begin deeply, and that he seriously contemplated resigning from all his political offices to join a law firm. He had not expected this ingratitude from the nation so soon after the glorious Irgun struggle and victory.

But there were demographic explanations for this result, which did not imply that the country was rejecting either Begin or Herut. Mass immigration had brought hundreds of thousands of newcomers to the country from Iraq, Yemen and North Africa. They may have heard something about the Irgun and its leader, but it was Ben Gurion who had brought them to the Promised Land "on the wings of an eagle."

Moreover, the economy was already in a perilous state. The days of austerity had arrived. The Government was able to persuade a large part of the electorate that their only hope of moving from tent or tin hut towns to apartment blocks was by re-electing Labor to office. Some old-timers had even begun to long for the "fleshpots of Egypt," recalling the relative comfort and ease of the days of the British Mandate.

Cynics summed up the situation in the following joke:

QUESTION: Why did Herut get 14 seats in the first Knesset election in 1949?
ANSWER: Because they kicked out the British!
QUESTION: Why did Herut get only 8 seats in the second Knesset election in 1951?
ANSWER: Because they kicked out the British.

That was the last time Herut declined. In the 1955 election,

Herut recovered, rising from 8 to 15 seats. In retrospect we now know that was their turning point, from decline to ascendancy.

On that occasion, Menachem Begin telephoned me in Johannesburg to share the glad tidings. "People are dancing in the streets for joy," he said with great emotion in his voice.

Chapter 9

WIEDERGUTMACHUNG

The first years of the State of Israel were dominated by the national effort to complete the war, massive immigration, and Herut's fight to loosen the monopolistic hold of the Histadrut (Israel's principal labor union) on the economy of the country. In addition, an event occurred in 1952 which, because of the deep emotions it aroused, reverberated throughout the Jewish World.

Less than seven years after the end of the World War II – in which 6,000,000 Jews – 1.5 million of them children – were barbarically and systematically murdered in the most horrific genocide known to man, the Government of Israel and world Jewish leaders entered into negotiations with the Federal Republic of Germany, headed by Chancellor Adenauer, for the payment of reparations totaling us$600 million for the pain, suffering and loss of property endured by the Jewish people.

No other development inflamed feelings as this did. Protests mounted in Israel and abroad. Begin was in the vanguard of the opposition, vehemently denouncing this *Wiedergutmachung* (or "reparation"; literally, making good again) with a nation responsible for the destruction of one-third of the Jewish people. As Lord Shawcross, chief counsel for the prosecution for the United

Kingdom at the Nuremberg Trials, had said: "History holds no parallel to those horrors."

Begin cited the fact that a *cherem* (act of excommunication) still applied to Spain, some 460 years after the Inquisition. He rejected the argument that no reconciliation was implied in the acceptance of reparations. "You cannot have dealings with the murderer, accept money from him and continue to claim that you will never forgive him his crimes," he insisted.

He argued that Germany was ostracized and outcast by the world and was seeking acceptance into civilized society. "We Jews will pave the way for them by whitewashing their crimes. We will start with reparations; then our country will be flooded with German goods; then we will welcome German Ambassadors – and even have to listen to the German anthem being played here in Eretz Israel."

Throughout Israel huge protest rallies were held, in which tens of thousands of Holocaust survivors participated. Feelings were sharply divided. Families split between sentimentalists and pragmatists. By the time the agreement was to be debated in the Knesset, feelings had reached fever pitch and thousands converged on the Knesset in angry mood. Menachem Begin, who had become the symbol and spokesman of the anti-reparationists, addressed them outside the Knesset and then, as the stormy debates got underway in the Knesset Chamber, the emotion-charged crowd advanced on the Knesset building, pelting it with stones. There had never been anything like it before, nor has there been since. But then, the issue was unique in world and Jewish history.

The decision to enter into the agreement was ultimately accepted by the narrowest of majorities – 61 Knesset Members (including 5 Arabs) supported the Government. Fifty voted against, five abstained and four were absent. In other words, of the Jewish Knesset Members, 56 voted in favor, while 59 did not. Obviously, every vote counted; Begin's friend and lieutenant Aryeh Ben Eliezer was brought by ambulance from the hospital, where he was recovering from a heart attack, to cast his vote.

The pragmatists' victory turned out to be only a formal one. Though they now had the authority to proceed with the reparations agreement, the moral victory went to Begin when the world news media reported that the decision was taken "against widespread opposition in Israel." Begin felt that honor was at least partly redeemed, and that history would record that "this shameful decision," as he described it, had been taken only in the teeth of strong opposition. Over the years, the sum of German reparations payments increased and, indeed, the country was flooded by German goods. But economic experts remain divided to this day on the efficacy of this influx.

Matters relating to Germany surfaced several times more, including the arrival of that country's first Ambassador in Israel and the prospect of purchasing arms from Germany and of supplying Israeli weapons to them.

Wiedergutmachung, as Begin had predicted, led to bizarre circumstances.

Several years after the reparations episode, Begin made a public issue of the covered-up story that German scientists were building lethal rockets for Gamal Nasser, the Egyptian ruler. The subject caused a deep rift between Ben Gurion and the country's Chief of Intelligence, Isser Harel, who advocated urgent countermeasures and public exposure of this plot.

A fraction of the terrible anguish of the 1952 debate over German reparations was revived in 1961 when Israel kidnapped Adolph Eichman from Argentina and put him on trial in Jerusalem. It was one of the most sensational experiences of the post-war period, and the eyes of the world were focused on that man in the glass cage in the Jerusalem courtroom. The evidence given by survivors tore at the hearts of the nation; the younger generation, "that knew not

Pharaoh," was bewildered by the horrific details. In and outside the courtroom, I heard some of them ask the very questions that Begin had raised in his criticism of the Government at the time of the reparations agreement. "If such terrible things were done to us, how can we forgive them?" Others recalled the story of Amalek and of the Spanish Inquisition, but again, pragmatists argued that a new generation had grown up in Germany as well, and that it would be wrong to "visit the sins of the fathers upon the children." After months of examination, the court found Eichman guilty and sentenced him to death according to a law providing for the death penalty for war crimes against the Jewish people. Eichman was hanged, his body cremated and the ashes scattered into the sea.

Today, relations between Israel and Germany have normalized – too much, according to some. In the years immediately after the war, German authorities felt that the need for contrition dictated a special attitude towards the Jewish State. But in the early 1970s they felt free to discard "the special attitude." Having paid their debt in hard cash, they claimed they were under no further obligation to Israel or to world Jewry. In fact, part of the younger generation in Germany, refusing to accept responsibility and resenting the moral stigma of the reparations agreement, denies that the Holocaust ever happened.

Another result of this "normalization" is that Germany felt free to liaise with Israel's Arab enemies and to support their political demands if they so chose.

On a non-governmental level, neo-Nazis and other enemies of the Jews are responsible for Holocaust Revisionism – a world-wide publicity campaign devoted to denying that the Holocaust occurred and implying that it was a figment of Jewish imagination, if not a deliberate plot to gain world sympathy for Jewish Statehood after World War II.

Not surprisingly, these nefarious activities had financial backing from Arab elements seeking to undermine the Jewish State.

It suited them well. If they could prove that the Holocaust never occurred, they might convince the United Nations that Western support for the creation of the Jewish State had been extracted by false pretenses and should, therefore, be withdrawn. They tried, each year, to get the United Nations General Assembly to adopt a resolution that would have delegitimized Israel. Their attempts were unsuccessful. But in 1975, these elements, together with the Communist world, did succeed in getting the UN to adopt a Resolution equating Zionism with racism.

The neo-Nazi danger is not yet over; periodically, evidence surfaces of its presence and proliferation in Germany and elsewhere. With the reunification of Germany there has been a recrudescence of xenophobia against Jews and other foreigners, and vigorous efforts by the German authorities to stem this dangerous tide have been met with partial success at best.

Upon assuming the premiership, Menachem Begin faced some agonizing decisions. One of these was, of course, the attitude he should adopt towards West Germany, which had established normal diplomatic relations with Israel. Subduing his personal feelings to the national need, he announced that he would maintain relations in the correct manner. But he did not refrain from reminding the European states, and Germany in particular, of their special responsibilities to the Jewish people when these states came out in favor of an Arab Palestinian homeland. "Europe, whose rivers flow with Jewish blood, has no right to lecture Israel on matters which could involve its life and death and the safety of every woman, man and child in our country."

When he received the German Ambassador to Israel for the first time, he still refused press requests for photographs of the two together at the start of their meeting. Yet, according to aides, the talks were conducted "without any hint of tension."

Chapter 10

WARDING OFF AGGRESSION

When gamal abdel nasser took control of Egypt after Farouk's degenerate regime had been swept away, he commenced preparations for another round of war against Israel. As a first move, the operations of *fedayeen* (terrorists) were sharply stepped up. Day after day, night after night, they crossed at undefended points of Israel's long-winding borders, to attack kibbutzim, raze farmlands and strike at defenseless civilians traveling on isolated roads.

At the same time, Egypt was seeking superpower aid to build the High Aswan Dam. When the United States refused their request, Nasser turned to the Soviet Union, eagerly waiting in the wings. The thrust to the Mediterranean had been the ambition of Russian rulers before the Bolshevik Revolution and since. Now, using Nasser as their tool, they penetrated the Middle East and established their foothold in Africa. For such a prize they agreed to sell modern weapons to Egypt and help train and develop Egypt's armed forces.

After 1955, Israel's military position suddenly deteriorated. The number of *fedayeen* attacks increased, and the number of Israel's complaints to the United Nations rose proportionately.

The threat to the Jewish State had become very grave. Menachem Begin urged forceful action against the *fedayeen*, going

so far as to advocate a policy of "hot pursuit" (following the terrorists to their bases across the border or launching attacks at
Israel's discretion), and demanding that the Arab-Soviet menace
be broken by destroying their military capacity before it became
unmanageable.

In their search for an arms supplier other than the United
States – which had begun laying down conditions – Begin's Herut
turned to France, where they found a host of eager friends, a
friendly press and a distinctly anti-Arab, pro-Israel public which
recognized the common interests of the two countries.

France itself was embroiled in the Middle East with its Algerian
commitments, and it suited France well to support another active
anti-Arab factor. At first the Israeli Government reacted negatively
to Herut's political initiatives but, before long, saw the potential;
the Herut-sponsored France-Israel Alliance committees, which
had attracted some of France's most distinguished public figures,
eventually provided an opening for the Israeli Government's entry
into this field, and for strengthening the Franco-Israeli relationship
at the official level.

Soon, French weapons were reaching Israel to counter the
Soviet arsenal in Egypt. Israeli pilots were flying French Ouregan
and Mystere planes. Israeli gunners were using French artillery.
Hope was revived that the mortal threat to the Jewish State could be
averted; Begin now urged a preventive war. Quoting Churchill that
"to ward off aggression" a preemptive strike was an act of "legitimate
national self-defense," he called on the Government to act.

At first, Mapai and the Communists were horrified at the
thought and, denouncing him as a war monger, turned on him
ferociously. But they soon conceded the validity of his proposal and
adopted it as their own policy. Nasser was deploying considerable
forces in Sinai in a manner that indicated a calculated plan for aggression against Israel. He tightened the illegal Egyptian blockade
of the Suez Canal and arrested ships of other nations carrying

cargo to or from Israel. Egyptian guns were mounted on the two tiny rock islands commanding the entrance to the Straits of Eilat, and also threatening Israel's air route to South Africa.

And so, on 29 October 1956, in response to mounting aggression and provocation, the Israeli Army, under the command of Moshe Dayan, crossed into Sinai and swept through the desert, thrusting towards the Suez Canal, which they reached within 100 hours, smashing all Egyptian military installations in their way. "Operation Kadesh," as this Sinai campaign was code-named, was a brilliant military success. Egypt's aggressive designs were thwarted and its Soviet arms humiliated.

In collusion with Israel, Britain and France intervened at a critical moment by sending a joint force to separate the combatants at Suez and impose a cease-fire. Within a few days, U.S. President Eisenhower and his Secretary-of-State John Foster Dulles demanded Israel's withdrawal from the Suez and Sinai.

Prime Minister Ben Gurion for the first time invited the Opposition leader, Menachem Begin, to his home and, after briefing him fully on developments, requested – and was immediately given – the Opposition's full backing and blessing for what was to come.

In a democracy, such inter-party consultation is perfectly normal. Certainly, in times of war, there is a readiness for bipartisan foreign and military policy. But in Israel this was a most extraordinary occurrence because of the strained relationship between the Government and Opposition, dating virtually from the birth of the State. Ben Gurion wanted nothing to do with his main political rival, and actively sought to undermine and ostracize him. He hardly ever spoke to Begin, and even when necessity obliged him to refer to him in the Knesset, he refused to mention Begin's name or title, but described him as "that man sitting next to Knesset Member Bader." Most times when Begin rose to address the Knesset, Ben Gurion would demonstratively walk out.

It was, therefore, quite clear that something unusual was happening when Ben Gurion initiated these discussions with Begin, who responded without any trace of malice.

The idyllic situation was short-lived. At the first signs of American pressure and Soviet threats, Ben Gurion caved in, it being "officially rumored" that he had been influenced by the tone and contents of a letter from Bulganin of the Soviet Union and the recall of the Soviet Ambassador. In his subsequent "Diary of the Sinai Campaign," Dayan, Chief of Staff of the victorious Israel Army and a great admirer of Ben Gurion, set out to show post factum that he had not panicked. "Ben Gurion did not hide his deep concern over the Soviet stand, nor did he seek to ignore the full gravity of its significance; but his reaction was not a trembling at the knees. He was not seized with panic. On the contrary, the emotional effect of the Soviet ultimatum was to spur him to struggle." And yet, at the time, the Russian threat was advanced as the cause for the Israel Government's capitulation.

Menachem Begin was infuriated by Ben Gurion's hasty action and accused him of a breach of undertaking. Begin was off to the United States in an attempt to mobilize public opinion for Israel's stand and, before leaving, visited Ben Gurion, who assured him that nothing would change during his absence from the country. However, while in New York, Begin learnt, to his astonishment, of Ben Gurion's announcement that Israel's forces would be pulled out of Sinai and Gaza. Rushing back, he undertook country-wide public activities to mobilize the nation against the Government's retreat.

As a visitor to Israel at the time, I saw Menachem Begin in a new role. No longer merely the leader of a Party, Begin had become a powerful national figure around whom hundreds of thousands of citizens – including a large part of the Army – were rallying.

Standing in the midst of large crowds at huge outdoor protest rallies – such as the one in Tel Aviv's Mograbi Square, which attracted some 50,000 people – I could sense the spellbinding effect of Begin's oratory and his rapport with the masses, who chanted *"Aza shelanu – Begin lashilton!"* ("Gaza is ours – Begin to the Government!"). This may well have been the beginning of his emergence as the populist leader, as Israel's strongman, a symbol of belief and hope.

Nine years later, in October 1965, former U.S. President Dwight D. Eisenhower told Max Fisher, the doyen of American Jewish leaders, who came to visit him in Gettysburg: "You know, Max, looking back at Suez, I regret what I did. I never should have pressured Israel to evacuate the Sinai."

Another former President, Richard Nixon, confirmed this fact. "Eisenhower told me many years later – in the 1960s – and I'm sure he told others – that the action that was taken [at Suez] was one he regretted. He thought it was a mistake."*

A mistake. Yes, even presidents of the United States are capable of committing grave blunders that can cost small nations, like Israel, decades of hardship and danger. But we now know that Israel's Prime Minister at the time, too, blundered by submitting to pressure, even from the country's closest ally.

---

* From *Quiet Diplomat*, the biography of Max Fisher by Peter Golden.

Chapter 11

THE SIX-DAY WAR

ANOTHER TEN YEARS were to pass before the flag of Israel again flew over Gaza.

Egypt, recovered from its defeat in the Sinai campaign, its arms more than replaced by the Soviet Union, renewed their threats against Israel's existence. In May 1967, the Arab countries neighboring the Jewish State coordinated their strategy and placed their military forces under unified command – always a signal that they intended to make war without provocation. Nasser again tightened the blockade on the Suez Canal and demanded the immediate withdrawal of the United Nations' force from Egyptian territory; this was accompanied by increasing anti-Israeli rhetoric in Cairo and Damascus. As emotions in Arab countries were whipped into a frenzy, huge Egyptian forces advanced in Sinai, and the Syrians mobilized their troops on the Golan Range.

The signals were unmistakable for Israel: another war. The reserves were called up and sent to the fronts. Levi Eshkol's Government was cautious, and set about exploring diplomatic channels to relieve the danger. At the time of the withdrawal from Suez and Sharm-el-Sheikh in 1956, the United States had guaranteed free passage through the Suez Canal. Now the U.S. appeared unwilling and proposed without conviction an international naval task force to clear the waterway. It was an abortive plan.

Israel faced a painful choice, understandably reluctant to become involved in another war and afraid of preempting it. But, while trying to arrive at a decision, the Government learnt that Nasser was planning to attack.

Israel's Army, meanwhile, was "eating sand," as the soldiers put it – waiting in the desert, listening to the threats from Cairo on their transistor radios and hearing of the indecisiveness at home. Morale fell as fears were expressed about the mortal danger to the Jewish State.

Begin broke the silence and indecisiveness by urging Prime Minister Eshkol to wrest the initiative from the Arabs and, in view of the grave national crisis, he proposed the creation of a Government of National Unity. Then, in a remarkable act of patriotism, Begin visited his old opponent, Ben Gurion – now living in retirement in his Sde Boker desert retreat – to suggest that he come back to the Premiership. He then proposed to Eshkol that he resign as Prime Minister in Ben Gurion's favor or, alternatively, that there be two Prime Ministers: one for foreign affairs (Ben Gurion) and the other for domestic matters (Eshkol).

After briefly pondering the proposition, Eshkol (himself a victim of Ben Gurion's animosity) replied: "As far as I am concerned, these two horses can no longer pull the same cart together." However, he did agree to the proposal for a Government of National Unity – which had become a popular cry in the nation – and to resign as Defense Minister in favor of Moshe Dayan. Menachem Begin and Yosef Sapir, his colleague in the Herut-Liberal Bloc, were invited to join the Cabinet along with Dayan.

The announcement had an electrifying effect in Israel. Morale improved overnight. The soldiers at the front responded warmly to this stiffening of national resolve as a stronger, more resolute leadership took the helm.

On the morning of 5 June the Israeli armed forces went into action. In a brilliant surprise move, the Air Force, under the command of General "Mottie" Hod, attacked the air forces of Egypt, Syria and Jordan, rendering them completely inoperative. With the full advantage of unchallenged air cover, Israel's ground forces advanced swiftly through Gaza to the Suez Canal and Sharm-el-Sheikh.

Jordan's King Hussein at first hesitated, but then, having been persuaded by Arab propaganda and by private assurances from Nasser that victory was inevitable, ordered his troops to move forward to attack. On Monday night, his artillery began to shell Jerusalem. This was Israel's hour of opportunity. To defend her territory and repel the attack, her forces advanced into areas Jordan had occupied for 19 years, sweeping to victory in Judea and Samaria, entering Bethlehem, Jericho, Shechem (Nablus) and Hebron. On the morning of 7 June 1967, the Old City of Jerusalem was liberated by a paratroop unit.

Only when that was safely in hand did Israel turn her attention to the third front: the Golan Heights, from which the Syrians had, for years, been shelling the Israeli kibbutzim in the valley below. This was the most difficult part of the war. As the Air Force pounded the Syrian bunkers, Israeli units ascended the steep, rocky mountain range and overwhelmed the Syrians in difficult hand-to-hand combat for every trench, pillbox and bunker.

Though the days passed with painful slowness, it was all over in six days. Israel's sons proved themselves, as their glorious ancestors, "swifter than eagles and stronger than lions." Israel emerged with 700 casualties and 2,000 wounded – and also with a nation transformed and a radically altered geopolitical position.

The crowning achievement of the war was the liberation of Jerusalem, which had been under enemy occupation for 19 years and from which the Jewish people had been expelled 1,900 years earlier.

"We have returned, never to be separated again," said Moshe Dayan on his first visit to the Western Wall.

Menachem Begin played a significant role in the war and its outcome. When he entered the Cabinet he learnt of the military plans, which he regarded as inadequate, and he sought an immediate reappraisal.

He helped shape the course of the war and the country's political posture in the face of superpower pressure and threats. Once again the Soviet Union saw her arms destroyed and humiliated. The United States was nervous and General De Gaulle haughty because Israel had not heeded his advice and warning against a preemptive strike. Begin's role stiffened Israel's back and strengthened her leaders' spirit. Above all, he influenced the decision to liberate Jerusalem and, to some extent also, the Golan. The story of the liberation of Jerusalem has been told and should be recorded again.

From the first day of the war, Begin felt that it was time to achieve Jerusalem's liberation. He went quietly from Minister to Minister, urging them to vote for a proposal that would come before the Cabinet on the first evening of the war, resolving that Israel would advance on the Old City. Yigal Allon was in complete agreement with Begin, and both sought to make the liberation of the Old City one of the war's principal aims.

Thirty-six hours later, the decision could no longer be delayed; a new and pressing factor was introduced into the debate.

It had been Menachem Begin's custom to rise at 5 AM each day to listen to the radio (local and foreign stations) and read the newspapers. In the early hours of the morning on 7 June 1967, while listening to the BBC, he learnt that, minutes earlier in New York (it was 11 PM of the previous day there), the UN Security Council had called for an immediate cease-fire. Begin knew instinctively that if it were carried into effect, the war would be half-finished again, and Israel would lose the opportunity to liberate Jerusalem.

Begin telephoned Prime Minister Eshkol, reported what he

had heard and urged immediate action for the liberation of Jerusalem. Eshkol did not require much persuasion. "I agree," he said. "Speak to Dayan. If he agrees, we shall go ahead." Begin did as requested; within minutes the two reached agreement.

At 7:30 that morning the IDF senior staff met. Dayan reported that Hussein's forces had brought up a unit of Patton tanks and had concentrated additional forces. The battle would be difficult. Many were being injured. The deputy chief of staff was on the spot to expedite the capture of the city.

At 9 o'clock the Prime Minister called a special session at which the question on the agenda was: Should the encirclement continue, or should forces break into the Old City and compel its immediate surrender? At 9:40 an air-raid alarm was heard. The discussion was interrupted and the Ministers descended into the bomb shelter. When the all-clear sounded, the discussion was resumed, and it was decided that the troops would enter the site of the Temple through the Lion's Gate, that the mosques would not be touched, and that all holy places would be safeguarded. In the midst of the discussion, Dayan received an urgent telephone call; a few minutes later he returned to announce: "The Old City is in our hands."

It was only after the Israel forces had liberated Jerusalem, taken control of Judea and Samaria and conquered the Golan Heights that the Government of National Unity agreed to a general cease-fire.

From that point on, Menachem Begin saw it as his task to protect the liberated areas from foreign pressure and internal weakening. First and foremost, Jerusalem had to be secured. He advocated, as an initial step, that the Old City be incorporated within the Jewish State. This was a complex problem; there were differences of opinions, fears, dismal warnings about what the major world powers might do and how the Christian world would react. But Begin stood his ground and, towards the end of June, the Government of Israel published a policy declaration in Jerusalem and at the United Nations saying that Jerusalem must be a unified city. Begin opposed an original draft that gave only technical and administrative convenience as the reason for this historic step; he suggested wording for the final official statement, which spoke in moving terms of the 1,900-year Jewish longing for the return to the Old City, of the efforts and sacrifices that were made over the centuries for this goal and of the fervent prayers of generations that were inextricably bound up with Jerusalem.

On his first visit to the Western Wall in the Old City, Begin, accompanied by the leaders of Herut and former commanders of the Irgun, recited the following prayer, which he had written for the occasion:

> God of our fathers Abraham, Isaac and Jacob, Lord of Hosts, be Thou our help. Our enemies encompassed us about, yea they encompassed us about and arose to destroy us as a people. Yet has their counsel been destroyed and their schemes will not be accomplished. For there has arisen in our Homeland a new generation of warriors and heroes. And when they went forth to engage the enemy there burst forth from their hearts the call which echoes throughout the generations, the call from the father of the Prophets, the redeemer of Israel from the bondage of Egypt: Arise, O Lord, and let Thine enemies be scattered and let them that hate Thee be put to flight.
>
> And we scattered and defeated them and flee they did.
>
> The defeated enemy has not yet laid down his arms.
>
> The Army of Israel continues to pursue and smite them.
>
> Lord, God of Israel, guard Thou our forces who with their arms are forging the covenant which Thou didst make with Thy chosen people. May they return in peace, children to their parents, fathers to their children and husbands to their wives. For we are but the surviving remnant of a people harried and persecuted, whose blood has been shed like water throughout the generations.

Today we stand before the Western Wall, the relic of the House of our Glory, in Jerusalem, the Redeemed, the City that is now all compact together, and from the depths of our hearts there arises the prayer that the Temple may be rebuilt speedily in our days.

We shall yet come to Hebron, the city of the Four Couples, and there we shall prostrate ourselves at the graves of the Patriarchs of our people. We shall yet be on the way to Ephrath as thou comest to Bethlehem of Judah. We shall pray at the Tomb of Rachel and we shall bring to mind the prayer of the prophet: "A voice is heard in Ramah, wailing and bitter lamentation, Rachel weeping for her children, she refuseth to be comforted for her children, for they are not. Refrain thy voice from weeping and thine eyes from tears, for there is a reward for thy labor, saith the Lord, and they shall return from the land of the enemy. And there is hope for thy latter end, and thy children shall return to their borders.

From the June War on, all the Zionist parties in Israel, on both the left and the right, went on record as saying: "whatever future peace treaty, Jerusalem will never be given up."

However, there was no similar consensus regarding Judea, Samaria, Gaza and the Golan, which some regarded as expendable.

Like Ze'ev Jabotinsky before him, Menachem Begin became the proponent of the belief in the Jewish people's inalienable right to all of Eretz Israel. He had given expression to that simple belief in his historic broadcast to the nation at the end of the Underground war, and consistently adhered to it throughout his life.

This was not a blind loyalty to an old doctrinaire concept for its own sake, but Begin's unreserved and genuine acceptance of the Divine Promise to His people, from which there can be no deviation. The Jewish people had been driven out of their land but remained faithful to it in their prayers, yearnings and aspirations. Moreover, in recent generations that right was accepted by the civilized world, which accorded it the necessary international and legal recognition. In addition, he explained, practical experience from 1948 to 1967 had shown that the former borders of Israel were indefensible, and that the retention of Judea, Samaria, Golan and Gaza was a matter of basic security for the country.

Begin served as a member of the Government from the first days of June 1967 to the first days of August 1970 – 37 months. Within that period his friend, Levi Eshkol, died, and he was succeeded as Prime Minister by Golda Meir. An election was held on 28 October 1969, giving Gahal (the Herut-Liberal Bloc) 26 Knesset seats and 6 Cabinet Ministers in the Government that Mrs. Meir created. Begin and Sapir were now joined by Haim Landau as Minister of Development and Ezer Weizman – former Commander of the Israel Air Force – as Minister of Transport (both of Herut), and Arye Dulzin (Minister Without Portfolio) and Elimelech Rimalt (Minister of Posts and Communication), both of the Liberal Party.

This coalition was short-lived. American pressure on Israel mounted. At the height of the War of Attrition, the U.S. demanded compliance with Security Council Resolution 242, which in its preamble emphasized "the inadmissibility of the acquisition of territory by war." U.S. Secretary of State William Rogers pressed for his plan requiring prior acceptance by Israel of the principle of withdrawal from the "occupied" territories.

Menachem Begin would not concede this principle nor be party to any such decision and, therefore, declared his intention of resigning from the Cabinet. To save the Coalition, various compromises were proposed, including an offer by Pinhas Sapir (Minister of Finance) that Begin and his Gahal Ministers be given the right to vote against the proposal in the Cabinet and Knesset, where the required majority would, nevertheless, approve the Rogers principle. The suggestion was firmly rejected. "That would be dishonest," Begin said. "If we are part of a Government we must accept our full share of Cabinet responsibility. If we are unable to do so, we have no place in such a Government."

The issue was painful for Begin. He was standing firm on principle. Gahal was divided. Even his own Herut Party was split on the question, and when the matter was eventually brought to a vote at a joint meeting of the Councils of the two parties (Herut and Liberal), Begin's view secured only the narrowest majority. I was with him that night and heard him say that, in a democracy, a majority of one was sufficient to express a movement's or a parliament's will.

The next morning he tendered his resignation from the Government, with his Gahal fellow-ministers following suit – some of them most reluctantly.

It was the first time in Israel's history that a Minister had voluntarily resigned his seat on a matter of principle. Even critics agreed that Menachem Begin had displayed consistency and had given a rare example of political integrity.

By his unique stand on principle, Begin may well have prevented or, at least, delayed the return of any portion of liberated Eretz Israel. He had become the conscience of the nation. Were he not there – had he not made the right to the land a matter of high national principle, the previous Labor Government would have felt free to negotiate the surrender of territory in their mistaken belief that, by doing so, they could achieve peace. They had to be reminded periodically that, in 1967, Israel did not hold the so-called "occupied territories" – Nasser was in Sinai and Gaza, the Syrians commanded the Golan and Hussein ruled in Jerusalem, Judea and Samaria. So what were these Arab nations' true plans? To liberate the "occupied areas," or simply to attempt Israel's destruction yet again?

Begin always distinguished between land that was conquered in the war and liberated parts of ancient Eretz Israel; the latter was land to which the Jewish people had an inalienable right and which would, therefore, not again be returned to foreign rule, not even when, one day, there was a prospect for real peace.

Chapter 12

THE YOM KIPPUR WAR

BEGIN WAS SUMMONED FROM THE SYNAGOGUE where he was at prayer on Yom Kippur, 1973, with the news that the Prime Minister wanted to see him at once. He immediately realized that something of the gravest nature had occurred, and that Israel faced peril once more. Like everyone else in Israel, he was stunned but, acting with characteristic responsibility and patriotism, refrained from comment and criticism in the first tragic and crucial days of the war. Only when the enemy was stopped did he rise in the Knesset and, as Churchill had done in the Commons in 1939, demand to know what had gone wrong and warn that those responsible would be held accountable.

At the same time, he pledged the total support of the Opposition for the war effort. A week later, when the initiative had passed to the Israelis on both fronts (Egypt and Syria) and the magnificent Israeli Army had transformed the enemies' advance into a rout, Begin demanded explanations. As he was then being kept informed by the Prime Minister on military and political developments, he argued against the Government's decisions – especially the one accepting the Russian-dictated cease-fire when Israel's Army was approaching Cairo and Damascus and the Egyptian Third Army was encircled and trapped after the daring and brilliant strategic maneuver directed by General "Arik" Sharon. He was particularly incensed that Israel had not even been consulted about the text and nature of the cease-fire proposals, but merely instructed to accept them. Again he endeavored to strengthen Israel's resistance to U.S. pressure – this time from Kissinger – but to no avail. The Government was still suffering from the Yom Kippur trauma, and declared its readiness to withdraw – as Ben Gurion had done in 1956 – and even to yield some of the fruits of the 1967 victory.

Eventually, the Suez Canal was handed back to Egypt. On the Syrian front, Israel's forces were withdrawn from the outskirts of Damascus, and later Kuneitra was handed back to the Syrians. This was one of the rare examples in history when an aggressor – who had set out to destroy his neighbor – was rewarded in order, as Kissinger put it, that the aggressor's honor be restored!

Now the political struggle for Israel's right to the ancient Land began in earnest. Begin, his colleagues and his followers in Israel and throughout the world worked unceasingly to enlighten, to explain that Israel was not bent on expansionism, but that her claim to the Land was just and righteous, that it had been recognized internationally and that it was indispensable for the nation's security.

Whenever I was with Menachem Begin in the Members' Restaurant in the Knesset, he took his usual table next to a window through which one could see the Hills of Jerusalem. He used to dine at that table with visiting senators, congressmen and parliamentarians from all over the world. When explaining Israel's circumstances, he always asked them to look through the window at a nearby hill, on which, before 1967, the enemies' guns were directed at the Knesset building.

"Do you expect us to give that hill back to the enemy?" he asked his guests. "Would you agree to have Soviet guns stationed a few kilometers from Capitol Hill in Washington?" he asked an American Senator. "No, no," came the instant reply. "Then why do you expect us to sacrifice our security and endanger our future?" he asked. Usually there was no answer.

On a visit to the United States he explained to Zbigniew Bzrezinski, President Carter's National Security Adviser, other prominent personalities and the news media that the creation of a Palestinian State on Israel's eastern border within rocket range of Jerusalem, Tel Aviv, Netanya and Petach Tikvah would not only threaten the existence of Israel, but also introduce a Soviet base into the heart of the Middle East, thus endangering the whole Western world.

Chapter 13

SOVIET JEWRY

THE YOM KIPPUR WAR produced grave and far-reaching consequences. Nearly 3,000 Israeli soldiers were killed – many of them youngsters; thousands more were wounded and maimed. These losses almost broke the nation's spirit. Israel had never experienced anything like it before. For the first time, the quality and capacity of Israel's army was questioned. The political leadership had blundered, and the nation paid a terrible price. Later, in her autobiography, Golda Meir, who as Prime Minister bore the main responsibility, admitted that she should have listened to the warnings of her heart and ordered an early mobilization.

> For me, that fact cannot and never will be erased, and there can be no consolation in anything that anyone else has to say or in all of the common-sense rationalizations with which my colleagues have tried to comfort me.
>
> It doesn't matter what logic dictated. It matters only that I, who was so accustomed to making decisions, failed to make that one decision.
>
> But I know that I should have done so, and I shall live with that terrible knowledge for the rest of my life. I will never again be the person I was before the Yom Kippur War.

Menachem Begin was at great pains to reassure the nation that there was little wrong with the Israeli Army, which had proved its caliber after the first week when, by sheer guts, improvisation and ingenuity, the men turned the tide of battle and went on to achieve one of the greatest military victories in the country's 25-year history.

A by-product of this blunder was a sharp decline in investment, in tourism and in *aliyah* (immigration) – including the blessed flow from the Soviet Union.

This *aliyah* from the Soviet Union was one of the most exciting developments of modern Israel. After at least two generations of Communist rule and indoctrination, a large part of the Jews of the Soviet Union still retained a spark – and often much more – of Jewish consciousness. Led by Zionist activists, they began to demand the right to emigrate to their ancestral home or to be reunited with their family there. Following the Six-Day War of June 1967, the trickle of Soviet Jews emigrating from the U.S.S.R. swelled to the proportions of a flood.

For years, Zionist activists had nurtured this spark of Jewish nationalism by, among other things, distributing handwritten copies of Zionist literature, including naturally the writings of Jabotinsky, and especially the famous feuilletons that he had written in Russian at the turn of the century.

In the years between Israel's last two wars, the struggle of and for Soviet Jewry became one of the nation's dominant themes. For obvious reasons, Menachem Begin was always in the forefront of the campaign for Soviet Jewry. After all, he had experienced Soviet rule and oppression. Two factors guided him: the urgent need to rescue the Soviet Jewish community and the fact that Soviet Jews constituted a vital source of *aliyah*.

Therefore, he and his movement gave impetus to the "Let My People Go" campaign. Begin frequently traveled abroad to meet with statesmen, to address large rallies, to explain through the various media what was involved in this great struggle and to mobilize Jewish communities for it.

He used to tell me: "We have great influence in the United States, and we must use it. If only our people had used that power in 1939, we might have prevented the Destruction. This time we must not fail."

When the first Conference on Soviet Jewry was held in Brussels in 1971, Begin was one of the principal speakers. I witnessed the spellbinding effect of his message on the large assembly. We subsequently learnt that it inspired the Jews behind the Iron Curtain, reverberated through the West and gave added impetus to the struggle. In a particularly moving passage, Begin struck out at the evil of the Soviet bureaucratic machine:

> Our generation witnessed the renewal of Jewish heroism – in the continuous endangering of personal freedom and life in the Underground, on the battlefield, in the prisons, in the concentration camps, in the purple garb of those in the death cell and in the long march to the gallows.
>
> Is there a heroism higher than these? We dare not reply too hastily to that question – for not all the trials are behind the heroes, the fighters for Zion, who are still in the U.S.S.R. Even today we may say that we are standing before a new peak of renascent Jewish heroism.
>
> Even we who fought, the few against the many, acknowledge that far more difficult than our way is that of those who are fighting in Communist Russia, without arms, for Zion.
>
> They are not only the few against the many. They are the few to stand against the NKVD – and they stand up against it even when they sit in jail. The Soviet secret police has many names – Cheka, NKVD, MVD, KGB…but it has one essence: machinery of oppression. Stalin called his agents engineers of souls. They break bodies to destroy souls. They crush souls

to make a man a non-man. There is no depth to which this machine, the most terrible on earth after the Gestapo, cannot descend to achieve its purpose.

Against all this, our brethren stand – young fighters overcoming the terror which is without comparison on earth. It is possible to say, without the slightest exaggeration, that in our day they are the bravest of all of those fighting for human freedom and dignity.

In the name of those who fought in days gone by in Eretz Israel, may I be permitted to say to you from far and near: We bow our heads before you, our brothers, heroes of the revival.

Later he referred to the story of Sylvia Zalmanson, the young woman who, with her brothers and husband, Eduard Kuznetsov, was sentenced to a long term of imprisonment by a Leningrad court. When sentence was pronounced against her she rose and proclaimed in Hebrew the imperishable words: "If I forget thee O Jerusalem, may my right hand wither…" This provoked the judge, who reprimanded her with great irritation and declared that foreign languages were not permitted in a Soviet court, whereupon the young heroine translated her proclamation into Russian.

"That was heroism of the highest order," Menachem Begin declared. "We know from our history that when Jews are ready for Kiddush Hashem, they may not yet be victorious, but they become invincible."

Menachem Begin (center) with his parents and sister, Rachel, and brother Herzl.

Menachem Begin standing at the left of Ze'ev Jabotinsky as he reviews members of Betar, Pinsk, 1933.

Menachem Begin as "Rabbi Sassover" with his wife,
Aliza and son Benjamin.

Honoring the flag of the Irgun Zvai Leumi at Menachem Begin's
first public appearance after the underground struggle
of more than four years.

As Jona Konigshoffer, a Tel Aviv bookkeeper.

Eytan Belkind, one of the survivors of the World War I
spy ring NILI, Rivka Aronson, sister of Sarah Aronson of NILI
fame and Mrs. Helen Friedman, sister of Dov Gruner.

With Reb Arye Levin, the beloved, saintly rabbi
of the prisoners of the Underground forces in
the days of the Revolt.

A rare luncheon – David Ben Gurion,
Ezer Weizman, Menachem Begin.

Carrying the caskets of Ze'ev and Johanna Jabotinsky.
The front bearers are Zvi Propes, Menachem Begin,
Aizik Remba and Aryeh Ben Eliezer.

Begin (right) with Prime Minister Levi Eshkol (center) in the
Sinai during the Six Day War, June 1967.

Prime Minister Begin with his long-time friends from
South Africa, Freda and Harry Hurwitz.

Menachem Begin at the Kotel reciting a special prayer before
he presented the government to the Knesset.

Menachem Begin speaking in the main synagogue of Bucharest, Rumania, during his important visit to that country. His meeting with the Jewish community was an emotional experience for them – and for him.

Prime Minister Begin bows in tribute to the Standards of Israel, as he is about to leave for the United States.

Prime Minister Begin receiving the blessing of the Lubavitcher
Rebbe in New York prior to his visit to Washington
to meet President Jimmy Carter.

At the White House ceremony where the Peace Treaty
between Israel and Egypt was signed.

Rosalyn and Jimmy Carter and Aliza and Menachem Begin
at a private dinner in the Prime Minister's official
residence in Jerusalem.

Prime Minister Begin's welcome on the US aircraft carrier,
the Eisenhower.

During a visit to Aswan for three days of talks with
Anwar Sadat, Begin visits Luxor.

In London, reviewing the Grenadier Guards.

Begin and Barbara Walters during one of their several
television interviews.

Taking the call from Oslo in his office when he was advised
that he had been awarded the 1978 Nobel Prize for Peace
together with President Sadat.

Receiving the Nobel Peace Prize medal from the chairperson
of the Nobel Committee.

In Egypt, at the funeral of President Sadat. Because it was Shabbat, Menachem Begin walked to the burial place from the hotel where he stayed. Ariel Sharon and Yitzhak Shamir are nearby to his left.

Watching the Israeli Army in action.

With Chief-of-Staff General Rafael Eytan at the air base where
Begin honored the pilots who participated in the strike at Osiraq.
(One of the pilots was Ilan Ramon, Israel's first astronaut
who perished in the Columbia disaster.)

Begin arrived in Washington to meet President Reagan soon
after he underwent a leg operation.

Menachem and Aliza Begin with their children and grandchildren, 1982.

Announcing his resignation as Prime Minister to his government colleagues.

Menachem Begin heard the news of Aliza's death while he was in the USA. He at once flew back and led mourners at her funeral. He is pictured here with his daughter, Leah.

The fresh grave of Menachem Begin on the Mount of Olives next to that of Aliza and, in front, the graves of Moshe Barazani and Meir Feinstein.

Chapter 14

EARTHQUAKE

MENACHEM BEGIN'S MOMENT OF DESTINY came in the early hours of Wednesday, 18 May 1977, when it was certain that Likud had emerged as the leading party in the election to the ninth Knesset and would, therefore, be called upon to form the next Government of Israel.

The polling stations closed at 11 PM. Within minutes an Israel television computer team that had polled the voters announced its result: Likud would win; Labor was to suffer a heavy loss.

At midnight I heard the BBC report that "an unofficial prediction by Israel Television showed a shock result in today's parliamentary election. The ruling Labor Party has lost a substantial number of votes, and the right-wing Opposition Likud had gained sufficient seats to enable it to establish the next Government."

Why "shock result"? Is it not the essence of British parliamentary democracy that an opposition party can win control of the government in a popular election?

The reaction among the traditional opponents of Jabotinsky's Revisionist movement was similarly confused and hysterical; they were flabbergasted, dismayed, stunned. Golda Meir called the result "a catastrophe."

She was implying, of course, that it was a tragedy for the people of Israel. But it was apparent from their mournful expressions that it was a catastrophe primarily for those in Israel's Labor establishment who had held power for so many years, who had borne out Lord Acton's profound statement that "power corrupts and absolute power corrupts absolutely."

The attitude of the so-called democrats – who preached democracy for all the world but could not tolerate it in Israel – was amusing and bemusing. It appeared as if they actually believed that the Socialists were born to rule Israel forever, or that the country was their private domain.

When the initial shock wore off, the second reaction set in: "It was an accident."

A subsequent scientific survey of the result of the election on 17 May proved conclusively that this was no accident, but the genuine expression of the will of the people of Israel. Likud emerged as the front-runner party in every major city of the country – in Jerusalem, Tel Aviv, Ramat Gan, Beersheba, Bat Yam, even "red" Haifa – all told, in 95% of the towns and villages of Israel. It commanded the most votes among the younger generation and was supported by 50% of the men in the armed forces.

No, there was nothing gratuitous in the dramatic success of Likud. It was the result of an inevitable historic process. One of the documents prepared by the Likud publicity people was a graph showing the steady decline of Labor's popularity from the first election in 1949 until the one in 1973, and the relative and steady rise of the forces now constituting Likud.

In retrospect, Begin's patience and astute political strategy was recognized. Of course, he would have preferred his own Herut party to gain sufficient electoral support to constitute a government on its own – but as a realist he knew this was not possible, or at best would take a long, long time. He therefore worked assiduously to consolidate the opposition forces.

In the early 1960s he initiated discussions with the General

Zionists (later to be known as the Liberals) with a view to forming a parliamentary alliance. At first they shunned his overtures.
The General Zionists were regarded as a "respectable" group. How
could they align themselves with Begin and his Herut extremists?
People were leaving Herut, they argued, not joining it.

But soon, the validity and logic of Begin's initiative began to
make sense. They, too, had little prospect of ever becoming the
principal factor around which a Government would be constituted.

A number of prominent General Zionists accepted the Herut
leader's thesis and promoted the idea within their party. The
negotiations, which Begin led personally, were complicated and
protracted, but eventually bore fruit when, in 1965, Gahal (Gush
Herut-Liberalim – the Herut-Liberal bloc) came into being with
Menachem Begin as the chosen leader of a parliamentary alliance
comprising 26 Knesset Members.

At first the two factions eyed each other suspiciously and
trod warily. They disagreed on the fundamental issue of the Jewish people's right to all of the ancient land. In fact, the preamble
of Gahal's first political manifesto emphasized that difference by
stating that the two parties had agreed to form a Parliamentary
Bloc as the alternative to the Mapai (Labor) regime, and that
"Herut continued to adhere to the view that the Jewish People had
an inalienable right to the Land." In all other matters of internal,
economic and social policy there was identity of interests between
them. They differed only on the territorial question.

However, as the years went by, the lines of differentiation
between the two partners grew dimmer. With his compelling personality, Begin emerged as the authoritative leader and dominant
figure of the Bloc, and he succeeded in holding the various factions
together even in times of great strain (such as in the mid-1970s,
when he pressed for Gahal's withdrawal from the Government).
While he could rely on the backing of the bulk of his own Herut

Party, he faced the solid opposition of the Liberal Party Council, with only a few of its members supporting his stand on principle. Yet, when the decision was taken by the narrowest majority, the Liberals avoided all temptation and pressures to break the alliance with Herut.

In the wake of the Six-Day War, they even dropped their opposition to Herut's "Land of Israel" policy, and henceforth Gahal acted in every way as a unified political party, even though its two wings continued to maintain their separate identities and administrations.

It did not go unnoticed in Israel and among opinion-makers abroad that the policy of Herut had attracted and convinced the leaders and members of an entire Party and had gained many adherents in other sections of the nation as well. Begin's Herut was no longer the political outcast but, in fact, was rapidly becoming the center of a large and growing political formation.

After the Six-Day War, Gahal also found support among influential elements of the Labor movement. The liberation of Jerusalem and other parts of Eretz Israel inspired Israelis from all walks of life and all shades of political opinion. Tens of thousands re-discovered their new/ancient land and fell in love with it all over again. To many it was simply inconceivable that any portion of it should be returned to the enemy or be sacrificed to political expediency.

A new multi-party ideological group, the Land of Israel Movement, arose spontaneously to educate the nation about its historic connection with the land. Its founders and leaders came from the Labor movement, Gahal and the Religious groups. Among them were the poet Natan Alterman, Rachel Yanait Ben-Zvi (wife of Israel's second President), Dr. Chaim Yahil, Eliezer Livneh, Prof. Harold Fisch, Moshe Shamir (the famous author whose origins were in Hashomer Hatzair), Shmuel ("Moekie") Katz (the well-known Revisionist and Herut leader) and General Avram Yoffe of Sinai Campaign and Six-Day War fame.

Though few in number, this group, by virtue of its individual and collective intellectual capacity and standing in public life, exercised considerable moral influence. At first they adopted a non-partisan stand, urging their followers only to give their support in elections to those parties that unequivocally stood for the retention of the liberated areas – which meant, principally, Gahal, for at that time even the National Religious Party was non-committal on the question. However, on the eve of the 1973 Knesset election, the Land of Israel Movement officially linked up with Gahal in the Likud and, as a result, Avram Yoffe was elected to the Knesset.

An alliance was similarly formed with a group of former Labor Party members who had followed Ben Gurion out of the Labor Party in 1965 to form the Rafi Party, but who had refused to return to Labor when the majority of Rafi decided to do so three years later. Now as the State List, they found common cause with Gahal and also joined Likud.

In the 1973 Knesset election, Likud was a parliamentary bloc, comprising Herut, the Liberal Party, the Land of Israel Movement, the State List and the Free Center (a group that had broken away from Herut but now returned as a separate entity). It was one of the most remarkable developments in Israel's political history that the disciples of Jabotinsky and some followers of Ben Gurion were now united under one banner and behind the leadership of Menachem Begin.

At the height of the Yom Kippur War, a political sensation was caused by the announcement that General Ariel ("Arik") Sharon, the hero of that war who was responsible for the crossing of the Suez Canal into Africa planned to leave the army and join Likud.

Though Likud did not win the election in 1973, it enjoyed a weighty presence, with 39 Knesset members. Menachem Begin's labors and persistence had been rewarded. The man who started out as the leader of a small group of his former Irgun Underground fighters and then founded the Herut Party in 1949 was the acknowledged and respected head of a large opposition party and a serious contender for the Premiership.

Some people claim that he had not expected to win the 1977 Knesset election and that the result came to him as a complete surprise. In fact, he was more than cautiously optimistic that this time he would succeed. In the first days of January 1977, at the time of the Herut National Convention, Begin expressed his confidence in victory to me. In the course of a lengthy conversation at his Tel Aviv home, he was analyzing the political developments and various trends and concluded with the words: "I think we have a chance this time."

Then he proceeded to tell me what he would say in his first statement after the election victory.

"We will invite all Zionist parties to join us in a Government of National Unity because of the grave problems facing our country and nation.

"We will offer to meet the Presidents of Egypt and Syria and King Hussein anywhere and any time to negotiate an end to the state of war and conclude a real peace treaty."

And indeed, in the early hours of Wednesday, 18 May 1977, when it was clear that Menachem Begin would be Israel's next Prime Minister, he appeared before the television cameras and made precisely the statement which he had indicated in our conversation more than four months earlier, when few shared his belief in victory.

The toppling of the Labor Party represented the final tremor of a political earthquake in Israel. In the year of Begin's election – 1977 – Israel was one of the few parliamentary democracies in the world. Only 28 out of the 160 independent states held regular democratic elections; the rest were one-party states or totalitarian or military regimes.

Yet the idea of a change of government was new to the people of Israel. For 29 years they were ruled by the Labor Party which, of necessity, coalesced with other groups to acquire a working Knesset majority. But there had never been a change from Government to Opposition; from one set of leaders to another; from one set of policies to another. Strange as it may sound, many in the brave Israeli nation had been afraid of the unknown and preferred, for decades, to stick with "the devil they knew" rather than risk change. Therefore, what happened on 17 May 1977 was variously described as a "revolution" or "earthquake," and in the context of Israel political life it was true. The old, familiar leaders were suddenly relegated to the background. There were new names, new faces, new voices. Israel acquired not only a new, but, for the first time, a starkly different Government, one whose basic policy guidelines differed fundamentally from those of the previous Governments.

Political analysts, searching for the causes of the "earthquake," found many. Any one of them might conceivably have brought down the Labor regime; it might have been a combination of all of them.

Without placing them in order of importance, I offer the following nine observations as the main contributory factors:

One: The people of Israel had at last become weary of their Government and its lackluster leaders. Nearly 30 years of its leadership was more than enough. Actually, Begin insisted in all his declarations that they had held sway for 46 years, from the 17th World Zionist Congress in 1931, when Labor took control of the World Zionist Movement and the Jewish community in Palestine.

Two: A wave of strikes produced Labor anarchy and economic hardship. Paradoxically, many of the strikes were directed against Labor and Histadrut enterprises, with the Government quite incapable of handling the situation.

Three: The Labor Alignment was riddled by internal dissension, with its leadership in open conflict. Several months before the Knesset election, Yitzhak Rabin was elected the Alignment's leader and candidate for the Premiership over his rival, Shimon Peres, by the narrow majority of 41 votes out of more than 2,000.

Four: Sharp internal criticism and disillusionment with Labor leadership and policy also found expression in the defection of some prominent personalities like Professor Yigal Yadin, Meir Amit, General Yariv and others who formed the Democratic Movement for Change, which made significant inroads into Labor's traditional base of support.

Five: Starting with Asher Yadlin – who was the unanimous choice of the Rabin Cabinet for the prestigious post of Governor of the Bank of Israel – several prominent Labor personalities were involved in sensational public scandals. Housing Minister Avraham Ofer committed suicide when his affairs came under investigation. Yadlin was found guilty and sentenced to imprisonment on charges of bribery and corruption. And Prime Minister Rabin resigned after it was found that, contrary to Israel's law, he and his wife, Leah, held a foreign currency account in the United States. The financial affairs of former Foreign Minister Abba Eban also came under suspicion, but no irregularities were established.

Six: Some observers maintained that Labor's defeat was the deferred punishment for the catastrophic blunders of its leaders on the eve of the Yom Kippur War. The people of Israel – like the citizens of the United States some six months earlier – had had enough of their former rulers and decided to punish them. Writing in the *Jerusalem Post*, Mrs. Rose Schaffer of Jerusalem put it this way:

> Israel has taken, with its last gasp of healthy breath, the first step to regeneration. If, as a bereaved mother, I could be said to have felt since the Yom Kippur War something akin to jubilation, it came on learning that the Labor Alignment had finally been toppled from its high and mighty chair of omnipotence.
>
> I trust and pray that our new leaders, whoever they may be, will gradually, if laboriously, lift Israel to the pinnacle of idealism it should never have fallen from.

Seven: Organization played an important part in the election campaign. High praise was lavished on Ezer Weizman, who was in charge of Likud's well-produced, modern, vigorous and inspired bid for power. He succeeded in mobilizing thousands of young and enthusiastic workers while, on the other hand, Labor's campaign lacked motivation and reflected a group of dull and tired men.

Eight: Menachem Begin emerged as a national figure of towering stature. His personal integrity and incorruptibility stood in marked contrast to the atmosphere of scandals that surrounded the Labor leadership. Even a heart attack only two months prior to the election did not damage Begin's public image or the nation's confidence in him. However, his illness and hospitalization limited his public appearances; accordingly, immense interest centered on his eve-of-election television debate with the Labor leader, Shimon Peres. If points had been awarded, there was little doubt that Begin had won. It was the triumph of the experienced and polished statesman.

Nine: Lastly, it was obvious that Likud's election program appealed to a large part of the nation, which found it appropriate to Israel's needs in the last quarter of the 20th century. Much of the text bore Menachem Begin's personal imprint and reflected the policies he formulated and advocated for three decades.

Prime Minister Begin was immensely proud of the practical expression of democracy that took place in complete peace and tranquility on Tuesday, 17 May. For years he had said that election day was "a beautiful day in Israel," for it was on that day that citizens had the power in their hands – with small slips of paper – to determine the kind of Government the country was to have.

Moreover, the transition away from the Government that had ruled for 29 years to the new and different Government was orderly and dignified. Begin graciously paid tribute to his predecessor, Yitzhak Rabin, for his cooperation in ensuring this smooth transition. Indeed, one commentator remarked that "democracy in Israel had reached maturity when its citizens realized that the State was not the private property of one party – the Labor Party – but that it belonged to the entire nation."

There were almost no strikes in Israel in the first months after the Likud Government was installed. Even a one-hour token work stoppage called by the Histadrut as a protest against the new Government's reduction of subsidies resulting in a 25% price hike was a flop. And a threatened merchant marine strike was averted by the intervention and negotiation of a Government representative, while an expected upheaval in El Al was postponed – and probably avoided – by the promise of Defense Minister Ezer Weizman to look into the whole position of the Israeli national airline, and the establishment of a government committee to consider and submit recommendations. And in November, the Histadrut's whipped-up frenzy against the Government's New Economic Program also soon petered out. On Friday, 28 October 1977, the new Finance Minister, Simha Ehrlich, announced revolutionary economic reforms – the first-ever free enterprise reforms of the Socialist system that had dominated Israel for decades. The New Economic Program accorded with the basic tenets of Jabotinsky's policies. Now, theoretical Revisionism was being put to the test of practical implementation.

For much of the nation, Begin was more than the chairman of the party elected to power. His sincerity, simplicity, humility and honesty had given him almost mystical appeal. It is noteworthy that the bulk of Likud's support came from the poorer, less privileged classes, who represented a large part of the country's labor force. They had given Begin his backing and majority and rallied around the Government in its confrontation with the Histadrut.

And lo and behold, a communist state, Rumania, invited Prime Minister Begin to pay an official visit, even though he was not an old-time colleague from the socialist world, as were Israel's previous leaders. The press subsequently revealed that Begin got on well with his Rumanian hosts, and his visit was expected to lead to the strengthening of economic and cultural ties between the two countries. Moreover, they said that it had been important for the President and Prime Minister of Rumania to hear Begin's views on the Middle East and other problems which they communicated to that part of the world from which Israel was cut off. The possibility of Rumania mediating between Israel and the Arab states was enhanced.

A few weeks later, the Prime Minister of Britain's Labour Party extended an invitation to Menachem Begin – who thirty years earlier had waged war against Britain – to pay an official visit to London. The wheel of history had turned full circle when Menachem Begin was honored at a state banquet in London early in December. And other governments likewise made it known that Israel's Prime Minister would be a welcome guest.

Chapter 15

THE MAN

Wʜᴀᴛ ᴍᴀɴɴᴇʀ ᴏꜰ ᴍᴀɴ was Israel's Sixth Prime Minister – the first in nearly three decades who did not come from the Labor movement?

Having known him throughout those three decades, I saw him as a considerate, kind, warm person. His stature did not affect his common touch, which made him the most beloved national figure in Israel. His solicitous inquiry of the soldier and kind word to the driver, the waitress, the porter, the student, the child, showed a real love of his fellow man, of *ahavat Israel* (love of Israel) and *ahavat Am Israel* (love of the People of Israel).

The affection and esteem showered upon him when he became Prime Minister was all the more remarkable because, from the days of the Irgun, he had been maligned by his adversaries among his own people and by his enemies abroad. His fiercest adversaries had relentlessly endeavored to portray him as an ogre, an insensitive, hard, cold, indifferent, intransigent extremist. He was denounced as an irresponsible and reckless demagogue, as an exploiter of labor, as a nasty capitalist living in the lap of luxury.

Anyone who had been to 1 Rosenbaum Street knows that all this was malicious misrepresentation. This "capitalist's" total possessions encompassed a few pieces of modest furniture in the simple rooms where he and his wife Aliza raised their three children, Benny, Chasya and Lea, rejoiced with their grandchildren and entertained their guests, including world statesmen. Significantly, this old apartment, which they occupied for more than 30 years, did not belong to the Begin family. It had been rented the whole time. I recall an occasion when, as an expression of gratitude for a successful mission abroad, some of us wanted to purchase a larger and more spacious dwelling for them. He declined with thanks, but firmly. We tried to persuade him to accept a motorcar which we thought would be fitting for the leader of the Opposition. He insisted that the small car and driver that the Movement had placed at his disposal were more than adequate. Eventually, he agreed to accept – instead of an apartment or motorcar – a gas stove for the kitchen. However, when it was delivered – to the astonishment of the delivery man and the store – it was returned with apologies. Ultimately, after further persuasion, he consented to accept the gift of an encyclopedia.

The Begin family was closely knit. He was strongly attached to his wife and children and doted on his grandchildren. Aliza was his true helpmeet, accompanying him along the difficult uphill road, encouraging him with a smile and her delightful sense of humor. He readily confided in her and listened to the opinions of his children and their friends, representatives of the younger generation. Benny was an intelligent young man and, to the delight of his father, eventually became active in the Herut Party. I once witnessed the father's satisfaction and pride when Benny delivered an impressive speech at a conference. Today, Benny is a highly respected Member of the Knesset with good prospects for important national office.

To my knowledge, Begin had no hobbies and few diversions from his all-absorbing work. As Prime Minister, he worked between 14 and 16 hours a day – and enjoyed it. He had no time for sport, although I saw him occasionally swim or play a game of chess (and a good game at that). He enjoyed, but admitted to not understanding music. He was a most avid reader, primarily of non-fiction works on politics and history.

One of his very few forms of relaxation was to watch a good movie; whenever possible, he used to "escape" – before he became Prime Minister – to the cinema with his wife on Saturday evenings. When we went to the cinema together, I had the impression that his concentration was not on the screen, that his thoughts were elsewhere, perhaps preparing a political statement or the outline of a forthcoming speech.

He enjoyed the company of friends, as was evident at the famous Saturday evening "Open House" salons.

But the character assassination – especially by way of innu-endo – never ceased. At times it touched the periphery of his own party as well. His refusal to be stampeded by pressure groups or to yield to ambitious or impatient individuals, brought him into the center of painful controversy on several occasions. But he always stood his ground, clenching his fists and carrying on for the sake of the cause which he held dear.

Once he told me: "We were ready to fight the British and challenge the Government, but this [a reference to an internal confrontation] is like a knife that goes deep into my heart."

Opponents, of course, capitalized on these internecine personality clashes by propagating their theory that Begin tolerated neither opposition nor criticism, that he refused to work with anyone who disagreed with his views or who was not a member of the "fighting family" (a reference to his former Irgun comrades). The truth is that he was simply not prepared to compromise the movement which he and his friends had built up with so much effort and suffering over the years. However, his leadership of Herut, Gahal and Likud amply illustrated his readiness and ability to work in close harmony with persons who came from different political backgrounds and held differing political views.

In the last six or seven years before he became Prime Minister, his political opponents gave the character assassination an ultimate twist. As long as Begin is there, they said, his Movement had no chance. Remove him, and you might win. This cry persisted and was eventually taken up by several cynics in his own movement who lacked faith in his eventual victory.

Many in Begin's camp could not recognize the origin and purpose of this particular brand of character assassination. As a visiting observer, it was always patently clear to me that *with* Menachem Begin – one of the few leaders of national and international caliber in Israel – his movement stood a chance of one day ousting Labor. Without him, that chance would be greatly reduced.

Labor knew it too, and therefore sought to separate Begin from the movement; as a result, some of his own faint-hearted supporters began to question his leadership – until the 1977 Knesset election took them completely by surprise.

His political opponents also made much use of the fact that he was "an eight-time loser." True. He led his Movement in eight elections – and failed, though he never gave up, and persevered with much tenacity, resoluteness and admirable patience. Begin had always gone to great pains to explain that, in the eight elections since 1949, the forces constituting Labor had dropped from 65 to 51 Members of the Knesset, while those of his Likud Movement had risen from 21 to 39; that the difference between them had been reduced to 12 Knesset seats and that the switch of some 80,000 voters would bring about the long-awaited change of Government.

One of the Labor Alignment's newspaper advertisements in the 1977 election campaign incorporated an illustration of a man taking a driving test with the caption: "He has failed his test 8 times. Would you let him drive?"

When I first saw it, I suggested to friends in Israel that they counter with this theme:

"This driver is to be admired for his tenacity and perseverance. Eventually, he will surely pass the test and get his license.

"But you have surely heard of drivers who, although they have had their license for many years, become reckless and irresponsible, or drive under the influence of liquor, endangering the public. Such drivers have their licenses revoked!"

Chapter 16

MAPS FOR PRESIDENT CARTER

MENACHEM BEGIN's visit to President Carter of the United States only a month after assuming office was of immense importance. While the talks revealed obvious differences in outlook, the ominously predicted breach never occurred. The two statesmen instead stressed the mutuality of their interests. Prior, during and after these talks with President Carter, the United States announced decisions to provide economic and military aid to Israel and, according to an Israeli military spokesman, U.S. arms deliveries continued on schedule.

And when, in the first days of October 1977, the United States Government joined the Soviet Union in a new policy declaration recognizing "the legitimate rights of the Palestinian people" and supporting the creation of a Palestinian homeland, the firm stand of Prime Minister Begin and his Cabinet and the strong reaction of American Jewry startled the Carter Administration, which quickly softened its stand.

President Carter had been well briefed about Menachem Begin and welcomed him to the White House with the warmest words:

This is a very important day in the history of our nation, and I think perhaps for the future of the Middle East and perhaps even for the future of the world.

Prime Minister Begin represents a nation which has just demonstrated again the importance of a true democracy where people in an absolutely unrestrained expression of individual preference in open elections can decide who their leader will be.

This has been a great test for Israel, and the orderly transition of authority and responsibility from one political party to another has been carried out not only with peace and cooperation, but I think with an enhancement of the confidence in the people of Israel in the future.

Having read the writings and biography of our distinguished visitor, I find a great parallel between what Israel is, what it stands for, and what Prime Minister Begin is and what he stands for. He is a man who has demonstrated a willingness to suffer for principle, a man who has shown superlative personal courage in the face of trial, challenge, disappointment, but who has ultimately prevailed because of the depth of his commitment and his own personal characteristics. And this is a strong parallel with what his nation has been and is. He is a man of principle and a man of independence, and the nation of Israel is a people of principle and independence.

One of the important personal characteristics of Prime Minister Begin which I admire is his deep and unswerving religious commitment. This has always been a guiding factor in his consciousness and in his pursuit of unswerving goals. There is a quietness about him which goes with determination and a fiery spirit in his expressions of his beliefs to the public, and this is as it should be.

Although there might be differences in perspective and viewpoint between him and me, his nation and the United States, the common goal of finding a path to permanent peace will inevitably bind us together.

We are honored by his presence. We welcome him and his wife as our visitors.

And I would like to close my comments of welcome to him by quoting from Isaiah, from the Bible, which he and I both read, given to us by God, Whom we both worship. Isaiah said: "And the work of righteousness shall be peace, and the effects of righteousness quietness and assurance forever."*

In responding, Menachem Begin first addressed the President in Hebrew, saying, "Mr. President, I have come from the Land of Zion and Jerusalem as the spokesman for an ancient people and a young nation. God's blessing on America, the hope of the human race. Peace to your great nation."

Begin then continued in English:

> In our time my people was thrown into the abyss. It had to extricate itself from the depths of the pits with the last vestige of its strength through an unequaled fight for national self-liberation of the few against the many, of the weak against the strong, of right against might.
>
> This, Mr. President is the reason why we yearn for peace, pray for peace and shall do everything humanly possible to bring about real peace between us and our neighbors. Peace is inseparable from national security.
>
> May I assure you, Mr. President, that to us that concept is no excuse for anything: neither is it a cloak of anything. To us, with the experience of physical annihilation and spiritual redemption, national security may mean the lives of every man, woman and child in Israel. Their lives can be, under certain circumstances, directly threatened and put in jeopardy.

* Isaiah 32:18

Mr. President, we in Israel see in you not only the first citizen of your great, mighty country, but also the leader and the defender of the Free World. However, the Free World has shrunk, indeed has been shrinking. It can be likened in our time to an island battered by winds, by stormy seas, by high waves. Therefore, all free women and men should stand together to persevere in the struggle for human rights, to preserve human liberty, to make sure that government of the people, by the people, for the people shall not perish from the earth.

I share your view that we stand together for human liberty and dignity. We may have differences of opinion, but we shall never disagree; we may only agree to differ.

In his discussions with President Carter, Begin took pains to explain what he saw as the elementary facts of the Jewish People's right to Eretz Israel, and to stress that Judea, Samaria and Gaza are not "occupied territories," but part of a unitary, indivisible ancient land. Begin saw this switch in emphasis as his first and main responsibility, for that issue has been and remains at the core of the conflict between Israel and her neighbors.

The much-publicized maps that the Prime Minister took to America with him were not of future borders, but of the pre-1967 situation, showing the narrow bottleneck around Netanya at which point the country could be cut in half. He explained that if a Palestinian state were created in Judea and Samaria, terrorists with medium-range rockets could strike at the civilian population of Jerusalem, Tel Aviv and Haifa with impunity. The second map showed tiny Israel surrounded by 20 Arab States.

At a press conference at the White House on 20 July 1977, Begin articulated this view in unmistakable terms:

> This demand (for a Palestine homeland), if it should come at any time into realization – I believe it will not – will create the

following situation: We would be nine miles from the seashore, ten miles from the seashore and, maximum, twenty miles from the seashore. Around Netanya, almost in the middle of the country we would be only nine miles from the seashore and there, by an onslaught of a tank column, the country could be cut in two in ten or fifteen minutes. Soviet artillery now has a range of forty-three kilometers eight hundred meters. So, in other words, from every point of what was in the past termed the Green Line, the conventional artillery possessed by our neighbors can reach every city and town and township. In fact, every house. In fact, every man, woman and child. To sum up, it would be a mortal danger to the State of Israel. It would mean the beginning of the end of our Statehood, independence and liberty.

Begin's Revisionist Zionist background and philosophy had given him the fervent belief in Israel's historic right – even duty – to hold and settle Jews in Judea, Samaria and Gaza which, as parts of the historic Eretz Israel, ought therefore not be given up. He and his colleagues always maintained that the dispute between Israel and the Arabs was not over this or that small piece of territory, but over the right of the Jewish People to exist as a nation in that region. The previous socialist Governments of Israel were, at one time, ready to freeze the borders at the 1949 armistice lines "for a thousand years," and offered to return 99% of the territories liberated in 1967.

Now Israel's friends were told that what they were asking of her was to give up part of the Jewish people's birthright – not to return some territory "illegally" taken from others. There are grave moral, political and historic implications in the difference between these two interpretations.

Menachem Begin and his Government made it clear that, while they were ready to negotiate an end to the state of war and real peace treaties with the neighboring sovereign Arab states, they would have no dealings with the Palestine Liberation Organization (which Begin called the Palestine murder organization). Speaking to the United Jewish Appeal leaders in New York, he said: "They proclaimed that they will recognize as Palestinians only Jews who were born or lived there until 1917. There were no more than 50,000 Jews in Palestine in those days. Now we have more than three million. So, in other words, 2,950,000 Jews – in our own country, in our own land – should take the stick and go to the *Galut* (the Diaspora), to Poland, to Germany, to other places of dispersion and persecution and Auschwitz and Buchenwald. This is their aim, this is their design."

He compared negotiating with them to "someone approaching me and presenting me with a sharp knife which he asks me politely to thrust into my heart. I ask: 'Why should I do such a thing?' and he tells me, 'for the sake of the friendship that exists between us.' For the sake of peace? Peace without me?"

Critics attacked his refusal to negotiate with the PLO by pointing to the fact that the Americans had eventually agreed to negotiate with the Viet Cong, the British with the Irish Sinn Fein and the French with the Algerian FLN.

"Yes," Menachem Begin responded, "I understand that. But the Viet Cong did not ask America to give up Washington, the Irish do not claim London and the Algerians did not demand Paris!"

Before leaving for the United States for his talks with President Carter, Begin asked the Knesset for consensus on two issues: refusal to negotiate with the PLO and rejection of the Palestine homeland idea. In putting the request he was able to claim that in the past his party had always supported requests for consensus from the Labor Governments if they were intended to strengthen Israel's position abroad.

His proposal received the votes of 92 of the 120 Knesset Members. Four members of the Communist Democratic Front cast the only negative ballots. There were six abstentions from the left-wing parties – four Mapam and two Sheli Knesset members. Therefore, when he addressed the American leaders he was able to speak in the name of the overwhelming majority of the Israeli nation.

Chapter 17

A NEW STLYE OF LEADERSHIP

In the first months of his premiership, Menachem Begin's greatest impact was on the morale of the nation, its mood, outlook, quality of life and values. Even before he officially took over, there was already a tangible difference in spirit. Begin established himself as the acknowledged authority in the country – a welcome change from what had been the case in the preceding months and years of the Labor Administration. He gained the respect and admiration even of fair-minded opponents, and on numerous occasions in the last days of June and the first days of July, I witnessed the unparalleled popularity he had achieved with the Israeli people.

His performance at the beginning of his term as Prime Minister was superb. Things were said and done that had been markedly absent from the country's political scene.

The difference first became apparent in the early hours of 18 May, when he made his first television statement to the nation. Wearing a yarmulke, he recited the *"Shehecheyanu"* prayer, "Blessing the Lord for bringing us to this Season," and then added appropriate Psalms. This was followed by his political evaluation and declaration. In conclusion he quoted from the Psalms *"Adonai Oz Leamo Yitein, Adonai Yevarech et Amo Bashalom"* ("The Almighty will give His people strength, the Almighty will bless His People with peace.")

Begin was the first of Israel's Prime Ministers to formally pay respect to the religion of his People, its institutions and symbols. Though a secular Jew and not a member of a religious party, Begin was a man of deep faith in the Torah and reverent respect for the heritage of his People. It was in this spirit that he visited the Western Wall on the day of the election, and again after the President had charged him with the task of constituting Israel's next Government. It was as an observant Jew that he went to the venerated Rabbi Zvi Kook to receive his blessing on assuming office and that he sought the blessing of the Lubavitcher Rebbe in New York before proceeding to Washington for his talks with President Carter.

His acknowledgment of divine intervention and guidance in the affairs of his people was revealed in his discussion with television reporters in America, who asked him whether his talks with President Carter were "fateful."

"Not fateful," he replied. "Important."

"The talks are of importance to Israel, the Middle East region, the Free World, and I venture to say, even for the United States. But fateful – no. You see the Jewish People is an eternal People, and its Fate has been determined by Someone else."

Commentators were quick to note his frequent use of the words *Be'ezrat Hashem* ("With the help of the Almighty"). David Landau, writing in *The Jerusalem Post*, said: "Perhaps Begin, with his mature, healthy Jewish attitude towards God – familiar and at the same time reverent – will be able to bring the secular modern Jewish State to terms with its God."

During his visit to Rumania, Begin's encounter with the Jewish community there was an especially moving experience – for them and for him. They were immensely impressed by the fact that the Prime Minister of Israel had requested the rulers of this socialist country to ensure that meals at the various state banquets were kosher.

Interestingly, not only the religious Jew was impressed by Begin's conscious and active respect for Jewish religion. Though not active practitioners themselves, they appreciated and, perhaps, expected the respect he paid to it. More enthusiastic citizens and visitors in Israel were heard to remark that "for the first time one senses that this is a *Jewish* country with a *Jewish* Prime Minister."

Begin also took pains to elevate the post of the President of Israel. Though the position is largely ceremonial, Begin believed that over the years the office and its incumbents had been taken too much for granted, or deliberately kept in the background. Accordingly, he proposed extending the President's authority in certain matters in the hope that the Head of State would become a unifying factor in the nation, above and apart from political conflict. When he accepted the charge to constitute the Government, Menachem Begin bowed graciously to President Katzir, and was applauded for this gesture. He also instituted the practice of calling on the President to brief him prior to, and report to him after, significant diplomatic missions away from Israel (Begin's visit to President Carter, for example).

In fact, from the moment he ascended to the post of Prime Minister, Begin's leadership style was characterized by a degree of statesmanship and respect rarely seen in modern politics. Shimon Peres, who became leader of the Opposition, was accorded all the respect and recognition due to his office and his status in the parliamentary life of the country. He was given an honored place at official functions and addressed by the Prime Minister as "my friend, the leader of the Opposition" – the closest approach to the British parliamentary tradition of "His Majesty's Opposition."

When Peres made his first speech as leader of the Opposition in the debate following the presentation of Begin's first Cabinet, the Prime Minister complimented him and then brought the house down when he added: "You made a good speech – not as good as the previous leader of the Opposition – but don't worry; you'll have lots of time to learn and improve."

As Prime Minister, Begin also invited the leader of the Opposition to meet him weekly for consultation on matters of importance. There are certain issues on which a bipartisan policy is critical – such as, for example, the national consensus that Begin achieved about the Government's refusal to negotiate with the PLO and its rejection of the Palestinian homeland idea. The practice was abandoned in the later stages of Begin's premiership, when Peres' attacks on the Prime Minister became more personal.

Another example of Begin's respect for the institutions of the State occurred as he was about to board the plane for the United States for his meeting with President Carter. The departure of the Prime Minister and his entourage was "official," meaning that the Cabinet, Knesset Speaker, heads of the Armed Forces and other dignitaries were on the tarmac to bid them farewell.

As the Prime Minister walked along the red carpet to the aircraft, the flags were raised and the honor guard presented arms. To the delight of all present, Begin turned off the carpet, walked towards the flags and bowed before the standards of Israel in tribute. This was the first time any leader of the nation had made such a gesture, and the press hailed it as a precedent for the future.

Begin's conduct was genuine and in accordance with the concept of *hadar* (honor, respect) that Jabotinsky taught his Betar youth movement through his writings, speeches and personal example. The fact that an Israeli Prime Minister was willing to so openly display this *hadar* signaled to the Israeli nation that a new era in Israeli leadership was underway.

Of course, there was no reason to expect dramatic and instant changes in all fields of endeavor. Menachem Begin and his determined – and comparatively youthful – team faced a task of almost overwhelming proportions. But the promise and the expectation of change was there from the day they took office. They inherited not only a 30-year- old set of entrenched policies and their effects; they inherited the legacy of an entire system of government and all its bureaucratic procedures, a one-party staff and all its diplomatic personnel.

At the outset, Begin established firm leadership and a sense of government authority. There was nothing ambivalent or indecisive about his early actions or statements. At his first press conference after the election, before hundreds of international and local newspapermen, radio reporters and television correspondents, he was asked the obvious question: "What about the occupied territories?"

Begin replied disarmingly: "What occupied territories?" and then he urged the journalists to call the areas by their correct name – "Judea and Samaria" – and not "Palestine" which, he lectured them, was originally a Roman name intended to embarrass the Jews at that time. Several days later, accompanied by General "Arik" Sharon, he visited the settlers at Elon Moreh (Kadum) to demonstrate his conviction that Jews had a right to settle in every part of Eretz Israel.

It will be recalled that, in his first post-election statement, Begin invited all Zionist parties to join Likud in a Government of National Unity. But the Labor Alignment, smarting from their unexpected defeat, rejected his overtures, and the negotiations with Professor Yadin's Democratic Movement for Change became deadlocked. Although he would have preferred to establish a broad-based coalition from the start, Begin was not prepared to delay the presentation of his Government any longer than necessary. Accordingly, his first Cabinet had the support of just more than half of the 120 Knesset Members. His main supporter, of course, was his own Likud Party, with 45 Members ("Arik" Sharon had officially joined Herut with his Shlomzion group, represented by 2 Knesset Members). The National Religious Party, with 12 Members, presented little difficulty in the negotiations and felt happier joining a Government headed by Menachem Begin than they had been under the leadership of the Labor Party. The Prime Minister was also assured the support of the 5 Agudat Israel Knesset Members, as soon as they were satisfied on various religious questions in the coalition agreement. This gave him a coalition backed by 62 Knesset members.

But the greatest political sensation of the moment came when Moshe Dayan defected from Labor to accept Begin's invitation to become his Foreign Minister (thus giving Begin's cabinet the support of 63 Knesset Members). This appointment caused an uproar in the country, and though there was initial dismay among some of Begin's followers, the storm abated. Most people came to admire Begin's political adroitness in this matter which, they felt, would prove effective on the "export market" even if less popular for local consumption.

Begin remained confident that the Democratic Movement for Change would, before long, accept his call. He therefore left three Ministries vacant in his Cabinet for them, and kept open his invitation to Yadin to become the Deputy Prime Minister.

Four months after the presentation of Begin's first Cabinet, the Council of the Democratic Movement for Change voted to enter the Coalition with their 15 Knesset Members, making the Begin Government the most widely-supported in 20 years of Israeli history. Now only the divided and weakened Labor Alignment, a few other small factions (of 1 or 2 Members), the Communists and the Arabs remained in the Opposition.

Explaining his party's last-minute switch, Professor Yadin said that Israel was facing one of its most severe political crises since 1948, and that there was sufficient consensus on the major questions to warrant their support of Begin's policy. Other matters were of secondary importance to Professor Yadin.

Some commentators took a less generous view, suggesting that

Yadin acted literally at the last minute, "before the door closed," for Begin was about to fill the vacancies in the Cabinet he had left for them; this could have precipitated in the Democratic Movement for Change bitter internal rivalry, a schism, or even eventual disintegration.

Begin urged his Cabinet colleagues to show proper deference to the Knesset, reversing the bad political relationship with the Knesset that they had inherited. He made every endeavor to be in the Knesset Chamber on all occasions, and hope that other Ministers would follow his example, thus setting a precedent that would encourage good attendance at Knesset sessions and, even edify representational government in Israel. He insisted that there would no longer be an empty Cabinet table in the Knesset Chamber, as in the past, and made appropriate arrangements with his colleagues.

Those who expected the immediate, wholesale dismissal of diplomats or civil servants were proved wrong; Begin told those in his own party who were unhappy about this that "we have come to serve, not to reap." In the first months of his term, few changes were introduced. Begin retained most of the personnel in the Prime Minister's office, but appointed a number of additional advisers. Shmuel Katz, Begin's one-time Irgun High Command comrade and author of the brilliant book *Battleground*, was appointed as Begin's adviser on external information. Another former member of the Irgun High Command, "Gidi" Paglin, who had parted from Begin's Herut Movement for more than a decade, was brought in as special adviser on countering terrorism. Dr. Moshe Sharon was appointed Begin's adviser on Arab Affairs. Naturally, Begin brought with him his trusted private secretary, Yechiel Kadishai, naming him Bureau Chief; Dr. Eliyahu Ben Elissar was appointed Director General of the Prime Minister's Office. Arye Naor, son of Esther Raziel (a veteran Irgun and Herut leader) was appointed Secretary to the Cabinet.

The permanent staff realized soon enough that they were dealing with a Prime Minister of vast political experience, one with a profound understanding of the Jewish communities throughout the world and their collective and specific problems. This Prime Minister required no prodding, for example, to become involved in the struggle for Soviet Jewry, but was ready to throw all the weight of his office and his personal prestige into that struggle.

Begin required no professional speech-writer. In fact, one of the men in the office who performed that role for previous incumbents said to me jokingly: "It looks as if I shall be either un-employed or on holiday." I heard Begin make hundreds of speeches in Hebrew, Yiddish, English, even Spanish and French. He was the finest orator in the Knesset. It was not only his oratorical skills that impressed, but the content of his speeches and statements and the logic of his argumentation.

In the years I had known him before he became Prime Minister, Begin rarely prepared more than skeletal notes; he had read a fully-written speech only twice in his life: the first time after his emergence from the Underground, when he addressed the nation over the Irgun's secret radio, and the second time in June 1977, when he presented his Cabinet and outlined his policy to the Knesset. Subsequently, as Prime Minister, he did write and read a number of major speeches. Usually he spoke without notes, or with only a few subject indications on a single sheet of paper. This does not mean that he appeared before his audience unprepared. Quite the contrary; his ideas and thoughts were carefully formulated in his few leisure hours, or while being driven from one function to the next, or on the rare occasions when he went to the cinema. His mind was always active and alert.

He also insisted on writing or dictating his own replies to letters of congratulation from Heads of State, Prime Ministers and some of his many personal friends and admirers, many of whom are the proud owners of hand-written letters which they had received from Menachem Begin over the years.

One of the changes that he introduced gave him particular pleasure. When he received me in his office for the first time, he pointed to the portraits of four Prime Ministers on the wall: David Ben Gurion, Moshe Sharett, Levi Eshkol and Golda Meir. "Now we will put up a picture of Yitzhak Rabin over there," he said, pointing to a spot next to the portrait of Mrs. Meir. "And here, facing my desk, will be pictures of Herzl and Jabotinsky," he added with a warm smile of contentment.

Begin had a "common touch" that went beyond attentive political representation. Private citizens found him accessible, courteous, friendly and ready to listen to their views, suggestions or complaints. Never aloof, he sometimes worried his security guards by stopping to chat with a man in the street or to shake the hands of people who stood aside to let him pass.

Television viewers were astounded by a program filmed on election day – but screened after the polling stations had closed – showing Menachem Begin walking through one of the poorest districts of the country. An old woman, her face showing the cares of a lifetime, was standing in the background and watching the interest that Begin's visit had stirred in the quarter. He suddenly turned to her, bent down to speak to her and then, taking her hand in his – as was his custom when he met a lady – kissed it. "The look in that old woman's eyes showed a love which only the rarest political leaders can acquire," a friend told me.

For years, Begin was the champion of the poor and underprivileged in Israel. Cleaving to Jabotinsky's concept of social justice, he regarded poverty as a blot on the nation. "We are the people of justice," he said. "How can we countenance this situation?" I heard him deal with this subject in his address at the festive opening session of the Herut Convention in Jerusalem's Binyanei Ha-oomah when President Katzir, Shimon Peres and other Cabinet Ministers of the Labor Government were on the dais. Turning to the representatives of the Government, he said: "You should be ashamed as socialists that in this country there are 50,000 families, totaling nearly 350,000 people, living in conditions of poverty. It is intolerable and undignified that in this day and age families should be living six or eight in a room. It disrupts family life. The children cannot study or do their homework. We must erase this blot."

True to his word, Begin initiated moves to deal with this problem in the first days of his premiership. At a reception honoring his friend Nessim Gaon, President of the World Sephardi Federation, Begin proposed a fund of $100 million to provide decent housing for poor families in place of their present slum dwellings. Later that week he called on the Jewish Agency Assembly to provide this sum over and above their normal fundraising efforts for Israel. When the American UJA's Prime Minister's Mission came to Israel the following month, they announced their readiness to adopt this project. Thus, in the first days of the Begin era, new hope was given to Israel's poor and underprivileged. Project Renewal, born in those early days, was to become "one of the most successful urban renewal programs in the world," as a research survey described it some years later.

Begin's rapport with the ordinary citizen was also evident at his unique "open house" on Shabbat afternoons, a tradition the Begins maintained throughout the 30 years they lived at 1 Rosenbaum Street in Tel Aviv. Every Saturday afternoon, a small group of family and close friends would visit them there. Guests from abroad knew that if they wanted to call on the Begins, that was the best time; they often arrived without even a prior telephone arrangement. The door was usually open, and the unexpected guest entered to warm welcomes and embraces from Aliza and Menachem Begin.

When he moved to the official residence in Jerusalem, Menachem Begin announced that their family tradition would be maintained. The security people were flabbergasted, but naturally acquiesced to the Prime Minister's wishes.

My wife and I were present at the first "open house" in Jerusalem. When we arrived at 3 Balfour Street, there was already a long line of people waiting for six o'clock but, as we were expected at 5:30, we were permitted by the armed guards to enter. By six o'clock, the line stretched around the block. Everybody was there. Mr. Citizen and his wife. Old-timers. Personal friends. Neighbors. Even tourists from nearby hotels who had read about the "open house" and were thrilled at the prospect of meeting Israel's Prime Minister.

Inside the reception rooms and courtyard there was much activity. The Prime Minister and his wife were marvelous hosts, offering their guests a slice of cake, a soft drink, or some wine for a L'Chaim. When I inquired why they were doing all this themselves, Aliza explained that they did not want to retain waiters on the Shabbat afternoon, when they should be with their families. Subsequently, a number of friends offered to assist with the preparation and the serving during the "open house" hours.

The courtyard became more crowded. A whole Yemenite family arrived – three generations of them, who gathered around Menachem Begin, singing, clapping hands and dancing. There, in another corner, a group of Chassidim. Now a small party of American tourists entered, some of whom were acquainted with Begin from his visits to the United States on behalf of the UJA or Bonds. Then, Chief Rabbi Casper of South Africa, who was visiting Jerusalem, arrived to greet the Prime Minister.

When the first three stars appeared, heralding the end of the Sabbath, the young son of Lily and Nathan Silver, who were close friends of the Begins, recited the *Havdalah* prayers with the Prime Minister at his side.

"Blessed art Thou, O Lord our God, King of the Universe, who distinguishes between the holy and the profane."

"Amen," responded the Prime Minister and his guests.

Surely, the most unusual things were happening at 3 Balfour Street, and the press was quick to recognize this fact. On the following morning, newspapers carried pictures of the long line outside the official residence, accompanied by comments from neighbors and guests. The most telling comment came from a nearby resident.

"I have lived here for years. That house was always closed up. No one – other than obviously official guests – ever went there. Now it is as if all the windows have been opened to let in the fresh air and send out warmth and love to us, the people outside."

Chapter 18

LEADER OF THE NATION

FOR MENACHEM BEGIN, the history of his nation did not begin on 14 May 1948. He viewed the modern state as the continuation of the long saga of an ancient people and stressed this fact in his speeches and articles. Nor did he recognize any division between Jews living inside Israel and those outside. On numerous occasions he declared that the citizens of Israel were the trustees in the Land of Israel for the whole Jewish People.

It was, therefore, significant that his first act as Prime Minister was to issue instructions for asylum in Israel to be granted to a group of 66 Vietnamese refugees who had been rejected already by a host of nations. Their little boat had been battered by storms, and their food and water supplies were dwindling dangerously low. When an Israeli merchant vessel captain sighted the boat, he radioed for instructions and was authorized – by the Israeli Labor Government – to rescue them.

But what to do with them?

By the time that this decision had to be made, the new Government had taken over. Begin, on his first day in office and in his first official act, ordered that the refugees be offered asylum in Israel.

He was proud of this humanitarian gesture which attracted much international interest and applause. Several weeks later,

President Carter, who had also been impressed by the action of the Israeli Prime Minister, referred to it specifically in his speech of welcome to Menachem Begin:

> I was particularly impressed that the first official action of his Government was to admit into Israel 66 homeless refugees from Vietnam who had been floating around in the oceans of the world, excluded by many nations who are their neighbors, who had been picked up by an Israeli ship, and to whom he gave a home. It was an act of compassion, an act of sensitivity and a recognition by him and his Government of the importance of a home for people who were destitute and who would like to express their own individuality and freedom in a common way, again typifying the historic struggle of the People of Israel.

Begin said in reply:

> It was natural for me as Prime Minister to give those people a haven in Israel. We remembered, we have never forgotten, that boat with 900 Jews that left Germany in the last weeks before the Second World War for Cuba. When they reached the Cuban shores, their visas were declared non-valid, and then they were nine months at sea, traveling from harbor to harbor, from country to country, crying out for refuge. They were refused.
>
> Eventually they went back to Europe. Some of them saved their lives. The majority went to the gas chambers. We have never forgotten the lot of our people, persecuted, humiliated, ultimately physically destroyed.

Begin's action also profoundly moved the people of Israel, who took the plight of the Vietnamese refugees to heart, and world Jewry, who were proud of this practical expression of Israel's concern for humanity. I saw an international assembly of Jewish leaders rise as one man to give the Prime Minister a standing ovation when he related the story again at a public function, asking them to remember Israel's gesture next time they heard Zionism equated with racism by the United Nations majority.

It is no secret that the Jews of the United States and of other countries were startled by Menachem Begin's election victory. They hardly knew him; what they did know of him was the product of the old character assassination campaign. They were familiar only with Israel's long-time Labor leaders, who frequently visited their communities, appeared at their conventions, at fundraising rallies and on television. They expected to find an irresponsible, doctrinaire ex-terrorist who would disturb the equilibrium. The situation was not helped by local press, radio stations and television commentators, who were churning out the usual alarmist verbiage.

Wisely, Begin swiftly dispatched Shmuel "Moekie" Katz to the United States, where his previous work had given him access to a number of U.S. Senators, Congressmen and reporters. Working ceaselessly for more than a month, he succeeded in creating a more balanced picture. By the time Begin arrived for his meetings with President Carter, the Jewish community was only slightly more receptive, but they quickly warmed to him. They were moved by his words, his deeds and his record of service, with which many of them were becoming acquainted for the first time.

In the first months of his Premiership, Begin succeeded in gaining the respect and support of the leaders and members of the large American Jewish community. Within days of taking office, the Prime Minister invited Rabbi Alexander Schindler, chairman of the Conference of Presidents (comprising the heads of some 30 major Jewish organizations), to Jerusalem for an exchange of views. The American leader was, at first, rather cautious and reserved, but after several discussions, Rabbi Schindler said, "I like what I see." When asked by a television reporter how he would advise the Prime

Minister to conduct himself when he meets the President of the United States, Rabbi Schindler replied: "Just let him be himself."

And following Begin's meeting with the Presidents' Conference in New York, Rabbi Schindler said: "Now we know why the People of Israel are excited about their new Prime Minister. The Jewish leadership sees in Begin what he truly is – the leader of the Jewish Nation."

Also characteristic of the eventual sentiment of American Jews was a full-page advertisement placed by a well-wisher in *The New York Times* on Sunday, 17 July 1977, the weekend prior to Begin's meeting with President Carter:

WELCOME, MENACHEM BEGIN
PRIME MINISTER OF THE STATE OF ISRAEL
Menachem Ben Zev-Dov Begin, Shalom!
When you walk into the White House
you will not walk alone!
Behind you walk forty centuries of the
History of the Jewish People;
>   Thousands of years of Jewish glory;
>   The majesty of the Kings of Judea and Israel;
>   the eternal wisdom of the Judges
>   and the vision of the Prophets of Israel.
Behind you walk twenty centuries of the Jewish Diaspora;
>   The blood-stained pages of a tortured
>   history of exile and dispersion,
>   discrimination and bigotry
>   and the fight for survival and revival
Behind you walk millions of victims of
>   Inquisitions and Persecution
>   genocide, pogroms, concentration camps
>   and crematoria
You will be walking as the representative of

a reborn nation.
> With the blessing and prayers of our
> eternal People everywhere.

Mr. Prime Minister:
When you walk into the White House
you will not walk alone!

And this is how the veteran journalist Robert St. John summed up Menachem Begin in an exclusive report from Washington:

> Men and women who report the news are by and large a cynical, sophisticated, not-easily-impressed lot of people. This is especially true of the Washington press corps. Most of the political, diplomatic and military correspondents here have, over the years, watched too many kings, queens, emperors, prime ministers, presidents and field marshals come and go to be anything but rather bored over the state visit of another of these miscellaneous VIPs.
>
> But this is to report that, whatever may have been the inner reaction of President Carter to Menachem Begin, the Washington press corps was obviously greatly impressed by this maverick from the Middle East.
>
> As I sat Wednesday afternoon in the crowded room in the old Executive Office Building close to the White House, where the Begin press conference was held, I paid close attention to how the almost 300 other reporters were reacting. Their questions were, for the most part, respectful. Not any was insulting. Of course they tried to pin him down, get him to commit himself, trap him in contradictions, force sensational headlines out of the confrontation. That's their business. But they soon discovered they were dealing with a professional; with a man who for Israel's entire 29 years has been practicing politics; a man who knows how to handle himself in a press conference;

a man who was not going to be tricked into saying either more or less than he wished to say for the moment.

The Washington press corps can scent honesty, sincerity and integrity, and it has utter contempt for the puny. Maybe that is why Begin came out of the encounter with the respect of most present. Before dashing off to telephones, or telegraph and cable offices to file their stories, they gave him indications of their great respect.

It is nothing new for an Israeli Prime Minister to be well received in Washington. Ben Gurion, Golda Meir and Rabin were three quite different people; each had a unique character. The Washington reporters I talked with late Wednesday agreed that Begin appears to have many of the strong points of his three predecessors, plus some positive characteristics all his own.

And White House correspondent Trude B. Feldman said:

After 15 years of covering White House state functions, I would rank Begin's visit as the most emotion-laden and drama-packed.

That evening, the atmosphere in the State Dining room was riveting during the exchange of after-dinner toasts. The 53 "working dinner" guests found themselves captivated as Premier Begin, in a low-toned voice, spoke about the moral greatness of America, about "little" Israel, about his own childhood and about the Holocaust. He seemed to transcend mere diplomatic polish and reached a level of heart-to-heart communication seldom displayed in the usual performance of a head of state.

At one point his words must have struck President Carter as particularly poignant. One could observe a mist appear in the President's eyes as he listened with rapt attention to Begin's touching, even painful description of the Holocaust. Begin's story was one of patience and courage that finally brought him to his present leadership role.

Later President Carter told her: "Before I met the Prime Minister, I learnt about him from his writings. Now that we have met and exchanged views face to face, we have come to like each other. In addition to his intelligence, strength and courage, he is a humble, gracious and sincere man.

"I was particularly impressed with his intimate knowledge, his unique and deep personal involvement with the people and the history of his country."

Chapter 19

AT THE RIGHT TIME

ON ASSUMING OFFICE as Israel's Prime Minister, Menachem Begin asked the nation to give him moral credit for one year. By and large, his request was granted by the citizens, the press, and even by many of his opponents. Most fair-minded people sensed that something had changed for the better in Israel. They liked the new style, new tone and new language. On 16 September the London *Jewish Chronicle* editorialized:

> Even the most severe Israeli critics of the policies of Mr. Menachem Begin concede that his Premiership has been marked by a new notion of strong leadership at the top. People talk of a "sense of direction," of "firm government," of someone being in command. Plainly, the contrast with the past years, and particularly the final months of the Labor administration, is sharp and tangible. Decisions, however arguable, are made. Policies, however unpalatable, are hammered out. There has so far been little of the internal political bickering and public display of petty jealousy, even open hostility among the nation's leaders which, over the previous few years, had agonized an Israeli public already plagued with many uncertainties. To this extent, Mr. Begin has already made his mark.

Israelis were impressed that their new Prime Minister spoke even to the mightiest without subservience or apology. As one commentator put it, Menachem Begin would offer the Arabs peace, but would not beg for it. Another praised Israel's relationship with the United States as being more firmly based on mutual respect and understanding. This was borne out in the first days of October 1977, when he and his Government stood firm in the face of the new American-Soviet policy statement that extended recognition to the "legitimate rights of the Palestinian people."

In his first actions Begin clearly indicated that, in the months and years to follow, he would strive to rescue the Jews of the Soviet Union, to increase and facilitate *aliyah* (immigration to Israel), to reduce and endeavor to stop *yeridah* (emigration from Israel), to eliminate the shame of poverty in his country, and to uplift and ennoble his people.

At his first appearances before the leaders of the World Zionist Organization, he called for vigorous efforts to provide Hebrew education for Jewish children everywhere as a means of linking them with the ancient Land and heritage and countering the erosive tendency towards assimilation. He also announced his intention of convening an Economic Conference that would address itself to Israel's grave economic problems.

Visitors to the country in the first months after Begin's election felt the new spirit; the depression and embarrassment of the post-Yom Kippur War years was being replaced by optimism and confidence. It was therefore not surprising that an opinion poll conducted in August indicated that, if another election were held in that week, Likud would emerge with an overall majority of 63 out of the 120 Knesset seats, and the Labor Alignment would be further reduced from 32 to 24 seats.

This indication of the nation's growing confidence was Begin's real victory. There were some who had suggested that the May 1977 Knesset election result was more in the nature of a vote against the Labor Alignment rather than a vote for Likud. But by August, only three months after the election, the people of Israel had taken their new leader to their hearts and were giving him their strong support and confidence.

His place in history was now recognized. Even a writer of a hostile piece in the *London Times* of 19 May 1977 found it necessary to describe him as one of Israel's Founding Fathers. "As the leader of the Irgun Zvai Leumi, he, and not Mr. Ben Gurion, was arguably responsible for the birth of Israel."

The change of Government had been a healthy development for Israel. The nation had approached and passed the test of democracy. Israelis were discovering that the Begin regime was good for Israel, for world Jewry and for Zionism.

Many regretted that the change had been so long in coming. Indeed, there were two previous occasions when Begin might have been elected Prime Minister. The first was immediately after the victorious conclusion of the revolt against the British. In many similar instances in countries of Europe, South America, Asia and Africa, it was the leaders of the active liberation struggle that were the natural choice for Government office. But in 1949, the new nation of Israel had other considerations and preferences.

The second occasion was the December 1973 election immediately after the Yom Kippur War, when it looked almost certain that the nation intended to punish the leaders responsible for the grave political blunders. Opinion polls in the weeks prior to the election showed Labor and Likud running neck and neck.

I was in Israel for the month preceding that election and knew that Labor was desperately worried and indulging in "war danger" propaganda against Begin and Likud. The tide was running against the Labor Government until it was saved by U.S. Secretary of State Henry Kissinger, who presumably preferred in Israel a pliable, weak-kneed Labor Government to firm Begin leadership. In pursuing his Middle East peace momentum, Kissinger hurriedly engineered the opening session of the Geneva Peace Conference, only 10 days prior to the Knesset election on 31 December.

The caretaker Government headed by Mrs. Meir ought to have refused to attend on the grounds that they were already out of office; there was no Government to represent Israel's views or to bind the nation to future arrangements. That might have been the decent thing to do, but, obviously, Kissinger's ideas (later proved wrong) also served Labor interests. To this day, I cannot escape the suspicion that there was collusion between them.

Israeli public opinion shifted overnight. On 20 December 1973 they were railing against the Labor leadership. On the 21st, after seeing Israelis and Arabs in the same hall in Geneva, and after listening to the words of Kissinger and Gromyko, their appraisal of Labor changed dramatically. So successful was the illusion that Israelis even disregarded the fact that none of the Arab participants had uttered the word "peace." A few days later, Israel went to the polls and again returned the old leadership to office.

Perhaps it was destined to be thus. A few years later, Menachem Begin emerged; he was the right man at the right time, both on the Middle East scene and in the history of the Jewish People. It was Israel's thirtieth anniversary year, and the very future of Eretz Israel was at stake. International and internal pressure was mounting for the surrender of portions of the territories, for recognition of Palestinian rights and for the creation of a Palestinian homeland. Menachem Begin, as Israel's Prime Minister during these tense times, would be called upon to respond to these pressures with strength, grace and consistency.

Chapter 20

FACE-TO-FACE WITH SADAT

FROM THE MOMENT he became Prime Minister, Menachem Begin stressed his yearning for peace between Israel and its neighbors. Less than six months after taking office, Begin – the "war monger" – was being mentioned as a candidate for the Nobel Prize for Peace, together with President Anwar Sadat of Egypt, because of their unprecedented efforts to achieve peace in November 1977, when the Egyptian leader responded to the Israel Prime Minister's invitation and came to Jerusalem for peace talks.

Technically, the two countries were at war, their armies on constant alert against each other. It required a special type of leadership in Israel, one of uncommon vision and strength, to give the Middle East peace efforts this entirely new dimension. The 44 hours of Sadat's sojourn in Israel as the guest of Prime Minister Begin changed the face of the Middle East.

Recognizing the great significance of the occasion, more than 2,000 news reporters from all parts of the world came to Israel for what was regarded as "the story of the decade." News correspondents were at pains to describe the sight of the Egyptian flag flying side by side with Israel's Star of David; the Egyptian anthem being played by an Israel military band, followed by "Hatikvah" and Israeli and Egyptian leaders smiling warmly at each other.

There was jubilation in Israel; people were dancing in the streets and excitement knew no bounds when the white Egyptian plane touched down at Ben Gurion Airport and the Egyptian leader stepped on to Israel's soil well after the Sabbath – as Begin had insisted – so that no one would have to desecrate the holy day. Of course, the joy was tempered by other feelings. It took great courage for Sadat to go to Israel, where 3,000 families still deeply mourned the dead of the Yom Kippur War, and where many thousands of young men were maimed as the result of his aggression in 1973. It required equal courage on the part of Israel's Prime Minister to initiate and authorize this unprecedented event. Only the pursuit of peace could justify such action.

It had all started on 4 July 1977, when Begin arrived at the home of the American Ambassador for the U.S. Independence Day celebration. Within minutes Begin asked if the Rumanian Ambassador was there. When the surprised envoy was brought to him, Begin told him that he wanted to visit Rumania as soon as possible. The request was conveyed to Bucharest and accepted. When the visit took place in August, the Israeli leader told President Nicolae Ceaucescu that he wanted to hold direct talks with President Sadat. Begin had always insisted on face-to-face negotiations with the Arabs in preference to the various third-party mediation efforts. Later that summer, when Sadat also visited Rumania, Ceaucescu told him of the Israel Prime Minister's wish to meet with him and, according to Begin, "an exchange of views took place there and then between the two men which was of great importance." President Ceaucescu indirectly confirmed his role when he remarked in a speech in Bucharest: "We have acted for the settlement of the Middle East issues through negotiations…"

Sadat subsequently used a public occasion to indicate that, for the sake of peace, he would be ready even to travel to Israel and speak to the people of Israel from the rostrum of the Knesset. Any suggestion that the Egyptian leader merely intended to embarrass Israel by presenting Egypt as the party seeking peace in the face of Israeli intransigence was speculation. Begin immediately replied by inviting the Egyptian leader to Jerusalem. He extended the invitation in a speech to a delegation of members of the U.S. Congress Armed Services Committee, then touring the Middle East and proceeding to Cairo the next day. When Begin heard that Sadat later told the same Committee that he had not yet received an official invitation from Israel, Begin hastened to transmit a formal invitation through the American Ambassador; more dramatically, he broadcast a special appeal in English directly to the Egyptian people:

> Citizens of Egypt, this is the first time that I address you directly, but it is not the first time that I think and speak of you. You are our neighbors and always will be.
>
> For the last 29 years a tragic, completely unnecessary conflict has continued between your country and ours. Since the time when the Government of King Farouk ordered to invade our land, Eretz Israel, in order to strangle our newly-restored freedom and independence, four major wars took place between you and us.
>
> Much blood was shed on both sides. Many families were orphaned and bereaved, in Egypt and Israel. In retrospect, we know that all those attempts to destroy the Jewish State were in vain, as all the sacrifices you were called upon to make – in life, in development, in economy, in social advancement – all these superfluous sacrifices were also in vain. And may I tell you, our neighbors, that so it will be in the future.
>
> You should know that we have come back to the land of our forefathers, that it is we who established independence in our land, for all generations to come.
>
> We wish you well. In fact, there is no reason whatsoever for hostility between our peoples. We, the Israelis, stretch out

our hand to you. It is not, as you know, a weak hand. If attacked, we shall always defend ourselves.

But we do not want any clashes with you. Let us say one to another, and let it be a silent oath by both peoples, of Egypt and Israel:

No more wars, no more bloodshed and no more threats.

Let us not only make peace, let us also start on the road of friendship, sincere and productive cooperation. We can help each other. We can make the lives of our nations better, easier, happier.

Your President said, two days ago, that he will be ready to come to Jerusalem, to our Parliament – the Knesset – in order to prevent one Egyptian soldier from being wounded. I have already welcomed this statement and it will be a pleasure to welcome and receive your president with the traditional hospitality you and we have inherited from our common father, Abraham.

And I for my part will, of course, be ready to come to your capital, Cairo, for the same purpose: No more wars – peace – a real peace, and forever.

It is in the Holy Koran that our right to this land was stated and sanctified. May I read to you this eternal surah:

"Recall when Moses said to his people, O my people, remember the goodness of Allah towards you when he appointed prophets among you. O my people, enter the Holy Land which Allah hath written down as yours."

It is in this spirit of our common belief in God, in Divine providence, in right and in justice, in all the great human values which were handed down to you by the Prophet Mohammed and by our prophets – Moses, Joshua, Jeremiah, Ezekiel – it is in this human spirit that I say to you with all my heart: Shalom – Peace – which in Arabic is *Sulkh*.

Later, Begin jokingly told a Herut Council meeting in Jerusalem that he hoped Sadat would in fact reciprocate the invitation and invite him to Cairo. "I would like to see the pyramids. After all, our ancestors built them – but you can assure the Egyptians that we shall not ask for compensation."

The mood in Israel was euphoric, and Prime Minister Begin had to caution his people not to exaggerate their hopes and expectations. It was asking a lot, because according to commentators "the public mood was almost as high as after the raid on Entebbe." Louis Guttman, Israel's foremost pollster, found that nearly 90% of the people believed that Sadat's visit had improved the prospects for peace, and 54% were convinced that there would not be another Middle East war. Only a month earlier, just over 10% felt that way.

Of course, this Begin-Sadat initiative did not produce instant peace, but in the words of the American astronaut who first reached the moon, it was "one giant leap" toward peace in the Middle East. It served to break down many of the psychological barriers in the relationship between Israel and her strongest enemy. In one dramatic move, the notorious three "No"s of Khartoum were erased. (Shortly after the Six-Day War of June 1967, representatives of all the Arab countries met at Khartoum and adopted a policy expressed in three negatives: "No recognition. No recognitions. No peace with Israel.")

Now, by going to Israel, the Egyptian President recognized the Jewish State literally overnight; he spent 44 hours in direct negotiations with its Prime Minister and other leaders, and the substance of the talks was peace.

If the first Sadat visit did not formally accomplish that, it came close to doing so. At a joint press conference at the end of the visit, Begin was able to state in the name of his guest and that of the Israeli Government: "We have made a solemn pledge in Jerusalem. There will be no more wars between us. This is a very great moral victory." The Egyptian ruler, who was at his side, added emphatically: "We agreed that the War of October 1973 will be the last war between us."

The practical outcome of these exchanges was an agreement to re-convene the Geneva peace talks under the auspices of the United States and the Soviet Union, and to remove some of the procedural obstacles that delayed such a conference up to that point. The two leaders, who apparently got on very well together in their five hours of private talks, also agreed to create permanent lines of communication and to create an ongoing process of discussion. As a result, Israeli Ambassador to the UN Chaim Herzog and his Egyptian counterpart met for the first time and held wide-ranging discussions, and a second round of talks between Israelis and Egyptians – this time in Cairo – was scheduled for mid-December.

Both Menachem Begin and Sadat were acclaimed by their people for their bold and imaginative peace effort. However, the Egyptian leader faced grave repercussions at home and in the Arab world. The moment he announced his intention of visiting Israel, his Foreign Minister Ismail Fahmi resigned and Mohammed Riad, who was appointed Acting Foreign Minister, resigned hours later. Moreover, the Begin initiative unwittingly split the Arab world, which was thrown into turmoil by Sadat's trip to Jerusalem. At a conference in Tripoli, Algeria, Libya, Syria, Iraq and South Yemen decided to freeze their relations with Egypt. Sadat immediately countered by severing diplomatic relations with those countries.

Whether Sadat would be strong enough to survive this upheaval remained to be seen. His country was near bankruptcy and his armed forces desperately in need of arms and spare parts, which were reaching him directly or indirectly from the Soviet Union. In fact, recognition of these problems might have prompted him to take the plunge.

A number of other factors brought about this remarkable historic development. First and foremost there was Menachem

Begin's passionate yearning for peace. Those who maligned him as a warmonger betrayed an abysmal ignorance of the man; he despised war with a fervor beyond imagination. The man who commanded the Irgun for nearly five years, whose decisions and orders sent men into action and to their death, whose policies as Prime Minister shaped critical Israeli military decisions, wanted no young man on either side of the border to die.

Some military experts have advanced the view that the danger of war in the Middle East receded the moment Likud took over. Even the Arabs realized that they would now be dealing with a different type of Israeli leadership, whose spirit was best explained by Menachem Begin himself in an airport interview on his return from the now-famous visit to Rumania. Reacting to the latest saber-rattling speech by the Syrian President, he warned Hafez Assad against threatening Israel. "We shall never initiate war," Begin said. "But if we are attacked we will defend ourselves, and such defense implies counter-attack. We will repel every act of aggression. In my Cabinet there are three generals who led great armies to victory – General Dayan, General Weizman and General Sharon. They, together with me and my friends, belong to a suffering – but to a fighting – generation," he declared.

A few weeks later he addressed a similar statement to President Sadat, who had again proclaimed his readiness to sacrifice a million men to regain the lands which Israel took from the Arabs in 1967. Begin warned Sadat that Israel might be obliged to launch a preemptive attack against the Arabs that would crush their armies for a generation. He reminded Sadat that all past Arab attempts to destroy the Jewish State had ended in failure and defeat. The Arab rulers must have realized that they faced a "no-nonsense" leadership across the border which was determined to prevent war and achieve peace through strength.

On his visit to the United States soon after his election, Menachem Begin made peace the main theme of all his addresses:

We want peace. We yearn and pray for peace. We want real peace based on security. We should start negotiating peace treaties immediately. We are late. Let us start at least now, with the delay of almost a generation, to negotiate and establish a real peace. When we say a peace treaty, we mean mainly a termination of the state of war, determination of permanent boundaries, diplomatic relations and economic relations.

With a sense of urgency, on the one hand, and some patience on the other, I think we can build a foundation for peace in the Middle East and a recognition of justice for all and fairness for all. We have started, by Israeli initiatives, the momentum for the peace-making process.

Of course not everything depends on us or the United States. We cannot read into the hearts of our neighbors, our enemies. I can only say: We have now placed on record that Israel wants peace, real peace, that Israel is prepared to go to Geneva. Israel is prepared to take part in sub-committees of mixed commissions and talk about all the conditions relevant to a peace treaty. The momentum is here...and we have laid the foundations for it.

Those were also the sentiments of his address from the rostrum of the Knesset after President Sadat had spoken.

Mr. President of Egypt: I am sure that I am expressing the consensus of all, the sense of the whole of this House when I say that there is one aspiration in our hearts, one desire in our minds; and all of us are at one in this desire and aspiration – to bring about peace, peace for our nation that has not known even one day of peace ever since we started returning to Zion; and peace to our neighbors, whom we wish well.

And we believe that if we make peace, if we make a real peace, we can help one another and a new period for the Middle East can be ushered in, a period of growth and blossoming, of development. It can flourish as in times of old.

We believe with all our hearts that the day indeed will come when we can sign a freely negotiated agreement with mutual respect. Then we shall know that the era of the war is over; that we have extended our hands to one another, we have shaken each other's hands and the future can be glorious for all the nations in this area.

Of course, the gap between Israel's national interest and Egyptian ambitions remained wide, the respective national aspirations apparently still irreconcilable. Yet the atmosphere had been transformed, the mood changed, the contact made and the way opened to an honorable and durable peace.

In the weeks following the Sadat visit to Jerusalem, Prime Minister Begin was urged to make "gestures" – to offer concessions (presumably territorial) in response to the Egyptian leader's courageous action, implying, of course, that Israel now had to pay the price for it.

But Begin would not be stampeded into anything that was not carefully thought out and in Israel's best interest. "Policy-making is not a question of gestures," he calmly told a London audience. "It is a serious matter. Israel's quid pro quo for Sadat's visit to Jerusalem was the hospitality that we accorded him.

"Now the negotiations will start. We shall negotiate sincerely. And we believe we shall reach agreement."

Chapter 21

THE VISION OF
ETERNAL PEACE

The process that began with Sadat's historic visit to Israel lasted nearly five years. The two leaders met eleven more times in Israel, Egypt and in Washington. Menachem Begin became the first Israeli leader to set foot officially in Egypt and to be received and honored by that country's leaders, and, more significantly, by its people; I was with him a number of times when, to the dismay of the security officers, he left the official car and approached large crowds lining the streets. As soon as they recognized him, they started chanting "Begin – Salaam! Begin – Salaam!" ("Begin – Peace!").

Both Sadat and Begin were conscious of the unprecedented role they were playing and of the profound meaning of their words and actions. In their earliest public appearances they set the tone and character of the mission on which they had embarked. "No more war. No more bloodshed. No more bereavement," Menachem Begin said with deep emotion. "Let the October War [Yom Kippur, 1973] be the last war," was Sadat's response.

Later, to dramatize their words, both leaders brought special delegations with them when they met in El Arish on 27 May 1979. Their official parties included representatives of bereaved families and groups of war invalids, most of them in wheelchairs or on crutches. Their encounter opened in a cold atmosphere as they eyed each other suspiciously from a distance. And then, step by step, they inched towards each other, slowly, slowly, faster until they almost ran to embrace each other – Egyptians and Israelis – shook hands and proclaimed together in the presence of the President of Egypt and the Prime Minister of Israel: "No more war. We shall never raise arms against each other." Begin was deeply moved by the scene and quietly asked: "Could there be more beautiful words than those simple words?" On a subsequent occasion, after describing the scene at El Arish, he said: "I'll never forget the proceedings. I don't think there has ever been such a meeting in the annals of other nations."

The personal relationship between Sadat and Begin grew and deepened. Before long Sadat began addressing him as "Menachem" and opened his letters with "Dear Menachem." He asked Begin to do likewise but he declined, saying modestly: "I am only a Prime Minister and you are a President." Nevertheless, they were soon on first name terms and their meetings, telephone conversations and letters became more frequent and covered a wide range of topics that extended beyond the Israel-Egyptian relationship.

During their three-day meeting in Aswan, they spent many hours alone sitting in the shade of a palm tree, far away from the hundreds of photographers and media people who were biting their fingernails in frustration. At one point Sadat rose, summoned an aide from a distance, who ran up to him, listened and ran back to their headquarters in the hotel. He returned a few minutes later with long rolls of maps. And, then to our surprise, Sadat and Begin got down on the ground and studied the map together for what seemed an eternity. The photographers craned their necks and got up to all sorts of acrobatic tricks to try to get a picture of the map with their telephoto lenses – but to no avail. Obviously, this incident became a talking point at the subsequent press conference, but neither man was prepared to reveal anything. Later, Begin told us that they had studied the proximity of Libya to Egypt. This was a matter of concern to Sadat because Libya's irrational leader, Qaddafi, had been mobilizing troops and moving them closer to his country's border with Egypt.

When Sadat visited Haifa, he was amazed and touched to find Jewish and Arab citizens intermingling as they lined the streets to welcome him to their beautiful city. While the two leaders were discussing issues of relationship and understanding, teams of experts were meeting to hammer out the details of the proposed peace treaty and the nature of the proposed autonomy for the Arabs living in Judea, Samaria and the Gaza district.

When these negotiations broke down because of sharp technical differences and Egypt's refusal to continue the dialogue in Jerusalem, U.S. intervention was required. At that point, President Carter became active as the facilitator in the process. He and U.S. Secretary of State Cyrus Vance tried to reduce the differences and to bring the two sides closer together.

Towards the end of August 1978, Vance arrived in the Middle East with invitations to Sadat and Begin to join President Carter at Camp David in an attempt to find an acceptable formula. Begin was very pleased with this development, and he took with him his Foreign and Defense Ministers, Dayan and Weizman, together with other members of his staff.

They spent 12 days and 12 nights in the camp, which had been sealed off from all outside contact. A cordial relationship developed between the members of the three delegations who moved about in casual dress, chatted, joked, jogged, played chess, and tried to persuade each other in a spirit of goodwill. Begin's only concession to the air of informality was to remove his tie and walk about without his jacket during the hot September days.

Carter shuttled between the Egyptian and Israeli bungalows, attempting to smooth over rough edges and to encourage general agreement. At several critical moments, Begin was ready to leave Camp David at once, without concluding anything. He felt that Israel was being unnecessarily pressured, and he was beginning to experience difficulties with members of his own delegation.

The most sensitive issue was, of course, Jerusalem. Begin had made his position clear at the outset – Jerusalem is the capital of Israel and its status and future are not open to discussion. The U.S. President proposed a compromise on the matter and asked Begin to "think it over for a day or two." At that point Begin emphatically reiterated his refusal and narrated the legend of the 12th century Rabbi Amnon of Mainz whom the local bishop had repeatedly tried to persuade to accept Christianity. After many refusals Amnon finally agreed to "consider the matter for three days." When he returned to his community he suddenly realized what he had done and failed to appear before the bishop three days later. He was then forcibly brought before the bishop, pleaded guilty and asked that his tongue be cut out for uttering the words that he would "consider the proposal for three days." Infuriated, the bishop said: "Not your tongue, but your legs which did not bring you here at the appointed time." Amnon's legs and arms were brutally amputated and salt poured on his wounds. He bore the torture with fortitude and was brought home just before Rosh Hashana. About to expire, he composed and recited the famous *"Unetaneh Tokef"* prayer which is a centerpiece of the Rosh Hashana prayers to this day.

"I shall not consider the fate of Jerusalem for a few days," said Menachem Begin, "but have to tell you here and now, Jerusalem was the capital of the Jewish State in the days of King David; so it is today and so it will be forever."

A few days later, he told an audience in Washington: "I don't know what is going to happen in Washington, DC. I live in Jerusalem, DC. Do you know the difference between the two DCs? Washington, DC stands for District of Columbia, and Jerusalem, DC for David's City!"

He also related the legend of Amnon to President Sadat at one of their subsequent meetings. "He understood it very well," Begin said, and revealed that Sadat repeated it to American officials, like Robert Strauss and Sol Linowitz, who came to the Middle East as special ambassadors to facilitate the negotiating process.

At a joint press conference following one of their meetings, Begin declared in Sadat's presence: "Jerusalem is one city, undivided and indivisible. Secondly, Jerusalem is the capital of Israel, since the days of King David, for eternity. There cannot be any division of any kind of Jerusalem and there cannot be two sovereignties in Jerusalem – the only sovereignty is that of Israel."

On 30 July 1980 the Knesset approved, by a vote of 69 in favor, 15 against, and three abstentions, a new Basic Law proclaiming that "Jerusalem united in its entirety is the Capital of Israel."

The world community was indignant. The UN Security Council unanimously condemned Israel. Twelve countries closed their embassies in Jerusalem and moved to the Tel Aviv area. Holland's ambassador wept as he left. The protest action was initiated by the Islamic states and their allies, who declared that "any Israeli action will be deemed as null and void." They also called for the end of Israeli occupation of all Arab territories, "including Jerusalem."

Responding to the conduct of the international community, a group of Christian friends in Israel, headed by Johan Luckhoff and Jan Willem van der Hoeven, decided to open an International Christian Embassy in Jerusalem, explaining that although they did not represent a specific country, they spoke for tens of millions of friends and supporters of Israel around the world.

Begin was deeply moved by their action, and at an early opportunity he thanked them for it: "We know that we are not alone! Your decision to establish your Embassy in Jerusalem at a time when we were being abandoned because of our faith was an act of courage and a symbol of the closeness between us."

A comprehensive agreement was achieved at Camp David, and

the Camp David Accords were signed at a unique ceremony in the East Room of the White House. The Accords comprised two parts: The Framework for Peace in the Middle East and a Framework for the Conclusion of a Peace Treaty between Israel and Egypt. These were supplemented by exchanges of letters between President Sadat, Prime Minister Begin and President Carter. In the Preamble the following was included:

> After four wars during 30 years, despite intensive human efforts, the Middle East, which is the cradle of civilization and the birthplace of three great religions, does not yet enjoy the blessings of peace. The people of the Middle East yearn for peace, so that the vast human and natural resources of the region can be turned to the pursuits of peace and so that this area can become a model of coexistence and cooperation among nations.
>
> The historic initiative by President Sadat in visiting Jerusalem and the reception accorded to him by the parliament, government and people of Israel, and the reciprocal visit of Prime Minister Begin to Ismailia, the peace proposals made by both leaders, as well as the warm reception of these missions by the peoples of both countries, have created an unprecedented opportunity which must not be lost if this generation and future generations are to be spared the tragedies of war.

The agreement called on Egypt, Israel, Jordan and the representatives of the Palestinian people to participate in negotiations on the resolution of all aspects of the Palestinian problem. The negotiations were to lead to a transitional period in which details would be worked out for full autonomy to the inhabitants, an elected self-governing authority, a withdrawal of Israeli armed forces and a re-deployment of the remaining Israel forces into specified security locations. "As soon as possible, but not later than the third year after the beginning of the transitional period, negotiations will take place to determine the final status of the West Bank and Gaza and its relationship with its neighbors and to conclude a peace treaty between Israel and Jordan by the end of the transitional period."

Letters were exchanged regarding Israeli settlements in the Sinai and regarding Jerusalem, about which Menachem Begin wrote as follows to President Carter:

> I have the honor to inform you that on 28 June 1967, Israel's Parliament (the Knesset) promulgated and adopted a law to the effect: "The Government is empowered by a decree to apply the law, the jurisdiction and administration of the State to any part of Eretz Israel (Land of Israel-Palestine) as stated in the decree.
>
> On the basis of this law, the government of Israel decreed in July 1967 that Jerusalem is one city indivisible, the capital of the State of Israel.

Begin never deviated from that simple, yet profound, statement: that Jerusalem is "one city, indivisible, the capital of the State of Israel."

The Camp David Accords also outlined the framework of a peace treaty between Israel and Egypt; detailed negotiations towards this objective were expected to take three months, from 17 September to 17 December. Begin agreed that no new settlements would be established in that three-month period but that "thickening" or consolidation of existing settlements would continue.

No sooner had he come out of Camp David when the "spinners" began circulating rumors that Begin had agreed to "suspend," "freeze," "abandon" settlement activity "indefinitely," "permanently," and so on. Begin responded vigorously and angrily to such suggestions no matter from which source they came – even President Carter himself. And indeed, anyone who knew Begin was convinced that he would never have agreed to anything that compromised Israel's claim to Eretz Israel.

Another half a year was to pass before agreement was achieved on the final text of the Israeli-Egyptian peace treaty. Differences were gradually narrowed down until 5 Articles remained in dispute. So near and yet so far! This prompted Carter to pay a personal visit to Israel and Egypt in early March 1979. In three days of difficult meetings, the American President saw Menachem Begin as the charming host, the man of principle and the tough negotiator who insisted on crossing every "t" and dotting every "i." Begin was not prepared to leave anything to chance for future interpretation, as had been the case, for example, with the Balfour Declaration. Every comma was important, every word and every phrase.

At the height of a particularly heated and frustrating discussion with the Israeli Cabinet, Carter presented the American version of the final text. After reading it, Menachem Begin said calmly and simply: "We will not sign this document." All eyes turned to Carter who, white with rage, responded: "You will have to sign," whereupon Begin answered: "Sir, I will not have to sign any document to which I do not agree. I take exception to this statement of yours."

After a silence of a few seconds that seemed an eternity to all of us in the room, Carter said in a low voice: "You are right, Mr. Prime Minister. You are right and I apologize."

But their best efforts still left a number of key paragraphs open, and Carter traveled to Egypt to try and persuade Sadat to soften his stand. A meeting was hurriedly arranged at the Cairo Airport.

Some hours later, my wife and I were at the Prime Minister's residence. He was alone, as Mrs. Begin was attending a function. The phone rang, and he asked my wife to answer. It was President Carter calling from Cairo. "We have an agreement," he told Prime Minister Begin. I saw his eyes mist over. "Thank God," he said, "we shall have peace."

This was one of the greatest moments in the life of Menachem

Begin. He had achieved a peace agreement with Egypt, the largest, most populous and strongest of all the Arab countries which had been Israel's principal enemy in five wars.

Begin addressed the nation on Independence Day: "A peace treaty is not a scrap of paper. This is the most important international agreement that a state can undertake and the peace treaty between us and Egypt also has practical results. On the eve of Independence Day, you saw one of the results with your own eyes from afar. This is the first time that a ship flying the Israeli flag – the blue and white flag – crossed the Suez Canal from its southern entrance at Suez City to Port Said and, on both sides of the canal, thousands of cheering Egyptians were happily greeting the ship and paying their respects."

The formal signing of the Peace Treaty took place on the lawn of the White House on 26 March 1979. The podium had a table with the Egyptian, American and Israeli flags behind it. As the three heads of government were announced, the many hundreds of distinguished Americans, Egyptians, Israelis and American Jewish leaders gave them a prolonged standing ovation. I sat in the fourth row facing the table and kept my eyes glued to the scene.

President Carter opened the proceedings: "Today we celebrate a victory, not of a bloody military campaign, but of an inspiring peace campaign. Two leaders who loom large in the history of nations, President Anwar Sadat and Prime Minister Menachem Begin, have conducted this campaign with all the courage, tenacity, brilliance and inspiration of any generals who have ever led men and machines onto the field of battle. Mothers in Egypt and Israel are not weeping today for their children fallen in senseless battle. The dedication and determination of these two world statesmen have borne fruit. Peace has come to Israel and to Egypt."

President Sadat spoke of "a new dawn emerging out of the darkness of the past, a new chapter in the history of coexistence among nations, one that is worthy of our spiritual values and civilization."

The address that Menachem Begin delivered at the signing of the Israeli-Egyptian Peace Treaty marked the high point in Begin's career, both as an orator and a statesman. It was remarkable for its attention to historical context, at once deepening and tempering the significance of the moment. But more, it was remarkable for its spiritual foundation; it was the proclamation of a man of faith, following on the heels of a treaty constructed by men and between nations of faith.

Conscious of the significance of the moment and of the fact that tens of millions of television viewers around the world would be listening to him, Begin made this one of the rare occasions when he delivered an address from a written text. He had worked on it for a week and chosen every word with utmost care:

> *Address by Menachem Begin*
> *at the ceremony of the signing of the*
> *Israeli-Egyptian Peace Treaty*
> *26 March 1979*

Mr. President of the United States of America, Mr. President of the Arab Republic of Egypt, Mr. Vice-President, Mr. Speaker of the House of Representatives, Mr. Speaker of the Knesset, Members of the Cabinet of the United States, of Egypt, of Israel, Members of the Congress and the Knesset, Your Excellencies, Chairman of the Board of Governors of the Jewish Agency, Chairman of the Executive of the Zionist Organization, distinguished guests, ladies and gentlemen:

I have come from the Land of Israel, the land of Zion and Jerusalem, and here I stand, in humility and with pride, as a son of the Jewish people, as one of the generation of the Holocaust and Redemption. The ancient Jewish people gave the world the vision of eternal peace, of universal disarmament, of abolishing the teaching and learning of war. Two prophets, Yeshayahu Ben

Amotz and Micha Hamorashti, having foreseen the spiritual unity of man under God – with His word coming forth from Jerusalem – gave the nations of the world the following vision expressed in identical terms:

"And they shall beat their swords into ploughshares and their spears into pruning hooks. Nation shall not lift up sword against nation; neither shall they know war anymore."

Despite the tragedies and disappointments of the past we must never forsake that vision, that human dream, that unshakable faith. Peace is the beauty of life. It is sunshine. It is the smile of a child, the love of a mother, the joy of a father, the togetherness of a family. It is the advancement of man, the victory of a just cause, the triumph of truth. Peace is all of these and more, and more.

These are words I uttered in Oslo on December tenth 1978 while receiving the second half of the Nobel Peace Prize – the first half went, and rightly so, to President Sadat – and I took the liberty to repeat them here, on this momentous, historic occasion.

It is a great day in the annals of two ancient nations, Egypt and Israel, whose sons met in our generation five times on the battlefield, fighting and falling. Let us turn our hearts to our heroes and pay tribute to their eternal memory; it is thanks to them that we could have reached this day.

However, let us not forget that in ancient times our two nations met also in alliance. Now we make peace, the cornerstone of cooperation and friendship.

It is a great day in your life, Mr. President of the United States. You have worked so hard, so insistently, so consistently, for this goal; and your labors and your devotion bore God-blessed fruit. Our friend, President Sadat, said that you are the "unknown soldier" of the peacemaking effort. I agree, but, as usual, with an amendment. A soldier in the service of peace you are; you are, Mr. President, even *horribile dictu* an intransigent fighter for peace. But Jimmy Carter, the President of the United States, is not completely unknown. Nor is his effort, which will be remembered for generations to come.

It is, of course, a great day in your life, Mr. President of the Arab Republic of Egypt. In the fact of adversity and hostility you have demonstrated the human value that can change history: civil courage. A great field commander once said: civil courage is sometimes more difficult to show than military courage. You showed both. But now is the time, for all of us to show civil courage in order to proclaim to our peoples, and to others: no more war, no more bloodshed, no more bereavement – peace unto you, Shalom, Salaam – forever.

And it is, ladies and gentlemen, the third greatest day in my life. The first was May the fourteenth, 1948 when our flag was hoisted, our independence in our ancestors' land was proclaimed after one thousand eight hundred and seventy-eight years of dispersion, persecution, and physical destruction. We fought for our liberation – alone – and won the day. That was spring; such a spring we can never have again.

The second day was when Jerusalem became one city, and our brave, perhaps most hardened soldiers, the parachutists, embraced with tears and kissed the ancient stones of the remnants of the Western Wall destined to protect the chosen place of God's glory. Our hearts wept with them – in remembrance.

"Omdot hayu ragleinu b'sha'arayich Yerushalayim, Yerushalayim habnuya k'ir sh-chubrah la yachdav."*

This is the third day in my life. I have signed a treaty of peace with our neighbor, with Egypt. The heart is full and overflowing. God gave me the strength to survive the horrors of

---

* "When our feet stood within thy gates, O Jerusalem, O Jerusalem built as a city that is compact together" (Psalm 122).

Nazism and of a Stalinite concentration camp, to persevere, to endure, not to waiver in or flinch from my duty, to accept abuse from foreigners and, what is more painful, from my own people, and from my close friends. This effort too bore some fruit.

Therefore, it is the proper place and appropriate time to bring back to memory the song and prayer of thanksgiving I learned as a child in the home of a father and mother that don't exist any more, because they were among the six million people, men, women and children, who sanctified the Lord's name with their sacred blood, which reddened the rivers of Europe from the Rhine to the Danube, from the Bug to the Volga – because, only because they were born Jews, and because they didn't have a country of their own, neither a valiant Jewish army to defend them, and because, nobody, nobody came to their rescue, although they cried out: save us, de profundis, from the depths of the pit and agony; that is the song of degrees written two millennia and five hundred years ago when our forefathers returned from their first exile to Jerusalem, to Zion.

*"Shir hamaʾalot bʾshuv adonai, et shivat Zion hayinu kʾcholmim. Az yimalei tʾzechok pinu ulshoneinu rinah. As yomru vagoyim higdil adonai laʾasot im eileh, higdil adonai laʾasot imanu hayinu sʾmeichim. Shuva adonai et shʾviteinu kaʾafikim banegev. Haʾazorim bʾdimah bʾrinah yiktzoru. Haloch yeilech uvacha nosei meshech – hazarah bo-yavo bʾrinah nosei alumotav."***

I will not translate. Every man, whether Jew or Christian or Moslem, can read it in his own language. It is Psalm 126.

**The following English translation of this Psalm, which Begin quoted in its entirety, is from the Jerusalem Bible:

1 When the Lord brought back the captivity of Zion, we were like men in a dream.

2 Then was our mouth filled with laughter, and our tongue with singing: then they said among the nations, the Lord has done great things for them.

3 The Lord has done great things for us; we are glad.

A month later, documents of ratification were exchanged; exactly three years later, on 25 April 1982, Israel completed her withdrawal from Sinai – including the withdrawal from the town of Yamit.

Yamit was a particularly bitter pill for Begin to swallow. He was proud that the painful operation was accomplished without bloodshed. In a subsequent interview, he confirmed that at Camp David he had not agreed "to evacuate our settlers from northern and southern Sinai." But President Sadat told Begin at their meeting in Ismailia that "if I should leave your people in the Sinai, my people will stone me." Begin commented that this was a very dramatic way of putting it. "Of course, I could have said, if I decide to evacuate them, my people will stone me. And may I say, indeed, there may now be some people of Yamit who perhaps are prepared to stone me. But, when you are elected to conduct the affairs of your nation, you sometimes have to make hard decisions." In fact, a group of disenchanted, irate members of his party criticized him angrily for surrendering territory to the Egyptians. They left the party and established their own, Techiya (Renaissance) Party, which stood to the right of Likud, and which lasted until 1992.

The Peace Treaty terminated the state of war between Israel and Egypt. Ambassadors were exchanged; now began the long and difficult process of ensuring that a true spirit of peace would evolve. This was not easy. Israel's first Ambassador to Egypt, Dr. Eliyahu Ben Elissar, had difficulty finding premises for the Israel Embassy and his residence. He and his wife Nitza were, at first, shunned by Egyptian officialdom and society. The media paid scant attention to him, and he was denied access to TV, radio and press. By and

---

4 Bring back our captivity, O Lord, like the streams in the Negev.
5 They who sow in tears shall reap in joy.
6 He who goes weeping on his way, bearing a bag of seed, shall come back with a joyful shout, carrying his sheaves.

large, this attitude has not changed to this day. By the time he left Egypt, however, Eli Ben Elissar had established good personal relations and contacts.

On the other hand, Egyptian Ambassador Bassiouny has stayed in Israel for 14 years. He is wined and dined, and all doors are open to him. He appears on Israeli TV, is interviewed by the press, and publicly celebrated his "bar mitzvah" year as Ambassador.

Some commentators have described the relationship as "a cold peace," but remembering the thousands of casualties on the Egyptian front in five wars, many Israelis retort that "a cold peace is still preferable to a hot war." No Israeli soldiers have been killed on the formerly volatile southern front since 1977.

One year after the Peace Treaty went into effect, Menachem Begin described it as a fundamental turning point in the history of the two nations. "We did not sign one more agreement on a cease-fire, or an armistice, or an interim accord, while at the same time the state of war remained intact, leaving a permanent opening for its activation, for attack, for bloodshed, for creating orphans, for bereavement. This time we put an end to the state of war. We signed a permanent peace and we said to one another: We shall never again employ our weapons, one nation against its neighbor."

Later he told the IDF radio: "True, there is an eastern front. Today it is no longer simple to declare war on us, everyone can see it with his own eyes. We made sacrifices for this peace. I would be the first to admit it. I will not deny it. Yet it was worth it – all these sacrifices."

In an interview with *The Wall Street Journal* on 30 July 1981, Menachem Begin said: "Cynics call the peace treaty a piece of paper. I am an old man, my friend – an old Jew, 68 years old – and I have worked for my people more than 50 years. In these 50 years I learned from experience that cynicism is not to be equated with wisdom. In my opinion, to the contrary.

"It is a very serious document and there are inherent guarantees, either by the objective situation or because two thirds of Sinai is demilitarized and there aren't going to be Egyptian troops in that part of Sinai (in the other third there are limitations to keeping forces and that wasn't the case in the past, in '56 and '57, when there was a withdrawal from Sinai after Suez and the Egyptian army came back to Sinai which was then remilitarized). Now it is demilitarized, so there are inherent guarantees."

In an address to the Knesset on Independence Day, 27 April 1982, Menachem Begin summed up as follows: "Three times we withdrew from Sinai, and three times the state of war remained intact…This time we have signed a peace treaty. No longer is there a state of war. Merchant ships and even warships pass freely through the Suez Canal. Freedom of passage through the Straits of Tiran has been assured for generations. There is no power that can remove the military unit of the United States of America that is stationed there in order to maintain freedom of navigation. That is the change; that is the revolutionary change."

Menachem Begin was the first – and thus far still the only – Prime Minister of Israel to have concluded a peace treaty with one of Israel's neighbors. He and his Government, backed by a substantial majority of the Knesset, paid a high price for the end of the state of war with Egypt and the conclusion of a peace treaty. Israel agreed to withdraw from all of Sinai, which would be demilitarized; to give up its air, land and naval bases there; to abandon the oil wells, which Israel had found and developed, in exchange for an Egyptian agreement to see oil to Israel and an American guarantee to make up for any shortfall. In addition, Israel agreed to withdraw from the town of Yamit and a cluster of settlements built in northern Sinai. This was perhaps the most difficult concession, and some of Begin's strongest supporters (such as Yitzhak Shamir and Moshe Arens) voted against it in the Knesset because they opposed the principle of abandoning Jewish settlements.

In monetary terms, the peace treaty cost Israel approximately $12 billion in abandoned and wasted infrastructure, compensation for the residents of Yamit and other settlements, rebuilding and relocating military bases, and oil to replace the supplies coming from the oil fields found and developed by Israel. But Begin considered all this worthwhile and necessary if it would provide his people with a long period of real peace. When he met with Sadat in Ophira (Sharm el-Sheikh) on 4 June 1981, he told the assembled international media with joy and satisfaction: "The Israeli-Egyptian border is the quietest corner in the world."

Chapter 22

NOBEL LAUREATE

In recognition of their remarkable and courageous efforts, President Anwar Sadat of Egypt and Prime Minister Menachem Begin of Israel were jointly awarded the Nobel Prize for Peace while the complicated negotiations were still in progress. I was in the Prime Minister's office when he received the first notification of the award. The news came late on a Friday afternoon as he was preparing to go home for the Sabbath. The world media wanted to interview him that night. He declined, saying that he would be making no comment until after the Sabbath. However, he did call President Sadat to congratulate him, and the two men had a very warm conversation.

That Saturday evening, there were many more guests than usual at the "Open House" in the Prime Minister's residence, including the great maestro Artur Rubinstein. After the Sabbath, the Prime Minister stepped forward and addressed the press in moving personal terms, saying that "the Prize belongs to all the people of Israel in recognition of their yearning, efforts, prayers and sacrifices for peace." He was the first Jew to receive the Nobel Prize for Peace in recognition of his efforts on behalf of his own people.

By the time the award ceremony actually took place, there were disagreements with Egypt, and Sadat did not go to Oslo, sending instead a Mr. Marei, a member of Sadat's family and one of his close advisers, to read his acceptance speech. In Israel, Begin's opponents started clamoring for him not to go, and even to give up the award, but it is clear in retrospect that such advice was motivated mainly by jealousy.

Menachem Begin, accompanied by his wife, members of his family, members of his staff and a small group of friends – the Silvers, Halevys, Gaons, Max Fisher, Reuben Hecht – was received with great warmth and honor in Oslo. The King of Norway invited the Begins to stay in the royal palace. It was an unforgettable occasion also for the small Jewish community of Norway.

In Oslo, Begin learned that Golda Meir, Israel's fourth Prime Minister, had died that day; naturally, he opened his address at the Award Ceremony with a brief tribute to her.

> Your Majesty, Your Royal Highnesses, Your Excellencies, Madam Chairlady and Members of the Nobel Prize Committee, Mr. Marei, representative of the President of Egypt, ladies and gentlemen,
>
> I ask for permission first to pay tribute to Golda Meir, my predecessor, a great leader and Prime Minister, who strove with all her heart to achieve peace between Israel and her neighbors. Her blessed memory will live forever in the hearts of the Jewish people and of all peace-loving nations.
>
> I have come from the Land of Israel, the land of Zion and Jerusalem, and here I stand in humility and with pride as a son of the Jewish people, as one of the generation of the Holocaust and Redemption.
>
> The ancient Jewish people gave the world the vision of eternal peace, of universal disarmament, of abolishing the teaching and learning of war. Two Prophets, Yeshayahu Ben Amotz and Micha HaMorashti, having foreseen the spiritual

unity of man under God – with His word coming forth from Jerusalem – gave the nations of the world the following vision expressed in identical terms:

"And they shall beat their swords into ploughshares and their spears into pruning hooks. Nation shall not lift up sword against nation; neither shall they learn war any more."

We mortals who believe in Divine Providence, when recalling those sacred prophecies, ask ourselves not whether, but when is this vision going to become reality? We remember the past; even in this century alone – and we know. We look around – and see. Millions of men of all nations are under arms. Intercontinental missiles deposited in the bowels of the earth or lying on the beds of oceans can destroy man and everything he has built. Not in Alfred Nobel's time, but in our own era, has mankind become capable of destroying itself and returning the earth to *Tohu Vevohu*. Under such circumstances, should we, can we, keep our faith in an eternal peace that will one day reign over mankind? Yes, we should and we can. Perhaps that very capability of total destruction of our little planet – achieved for the first time in the annals of mankind – will one day, God willing, become the origin, the cause and the prime mover for the elimination of all instruments of destruction from the face of the earth and ultimate peace, prayed for and yearned for by previous generations, will become the portion of all nations. Despite the tragedies and disappointments of the past, we must never forsake that vision, that human dream, that unshakable faith.

Peace is the beauty of life. It is sunshine. It is the smile of a child, the love of a mother, the joy of a father, the togetherness of a family. It is the advancement of man, the victory of a just cause, the triumph of truth. Peace is all of these and more and more.

But in my generation, Ladies and Gentlemen, there was a time indescribable. Six million Jews – men, women and children – a number larger than many a nation in Europe – were dragged to a wanton death and slaughtered methodically in the heart of the civilized continent. It was not a sudden outburst of human or rather inhuman cruelty that from time to time has happened in the history of mankind; it was a systematic process of extermination which unfolded before the eyes of the whole world for more than six years. Those who were doomed, deprived of their human dignity, starved, humiliated, led away and ultimately turned into ashes, cried out for rescue – but in vain. Other than a few famous and unforgettable exceptions they were left alone to face the destroyer.

At such a time, unheard of since the first generation, the hour struck to rise and fight – for the dignity of man, for survival, for liberty, for every value of the human image a man has been endowed with by his Creator, for every known inalienable right he stands for and lives for. Indeed, there are days when to fight for a cause so absolutely just is the highest human command. Norway has known such days, and so have we. Only in honoring that command comes the *regeneration* of the concept of peace. You rise, you struggle, you make sacrifices to achieve and guarantee the prospect and hope of living in peace – for you and your people, for your children and their children.

Let it, however, be declared and known, stressed, and noted that fighters for freedom hate war. My friends and I learned this precept from Ze'ev Jabotinsky through his own example, and through the one he set for us from Giuseppe Garibaldi. Our brothers in spirit, wherever they dwell, learned it from their masters and teachers. This is our common maxim and belief: that if through your efforts and sacrifices you win liberty and with it the prospect of peace, then work for peace because there is no mission in life more sacred.

And so reborn Israel always strove for peace, yearned for it, made endless endeavors to achieve it. My colleagues and I have gone in the footsteps of our predecessors since the very first day we were called by our people to care for their future. We went any place, we looked for any avenue, we made any effort to bring about negotiations between Israel and its neighbors, negotiations without which peace remains an abstract desire.

We have labored long and hard to turn it into a reality – because of the blessings it holds for ourselves, our neighbors, the world. In peace, the Middle East, the ancient cradle of civilization, will become invigorated and transformed. Throughout its lands there will be freedom of movement of people, of ideas, of goods. Cooperation and development in agriculture will make the deserts blossom. Industry will bring the promise of a better life. Sources of water will be developed and the almost year-long sunshine will yet be harnessed for the common needs of all the nations. Yes, indeed, the Middle East, standing at the crossroads of the world, will become a peaceful center of international communication between East and West, North and South – a center of human advancement in every sphere of creative endeavor. This and more is what peace will bring to our region.

During the past year many efforts for peace were made and many significant events took place. The President of the Arab Republic of Egypt expressed his readiness to come to Jerusalem, the eternal capital of Israel, and to address our parliament, the Knesset. When that message reached me I, without delay or hesitation, extended to President Sadat on behalf of Israel, an invitation to visit our country. I told him: You will be received with respect and cordiality. And, indeed, so he was received, cordially and respectfully, by the people, by the parliament and by the government of our nation. We knew and learned that we have differences of opinion. But whenever we recall those days of Jerusalem we say, always, that they were shining, beautiful days of friendliness and understanding. It was in this same atmosphere that the meetings in Ismailia were conducted. In the spirit of the Nobel Prize tradition we gave to each other the most momentous pledge: No more war. No more bloodshed. We shall negotiate and reach agreement.

Admittedly, there were difficult times as well. Let nobody forget that we deal with a conflict of more than sixty years with its manifold tragedies. These we must put behind us in order to establish friendship and make peace the beauty of our lives.

Many of the difficulties were overcome at Camp David where the President of the United States, Mr. Jimmy Carter, unforgettably invested unsparing effort, untiring energy and great devotion in the peace-making process. There, despite all the differences, we found solutions for problems, agreed on issues and the Framework for Peace was signed. With its signature, there was rejoicing in our countries and throughout the world. The path leading to peace was paved.

The phase that followed was the natural arduous negotiations to elaborate and conclude a peace treaty as we promised each other to do at Camp David. The delegations of both countries worked hard and have, I believe, produced a draft document that can serve, if and when signed and ratified, as a good treaty of peace between countries that decided to put an end to hostility and war and begin a new era of understanding and cooperation. Such a treaty can serve as the first indispensable step along the road towards a comprehensive peace in our region.

If, because of all these efforts, President Sadat and I have been awarded the Nobel Peace Prize, let me from this rostrum again congratulate him – as I did in a direct conversation between Jerusalem and Cairo a few weeks ago after the announcement.

Now, it is I who must express gratitude from the bottom of my heart for the great honor you do me. But, Ladies and Gentlemen, before doing so, permit me to remind us all that today is an important anniversary – the thirtieth anniversary of the adoption of the Universal Declaration of Human Rights. Let us always remember the magnificently written words of its first Article. It expresses the essence of all the declarations of the rights of man and citizen written throughout history. It says: "All human beings are born free and equal, in dignity and rights. They are endowed with reason and conscience and should act towards one another in a spirit of brotherhood."

Free women and men everywhere must wage an incessant campaign so that these human values become a generally recognized and practiced reality. We must regretfully admit that in various parts of the world this is not yet the case. Without those values and human rights the real peace of which we dream is jeopardized.

For reasons self-understood, but which every man and woman of goodwill will accept, I must remind my honored listeners of my brethren the prisoners who are deprived of one of their most basic rights: to go home. I speak about people of great courage who deserve not only the respect but also the moral support of the free world. I speak about people who, even from the depths of their suffering, repeat the age-old prayer:

Next year in Jerusalem.

The preservation and protection of human rights are indispensable to give peace of nations and individuals its real meaning.

Allow me, now, to turn to you, Madame President of the Nobel Peace Prize Committee and to all its members and say, thank you. I thank you for the great distinction. It does not, however, belong to me; it belongs to my people – the ancient people and renascent nation that came back in love and devotion to the land of its ancestors after centuries of homelessness and persecution. This prestigious recognition is due to this people because they suffered so much, because they lost so many, because they love peace and want it with all their hearts for themselves and for their neighbors. On their behalf, I humbly accept the award and in their name I thank you from the bottom of my heart.

And may I express to His Majesty, the King, our deep gratitude for the gracious hospitality His Majesty, on this occasion, bestowed upon my wife and myself.

Your Majesty, Your Highnesses, Members of the Nobel Peace Prize Committee, Ladies and Gentlemen:

Seventy-seven years ago, the first Nobel Peace Prize was awarded. Jean Henri Dunant was its recipient. On December 10, 1901, the President of the Norwegian Parliament said:

"The Norwegian people have always demanded that their independence be respected. They have always been ready to defend it. But at the same time they have always had a keen desire and need for peace."

May I, Ladies and Gentlemen, on behalf of the people of Israel, respectfully subscribe to these true and noble words.

Thank you.

The ceremony was followed by a state banquet for the distinguished Nobel laureate and President Sadat's representative, and afterwards Max Fisher, the Chairman of the Board of Governors of the Jewish Agency, gave a reception in his hotel suite in Menachem Begin's honor.

Begin's share of the Nobel Prize was about $85,000. He devoted the full sum to establish the "Menachem and Aliza Begin Nobel Prize Fund" to assist needy students. A board, chaired by their son, Dr. Benjamin Begin, receives recommendations from the presidents of the country's universities of deserving and needy students who are awarded a scholarship to cover their annual tuition fee. One condition is attached: the student must undertake to provide tuition to a little schoolboy or girl from the underprivileged part of the population. We were at the simple ceremony at the Prime Minister's residence when the first awards were made. The selected students arrived and found their little "partners" – all spruced up for the occasion – who came with their parents and members of their families. Dr. Begin explained the significance of the special fund (*Perach* – Flower) and then called up each student in turn. He or she walked to the table accompanied by their small "partners" to receive an envelope containing a check from the Prime Minister and Mrs. Begin.

Chapter 23

TROUBLED TIMES

My wife and i arrived in Israel as immigrants on Thursday, 18 May 1978, and I commenced my duties as Prime Minister Begin's adviser on external information three days later. In the first week, one of my new colleagues told me: "You should have been here in the first six months when unbelievable and wonderful things were happening almost every day."

By mid-1978, the situation was somewhat different. Begin's Government was subject to American pressure and shaken by internal dissension. American Jewish leaders were critical of the government's settlement policy. Some of them neither understood nor cared about the Jewish people's inalienable right to Eretz Israel, which one of them dismissed in my presence as "Biblical nonsense." They sent delegations to try to persuade the Prime Minister of Israel to yield and make major concessions "for the sake of peace." They were "uncomfortable" with the ongoing collision between their own government and Israel.

Some of Begin's ministers were trying to pull or push him in different directions. Disagreeing with the substance of Begin's autonomy plan and its procedural framework, Moshe Dayan resigned as Foreign Minister on 21 October 1979, and was replaced by Yitzhak Shamir, who had served with distinction as Speaker of the

Knesset since the start of the Likud Administration. Ezer Weizman, an unyielding hawk who had by now softened his stand, constantly quarreled with the Prime Minister, harassed him, shouted at Cabinet meetings and eventually also resigned. Until the appointment of a new defense minister, the Prime Minister himself served as acting defense minister. That interlude was to last several months, and he enjoyed the experience very much. In due course, General Ariel Sharon, one of Israel's best-known generals and strategists, was appointed Minister of Defense.

The Government did not have sufficient Knesset support to introduce the economic reforms outlined in its policy guidelines. This worried and frustrated Begin greatly, but there was little he could do about it.

He took great pains to explain at every opportunity that the Israeli withdrawal from Sinai must not be taken as a precedent for similar steps in Judea, Samaria, the Gaza district and the Golan Heights. "There is no comparison," he told an interviewer on the NBC program "Meet the Press" on 25 April 1982 – the day the last of Israel's troops left Sinai.

> We gave up Sinai, the Sinai Peninsula, 23,000 square miles, two sophisticated airfields, an oil well from which we already derived two years ago, 24 per cent of our annual consumption, which is 8 million tons, and then we had to evacuate our civilian people, which was a real trauma. You might have seen it on your television. And we carried out our commitment to the dot and to the date.
>
> But there is no comparison with the Golan Heights or with Judea and Samaria. We have in Sinai now 150 kilometers of completely demilitarized desert land, which can be photographed. We can see whether a breach took place. We can control it. You cannot do so on the Golan Heights, neither in Judea and Samaria. So let us not make any comparisons whatsoever.

Now we applied the law and jurisdiction of Israel to the Golan Heights. This law stands.

We want peace with Syria on the basis that on the Golan Heights we apply the law and jurisdiction of the State of Israel.

Q: Mr. Prime Minister, there are people who say that you're moving unmistakably to annex the West Bank and the Gaza Strip.

A: Well, first of all, I would like to say a word about the term annex, or annexation. You can annex foreign land. You cannot annex your own country. Judea and Samaria are part of the Land of Israel, or in foreign languages, Palestine, in which our nation was born. There our Kings ruled and our prophets brought forth the vision of eternal peace. How can we annex it?

He also stressed that he was offering the Palestinian Arabs autonomy, but under no circumstances would there be a Palestinian state in the area between Mediterranean and the Jordan River.

The Golan Heights Law was adopted by the Knesset on 14 December 1981 by a majority of 63 against 21. Eight members of the opposition Labor Party voted with the Government. Begin was ill at the time and surprised the Cabinet Ministers by summoning them to his sick bed. He told them emphatically that he had decided to pass a law annexing the Golan Heights that very day. He cited Syria's implacable hostility to Israel, the rejection a few days earlier by the Syrian president of any ties with Israel, and the continued presence of Syrian missiles in Lebanon. The Golan Law states: "The Law, jurisdiction and administration of the State shall apply to the Golan Heights."

This move was at once rejected by the United Nations. The

UN Security Council declared that the Israeli decision to impose its laws, jurisdiction and administration on the occupied Syrian Golan Heights is "null and void and without international legal effect." It demanded that "Israel, the occupying Power, should rescind forthwith its decision."

The Golan Law was but one of a series of events in a stormy period in Israel's history. From the beginning of 1981, Israel was caught up in a heated campaign for the election of the Tenth Knesset, which was to take place on 30 June 1981. The Likud won 48 seats and the Labor Alignment 47. Menachem Begin was able to constitute a viable coalition with the Religious parties and to continue leading the country. However, while he gave much attention to the election campaign, his mind was on another matter that he did not discuss with his Cabinet colleagues, nor did he share it with the United States administration, nor with his friend, the Egyptian President. This was one occasion when not even his wife knew what was in his heart.

For some time he was troubled by secret reports that Iraq's atomic reactor was about to "go hot." The reactor built at Osiraq near Baghdad was supplied by France and staffed by French and other European experts. It was reaching the perilous moment when it would contain the critical quantity of fissionable material.

Israel's Prime Minister left no diplomatic channel unexplored, appealing in vain to the French and the Americans to get the Iraqis to halt their work.

Iraq's ruthless dictator, Saddam Hussein, was about to acquire nuclear capability. Hussein tried to disguise the operation as a peaceful industrial development project. But Begin had decided some time earlier that, if his top-secret diplomacy failed, he would use military means to destroy the reactor – a totally unprecedented action. He consulted only with the Defense Ministry, the Chief of Staff of Israel's Defense Forces, and the officers who would be directly involved in such an operation.

On 7 June 1981, the eve of the Festival of Shavuoth in Israel, the carefully planned and long-prepared operation was carried out. Israel Air Force planes flew to Iraq over neighboring Arab territories, destroyed the reactor and returned safely to base. King Hussein of Jordan was on his royal yacht in the Gulf of Aqaba as the planes roared overhead. He counted eight F-16s and six F-15s providing an escorting umbrella. But he was left guessing as to their destination and purpose. Saudi Arabia's AWACS were not in the air at the time.

Begin was in the official residence in Jerusalem when the Chief of Staff Eytan telephoned to report that "the boys have set out." "Let's hope for the best," Begin replied pensively. He revealed afterwards that he prayed incessantly, and thought of his parents and family who had been killed by the Germans. His duty was to protect his grandchildren and all the children of Israel.

"I have lived with this problem for two years already," he said in a press interview the next day. "Sometimes I would go out and meet groups of children. They would make a circle around me, I would chat with them and they would ask me questions – and then it would occur to me: My God, what will happen to these children? They are now seven or eight years old. When they are ten or twelve years old, the atomic bomb might be dropped on them. What would happen to them? I don't deny it – there were many and very serious doubts until we took the decision with absolute determination."

The operation took place on Sunday on the assumption that the 100–150 foreign experts employed at the reactor would be absent on the Christian day of rest. This assumption was proved correct. Only one French worker who had remained on the site unexpectedly was killed.

At 4:30 on Sunday afternoon, shortly before the start of Shavuoth, much unusual activity was taking place at the Prime Minister's residence as the Ministers of the Government arrived in their official cars. They had been asked to gather without being told the reason, and assumed all sorts of things.

At five o'clock Prime Minister Begin addressed the assembled Ministers: "Welcome, my friends. At this very moment our planes are approaching Baghdad and the first one will be over the reactor in a very short time."

Suddenly there was total silence in the room as though the fate of Israel was hanging in mid-air. Begin explained that Israel had reliable information that the reactor would be active by July or September. It would then be too late for an attack because at that stage large amounts of radioactive material would be released over Baghdad, bringing death to hundreds of thousands of innocent people. "No Jew, no Israeli Government, would perpetrate such a deed. Therefore, we decided to act now and chose Sunday as a further precaution to prevent casualties."

Becoming very personal, Begin told his colleagues: "A few minutes ago my wife asked why I was so nervous. But I could not tell her. Nor could I tell my son, whom I trust implicitly. I have taken the responsibility, the anxiety and the decision, entirely upon myself. My soul-searching extended over many weeks. I knew that if I did not give the order today, that lunatic Saddam Hussein, who aspires to become the leader of the Arab world, will have two or three atomic bombs. Our experts believe that one Iraqi atom bomb could kill fifty thousand of our people instantly and cause the deaths of a further one hundred and fifty thousand subsequently. With three atomic bombs, the enemy could destroy Jerusalem and its vicinity, Tel Aviv and its suburbs, Haifa and its environs. Twenty percent of the Israeli population would be annihilated or injured. In the United States, such a ratio would equal 46 million casualties.

"Consequently, Iraq's manufacture of atomic bombs constitutes an existential threat to the State of Israel. It is the sacred duty of the Israeli government to act in good time to ward off the danger which threatens, at a single stroke, to destroy everything we have built up here over more than one hundred years."

He revealed that the actual operation was planned to last two minutes.

Shortly after 5:30 PM, Begin received a call in his library that the attack had been successful. "The target has been destroyed. The boys are on their way back. All are well."

Relieved and delighted, Begin shared the good news with his anxious Ministers. He later said: "A weight was lifted from our hearts. We embraced." Some Ministers wept; others laughed; some sat stunned, staring into space.

By seven o'clock the planes landed at their home base, and in the Prime Minister's residence the Ministers toasted the Air Force.

But for Begin, the joy ended quickly. He knew that Israel would be condemned for the raid, and so it was. I was then serving in Washington where the "skies were falling" around us. The Administration was in shock and Vice-President George Bush called for sanctions against Israel. Some Jewish leaders were horrified. In Israel, where the Knesset elections were only a few weeks away, Begin was accused of a "cheap election trick." Upset by such a charge, he immediately retorted that he would not endanger a single Israeli soldier or airman for the sake of an election.

He reminded the Americans of the words of President John F. Kennedy during the second confrontation with Cuba which was, in fact, a fateful confrontation between the United States and the Soviet Union. "The American President then said: In our times, with swift weapons, the moment of the greatest national danger does not necessarily come with the actual opening of fire. This is a principle applying to all nations. For reasons that need not be explained, it applies also, perhaps more so, to the State of Israel."

As Prime Minister and Acting Defense Minister, Begin led the publicity campaign, appearing at press conferences and granting interviews. He wrote to the President of the United States and to the heads of other governments. The Security Council of the United Nations "strongly condemned the Israeli attack" and called for "appropriate redress for Iraq for the destruction it has suffered." The United States suspended delivery of four F-16 fighters to Israel.

Begin took all this in his stride. He congratulated the Air Force and the unit that had conducted the operation. When the Air Force commander asked him to receive these men for a few minutes at his office, he insisted instead on visiting them at their base. At the ceremony, a week later, Begin said: "On behalf of the nation and its democratically elected government, I have come to thank you. We have come here because we wished to breathe the atmosphere in which you fly. Everything said here may, perhaps, be forgotten, but what you did shall be remembered by the generations to come. Thanks to you, we have been freed of a nightmare which has pursued us for two whole years."

The storm of protest subsided but it took another ten years for the world at large and the people of Israel to recognize the remarkable contribution that Menachem Begin had made by his bold decisions which even his harsh critic Abba Eban subsequently described as "one of the most dramatic decisions ever taken by a government in the nuclear age."

At the time of the 1991 Gulf War, in which a U.S.-led coalition of more than 30 nations was involved in a large-scale war with Saddam Hussein's military regime in Iraq, the highest tributes were paid to Menachem Begin – by then a withdrawn, sick man. Resolutions were proposed in the U.S. Congress "thanking Israel for destroying the atomic reactor." Senators and Congressmen came to Israel and proclaimed their gratitude with tears in their eyes. *The Miami Herald*, which had been particularly critical of Begin's action, apologized to him and put the record straight. All agreed that the Gulf War could have taken a terrible, tragic turn if Saddam Hussein had possessed an active nuclear capability. No one doubted that the brutal dictator, who used poison gas against his own people, would have used atomic weapons against the coalition forces in the "mother of all battles," as he called it.

But Begin's greatest satisfaction in this matter was a letter signed in 1991 by 100 of the 120 Knesset Members paying tribute to him for taking courageous unilateral action against Iraq. Several times he pointed out to me that among the signatories were some of his long-time political opponents. He was pleased that Yitzhak Rabin was among the signatories. But Shimon Peres, who as head of the opposition in 1981 had addressed "a last minute appeal" to Begin to stop the action and criticized it afterwards, refused to sign the tribute. Obviously, the Communist and Arab Knesset Members likewise did not sign the document.

Chapter 24

LOSS OF A FRIEND

Israel's action placed Anwar Sadat in a difficult situation. He had met with Begin at Ophira (Sharm el Sheikh) on 4 June – three days prior to the bombing of the reactor – and it was naturally assumed that Begin had briefed and prepared his Egyptian friend. In fact, the subject was not discussed. "I did not say a thing to President Sadat, and he did not know a thing about the action and its date. It was forbidden to tell him. It was a military secret of the utmost classification.

"And if the Americans today say that they did not know from the start, I confirm this. I did not tell them anything."

And yet my friend and publisher, Dr. Michael Neiditch, recalls that in January 1981, while serving as a Congressional foreign policy analyst, he and 11 American colleagues visited the chief of the Israeli Air Force, who declared: "You know the Iraqis are building a nuclear reactor" and he went on to explain Israel's concern about such a development that could one day endanger the country and threaten the interests of the Free World.

Sadat was severely criticized in Egypt, where different groups were actively plotting against him. "I could not expect Menachem to tell me about such an action when we met a few days ago," he said.

The two leaders met for the last time in Alexandria on 26 August 1981, where their talks covered a wide range of topics and resulted in agreement to resume the autonomy talks and the process of normalization in the relations between the two nations.

Six weeks later, on 6 October, marking the anniversary of theYom Kippur War, Sadat was assassinated in full view of the world's TV cameras as he stood on a podium, taking the salute at a military parade. As the armored vehicles rolled by and paused briefly before him, the "soldiers" in one such vehicle jumped off, turned their machine guns on Sadat and mowed him down. Pandemonium broke loose. Security personnel rushed to Sadat – but it was too late. The killers were apprehended, subsequently tried and finally executed. During their trial it was proved that they were members of an Islamic fundamentalist group.

Menachem Begin was deeply distressed by the death of his friend, and he decided that he would personally attend the funeral the following Saturday. Because of the Sabbath, he asked to be accommodated at a hotel near the burial place, and he walked all the way to the ceremony. It required tremendous physical effort from him and, considering the circumstances, was an act of great courage. In a statement after the assassination, Begin said:

> President Sadat fell victim to a criminal assassination. The people of Israel share in the mourning of the people of Egypt. We send our deepest condolences to Mrs. Sadat and the children. President Sadat was murdered by the enemies of peace. His decision to come to Jerusalem and the reception accorded to him by the people, the Knesset and the Government of Israel will be remembered as one of the great events of our time. President Sadat did not pay attention to abuse and hostility and went ahead with endeavors to abolish the state of war with Israel and to make peace with our nation. It was a difficult road. The President of the United States, Mr. Carter,

the President of the Arab Republic of Egypt, President Sadat, and I as Prime Minister of Israel and our colleagues resolved to do our utmost to reach the noble goal of establishing peace in our region. Unforgettable are the days of Camp David, and so is the hour in which the President of Egypt and the Prime Minister of Israel signed a treaty between our two countries, and the President of the United States attached his signature as a witness to that historic act. Millions of peace-loving people throughout the world rejoiced. During our many meetings personal friendship was established between us. I therefore lost today not only a partner to the peace process, but also a friend. The hearts of my wife and me go out to Mrs. Sadat and to all the bereaved family. May God console them in their grief. We hope that the peace process, despite the cruel act of his enemies, will continue, as we know President Sadat would wish with all his heart.

While in Cairo, Prime Minister Begin met with other world leaders who headed their countries' delegations to the funeral. There were the former U.S. Presidents Nixon, Ford and Carter, as well as Secretary of State Alexander Haig. Begin also met President Mitterand of France, the King of Belgium, Prince Charles of Britain, and many prime ministers and foreign ministers.

The most important meeting, of course, was with Egyptian President-elect Hosni Mubarak, who was to succeed Sadat and is Egypt's President today. They had met previously during Begin's various sessions with Sadat. This time, however, the moment was different and dramatic. When the two men extended their hands to each other both uttered the same words simultaneously: "Peace forever." Mubarak addressed the Israeli leader as "My friend, Mr. Begin," who responded with the same words.

Regrettably, the relationship between the two was not the same as the very special friendship between Sadat and Begin. In fact, they never met again, although there were occasional exchanges by letter and telephone. Ministers of the Israeli Government did pay rare visits to Cairo but, generally, the relationship was beginning to cool, causing anxiety in Israeli circles.

Nevertheless, President Mubarak has preserved the letter of the peace treaty with Israel, even if the spirit in which it was conceived has yet to become the accepted norm of the relationship. For the soundest pragmatic reasons the government of Egypt is honoring its treaty obligations, but the spirit of peace has yet to evolve among the people of that country and, strangely, especially among intellectual elements like the Lawyers Association and the journalists who continue to write in generally hostile terms about Israel and its leaders.

Chapter 25

IS ISRAEL A BANANA
REPUBLIC?

For MENACHEM BEGIN, the period of time following President Sadat's assassination was one of intensive diplomatic and political activity. He held frequent meetings with statesmen and leading journalists, and periodically he addressed the Knesset on foreign policy issues.

His adamant stand on Jerusalem, the Golan, Judea, Samaria and Gaza and his active support for a vigorous settlement program in the "territories" made him the target of Opposition attacks on him and on the Likud Party, and he took much sharp criticism from the U.S. Administration, European governments and certain Jewish organizations – some of whom advocated an end to the settlement program and the ceding of all or part of the territories in exchange for peace. Begin rejected such pressures firmly and vigorously.

He was particularly disappointed in Jimmy Carter, whom he had lauded in glowing terms at the time of the original negotiations and the subsequent Camp David Agreement; Begin had once gone so far, to the astonishment of his party associates and friends, as to compare Carter to his mentor, Ze'ev Jabotinsky. But more recently, Carter had abandoned his neutral posture in the

Arab-Israeli dispute. Now, in speeches, articles and books, Carter was misrepresenting the essence of the Camp David Accords, and accusing Begin of having reneged on an alleged commitment to stop the settlement development program. Begin's relationship with Carter cooled precipitously. Nevertheless, after Carter lost the 1980 election, Begin, on an official visit to the U.S., made a special detour to Plains, Georgia, to see his old friend. That was their last encounter. Some years later, when the Carters came to Israel and Begin was in retirement in Jerusalem, the ex-President had to be content with a telephone conversation with Begin from the residence of President Herzog.

The 1980 U.S. presidential election brought to Israel a host of hopefuls who obviously believed that being photographed with Israel's famous Prime Minister would prove helpful in their campaigns at home. Also, a new breed of security and foreign policy experts appeared; such types were expected to play a key role in the future Reagan Administration.

Upon his election, U.S. President Ronald Reagan and Prime Minister Begin exchanged the usual courtesies, and a good working relationship was established between the two leaders. But a great deal of tension soon arose, due both to the U.S. arms embargo following Israel's attack on the Iraqi atomic reactor and to Reagan's decision to supply AWACS to Saudi Arabia. Furthermore, there were sharp differences between the U.S. and Israel over the eight-point "peace plan" of Saudi Arabia's King Fahd. It became apparent that the Reagan Administration was not adhering to the staunchly pro-Israel policies enunciated by the Republicans during the election (among whom there had even been talk of moving the U.S. embassy to Jerusalem). But many Israelis had already dismissed such election promises as meaningless.

Begin was deeply concerned about the supply of U.S. arms to Arab countries who maintained a state of war against Israel. "It is a kind of avalanche," he said, "and we are perturbed because it may change the present balance of power."

In a statement to the Knesset on 11 May 1981, Prime Minister Begin dealt with the supply of U.S. arms to Arab countries. "The current U.S. Administration, while friendlier than many of its predecessors, has decided to sell F-15 assault equipment to Saudi Arabia, as well as AWACS planes, which are highly sophisticated aircraft, perhaps not to be found anywhere else in the world. These AWACS constitute a direct threat to the civilian population in the center of Israel. Should Saudi Arabia receive these aircraft, our every move would be transparent, in the air and on the ground. Some respected and important Americans have given this simple advice: What are you worried about? You have a marvelous air force. If they are stationed near the Israel Border – instead of in the eastern part of Saudi Arabia – you simply shoot them down. And at the same time they tell us that, for many years to come, there will be Americans and Saudis in those planes after the AWACS are sold to Saudi Arabia.

"What strange advice we get from Washington. We are supposed to shoot down the plane and kill not only the Saudis who are our enemies, but also the Americans who are our friends. Very strange advice indeed, and we cannot accept it. A second piece of advice: What are you worried about? We won't give them AWACS for another 5 years. Very well, but what will happen after five years? Does a people live on borrowed time?"

When told that Israel still had the qualitative edge over her enemies, Begin always responded that a point is reached when quantity outweighs quality and, therefore, the constantly growing quantity of arms at the disposal of the Arab countries could undermine Israel's qualitative superiority.

Menachem Begin met President Ronald Reagan for the first time on 9 September 1981. On his arrival in Washington, he was assured that the Reagan Administration did not wish to deal with recent events (i.e. the attack on the Iraqi reactor, the delay in delivery of U.S. arms or an Israeli attack on the terrorist headquarters in Beirut which had infuriated the U.S.), but rather to look to the future. In his welcoming remarks, President Reagan said:

> On behalf of the American people, Nancy and I are honored and delighted to welcome you and we are proud to stand beside you this morning.
>
> Mr. Prime Minister, your strong leadership, great imagination and skilled statesmanship have been indispensable in reaching the milestone of the past few years on the road towards a just and durable peace in the Middle East. You and the members of your coalition have earned our respect and admiration. Many cynics said Israel would never make peace with Egypt, but you did. Then they said you would not honor your commitment, but you did. Now they say you cannot go forward to work out a just and durable peace with all your neighbors. We know you will.
>
> Prime Minister Begin, I know your entire life has been dedicated to the security and well-being of your people. It wasn't always easy. From your earliest days you were acquainted with hunger and sorrow, but as you've written, you rarely wept. One occasion you did – the night your beloved State of Israel was proclaimed. You cried that night because, as you said, truly these are tears of salvation as well as tears of grief. Well, with the help of God, and us working together, perhaps one day for all the people of the Middle East, there will be no more tears of grief, only tears of salvation. Shalom, Shalom to Him that is far off and that is near.

In response, Menachem Begin thanked the President for his heartwarming remarks "about my people and my country, and touching words about my life. It is only one of the uncountable thousands and millions who suffered and fought and persisted and saw, after a long night the rise of the sun. Today I am one of them because this is our generation. Your appreciation of our motives, our efforts, our sacrifices is very dear to all of us. Mr. President, we see in you not only the President of the United States, but also the defender of freedom throughout the world."

After two days of talks in Washington, the Israel Prime Minister remarked at a press conference that a "turning point" had been reached in Israel-American relations when a formal agreement of strategic cooperation between the U.S. and Israel was concluded. Defense Minister Sharon and Secretary of Defense Weinberger later announced the creation of a joint working team to discuss strategic issues and other details.

But only three months later, after the passage of the Golan Law by the Knesset, the U.S. announced that it would be taking punitive measures against Israel. This infuriated Menachem Begin, who in an unprecedented move summoned the American Ambassador, Samuel Lewis, and read him a prepared statement which said, among other things:

> Three times in the last six months the U.S. government has "punished" Israel – after the attack on the Iraqi nuclear reactor near Baghdad; after we bombed the PLO headquarters in Beirut, and now you are punishing us after the Knesset passed on all three readings, by an overwhelming majority of two thirds, the "Golan Heights Law."
>
> What kind of expression is this – "punishing Israel?" Are we a vassal state of yours? Are we a banana republic? Are we youths of fourteen who, if they don't behave properly, are slapped across the fingers?
>
> You have no right to "punish" Israel and I protest the very use of the term.

You have announced that you are suspending consultations on the implementation of the memorandum of understanding on strategic cooperation and that your return to these consultations in the future will depend on progress achieved in the autonomy talks and on the situation in Lebanon.

You want to make Israel a hostage of the memorandum of understanding.

I regard your announcement suspending these consultations as the abrogation by you of the memorandum. No "Sword of Damocles" is going to hang over our head.

The people of Israel has lived 3,700 years without a memorandum of understanding with America – and it will continue to live another 3,700!

Now I understand why the whole great effort in the Senate to obtain a majority for the arms deal with Saudi Arabia was accompanied by an ugly campaign of anti-Semitism.

First the slogan was sounded "Begin or Reagan?" – and that meant that whoever opposes the deal – including Senators like Jackson, Kennedy, Packwood, and of course Boschwitz – is supporting a foreign prime minister and is not loyal to the President of the United States.

Then we heard: "We should not let the Jews determine the foreign policy of the United States." Let me say that no one will frighten the great and free Jewish community of the U.S. No one will succeed in cowing them with anti-Semitic propaganda. They will stand by our side. This is the land of their forefathers – and they have a right and a duty to support it.

Menachem Begin's defense of Israel's honor even against its most important friend, the United States, sparked a stormy debate in the Knesset, where the Labor party's no-confidence motion was defeated. Thousands of cables expressing support for Prime Minister Begin's action reached the Prime Minister's office from many places in Israel and abroad. Howard Squadron, the Chairman of the Conference of Presidents of Major American Jewish Organizations, cabled his appreciation for the Prime Minister's remarks about the American Jewish community; Lord Emanuel Shinwell, a former British Minister of War, said: "Thank God that someone had the courage to stand up to the Americans, and tell them what had to be told."

Despite this sharp clash, the basic relationship continued on a fairly even keel while efforts were made in Washington and Jerusalem to improve the atmosphere.

There was, however, one more disruption on 1 September 1982 when the U.S. Administration announced a peace plan which became known as the Reagan Plan. It was apparent that while the people in the State Department had consulted various Arab elements before announcing the Plan, they presented it to Israel as a fait accompli. Menachem Begin had taken a few days of leave in Nahariya in the north of the country. (In fact, this interlude was arranged to enable him to meet secretly with President-elect Bashir Gemayel of Lebanon.) Ambassador Lewis traveled to Nahariya to show the Plan to Begin who reacted: "It is the saddest day of my life," and he determined to reject the plan as not being even a basis for negotiation.

The American plan was, in essence, an endorsement of the principle of Israel giving up territory for peace and of "self-government for the Palestinians of the West Bank and Gaza in association with Jordan." What incensed Begin primarily was the fact that the United States had carefully constructed a Middle East peace plan in consultation with Arab governments, but not with Israel, whose very future was to be decided. He refused even to accept the document from the American Ambassador, and cutting short his Nahariya "vacation," flew by helicopter to Jerusalem where a specially summoned Cabinet session rejected the Reagan plan.

In a letter to Reagan, Menachem Begin explained that the plan contradicted and deviated from the Camp David Accords and he protested "the omission to consult us prior to forwarding your proposals to Jordan and Saudi Arabia, the former an outspoken opponent of the Camp David Accords and the latter a complete stranger to, and an adversary of, these accords." Begin continued:

> As there was not prior consultation, the United States government could have taken the position that the "West Bank" should be reassociated with Jordan. What some call the "West Bank," Mr. President, is Judea and Samaria; and this simple historic truth will never change. There are cynics who deride history. They may continue their derision as long as they wish, but I will stand by the truth. And the truth is that millennia ago there was a Jewish Kingdom of Judea and Samaria where our Kings knelt to God, where our prophets brought forth the vision of eternal peace, where we developed a rather rich civilization which we took with us, in our hearts and in our minds, on our long global trek for over eighteen centuries and, with it, we came back home.
>
> By aggressive war, by invasion, King Abdullah conquered parts of Judea and Samaria in 1948; and in a war of most legitimate self-defense in 1967, after being attacked by King Hussein, we liberated, with God's help, that portion of our homeland. Judea and Samaria will never again be the "West Bank" of the Hashemite Kingdom of Jordan which was created by British Colonialism after the French army expelled King Feisal from Damascus.
>
> Mr. President, you and I chose for the last two years to call our countries "friends and allies." Such being the case, a friend does not weaken his friend, an ally does not put his ally in jeopardy. This would be the inevitable consequence were the "positions" transmitted to me on August 31, 1982, to become reality.

I believe they won't.

"For Zion's sake I will not hold my peace, and for Jerusalem's sake I will not rest" (Isaiah, Chapter 62).

Begin was also concerned with the attitude of some European leaders towards Israel and with their pronounced support for the Palestinian cause. He did not hesitate to express his resentment in the strongest terms – especially in regard to the French and German attitude and the behavior of the European members of the UN Security Council which, for example, had condemned Israel after the attack on the Iraqi reactor. In an interview with French television, he conveyed his sentiments with biting sarcasm: "I will tell you something – but secretly. Don't tell your friends. I prefer to save the lives of our children and be condemned by a Security Council, than vice-versa. Clear?"

He was furious with the French for enabling the Iraqis to build the atomic reactor and, after its destruction, to assist them to rebuild it. He recalled that France and Israel were, at one time, real friends and allies.

"When Ben Gurion one day visited Paris, President de Gaulle greeted him and referred to Israel as "our friend and ally." Ally is a very strong word because it means mutual help, and there was a time when we fought together for our common interests.

I would like to tell the French people that since my boyhood I loved France with all my heart and soul. The time when we had friendship and alliance was a great time of great happiness for many in Israel, including myself.

Then came the change and the worst period was under the presidency of Giscard d'Estaing, when France helped the Iraqis to build an atomic reactor that may one day produce their atomic bombs.

After the election of François Mitterand as President of France, Begin described him as "a true friend of Israel."

> However, he talks about something close to a Palestinian State – and we will never agree to that. But, he said he would not allow Israel or its security to be harmed under any conditions. For him the State of Israel is something sacred. Why? The State of Israel is a Jewish State, and it demonstrates the historic continuity of the Jewish people. This is a very interesting philosophical idea.

Germany was another matter altogether. Begin had "a special attitude" towards that country and its leaders, and severely reprimanded Chancellor Helmut Schmidt for his statement on a visit to Saudi Arabia that Germany had obligations to various peoples, among them the Palestinians. He failed to mention the Jews.

Begin said that he had found the Chancellor's statements "astonishing," particularly so from the standpoint of the head of government of a nation which bears responsibility for the extermination of six million Jews, among them a million and a half little children.

When Schmidt demanded that Begin apologize to him, the Israeli Prime Minister replied: "I will not apologize to Mr. Schmidt. Rather, I counsel him, speaking as a free man who fought for the continued existence and the liberation of the Jewish people, that he take an example from his predecessor, Mr. Brandt, visit Warsaw, go to the site where the Jewish ghetto once stood, go down on his knees and ask forgiveness of the Jewish people and of all nations loving justice and liberty for what his countrymen perpetrated under the Nationalist Socialist regime against my people at the time when Mr. Schmidt remained faithful to the personal oath he had given to Adolf Hitler as a soldier and officer in the army."

Obviously, this statement further strained relations with Germany, which had become an important trading partner of Israel in Europe. Begin was severely criticized, but he remained steadfast, insisting that as Prime Minister of the Jewish State he could not ignore the contempt shown to his people, and that he felt fully justified on moral grounds, which in this case were more important than pragmatic considerations.

Chapter 26

PEACE FOR GALILEE

MUCH OF BEGIN'S ATTENTION was naturally directed at international affairs, but his main concern was always the security of the country and the safety of its citizens.

In the early 1980s, the Israeli civilian population in the north was again under attack by the PLO, which had virtually hijacked Lebanon to use its territory as the base from which to fire volleys of Katyusha rockets at Kiryat Shmonah and other northern settlements. For months on end, the residents rushed to underground shelters as the sirens wailed announcing another attack. The children slept every night in the underground shelters, and their worried parents and psychologists were concerned that this form of warfare would indelibly scar their young lives. Some families began to leave the area.

Begin summoned the Defense Minister, Chief of Staff and army commanders and instructed them to prepare elaborate plans to end this PLO terror. On a visit to the north he vowed: "No more Katyushas will fall here."

The problem was, of course, complicated by the proximity of Syria, whose ruler, Hafez Assad, had ordered increased military readiness and the advance of ground-to-air missile batteries towards the Israeli border.

This did not prevent a number of deep raids into Lebanese territory by the Israel Air Force, which pinpointed PLO headquarters and arms caches in Beirut for their attacks. Once again the international community of civilized and not-so-civilized nations sang out in protest against Israel, with calls for sanctions and other punitive measures.

The tension on Israel's northern border had been mounting since 21 April 1982, when Israel downed two Syrian MiGs over Lebanon and bombed terrorist bases in Sidon. On 9 May, Israeli jets attacked terrorist targets in southern Lebanon and, in response, northern and western Galilee were shelled by PLO artillery units in southern Lebanon.

On the second of June, PLO gunmen shot in the head Israel's Ambassador to London, Shlomo Argov, gravely injuring him as he was leaving the Dorchester Hotel after a reception. An emergency Cabinet meeting was held in Jerusalem the next morning. Begin spoke in grave terms about the event, declaring that an attack on an Ambassador was tantamount to an attack on the State. He called for retaliation. The previous night, the Prime Minister had authorized an air strike on PLO ammunition depots that had been identified under the Beirut Sports Stadium. Two hours later, the PLO opened artillery fire along the entire northern border of Israel, causing considerable damage. One Israeli was killed in the shelling, and two were lightly wounded.

The Cabinet was called to another meeting at the home of the Prime Minister shortly after the end of the Sabbath. Defense Minister Sharon and the Chief of Staff, General "Raful" Eytan sought Cabinet approval for the Israel Defense Forces to move into Lebanon in order to drive the terrorists out and put the PLO artillery and Katyusha rockets out of range of Israel's northern population – a distance of about 40 kilometers.

The Cabinet was seriously concerned about the possibility of Syrian involvement, and Prime Minister Begin stated emphatically that there was no intention to attack Syria (unless Syria struck first).

The Government of Israel decided to mount a large-scale operation code-named "Peace for Galilee" which they hoped would be of short duration. However, it became one of those massive military actions that generates its own momentum and continues well beyond the anticipated time.

And so, on 6 June, IDF units crossed the Lebanese border and, advancing along the coastal road to Tyre, reached Nabatiya in Lebanon. They moved into the area which had been under PLO control and which Israelis had appropriately named "Fatahland." It was 15 years to the day that an earlier Israeli Government, under Prime Minister Levi Eshkol, had ordered the IDF to attack Egypt in what was to become the Six-Day War.

That day, Menachem Begin became the fourth Israeli Prime Minister to preside over a Cabinet that launched major military operations that developed into war.

On the second day of the operation, Israeli forces captured the Beaufort Castle and clashed with units of the Syrian army. The Israel Navy landed tanks and infantry north of Sidon, while the Air Force continued bombardment of PLO bases. Coordination between Israeli ground, naval and air forces was superb.

On the third day, the Israel Air Force downed 6 Syrian MiGs and 22 more the next day – without losing a single one of its own. At the same time, the Air Force destroyed 19 Syrian ground-to-air missile batteries in the Beka'a Valley that were threatening Israel's command of the skies.

The "Peace for Galilee" Operation dragged on for days and weeks beyond the original prescribed time. Israel's forces advanced further north, encircled the Beirut airport and moved into portions of Beirut. Political pressure within the country began to mount. For the first time in Israel's history, the Opposition took a public stand against a war in which the nation's sons were involved and, as the number of casualties grew, they organized street demonstrations and rallies. In the previous five wars, the Herut-Gahal opposition parties gave maximum support to the Government and rallied around the fighting forces. Only when the actual physical battle-field dangers had passed in those earlier wars did Menachem Begin and his colleagues give public expression to their criticisms. The clearest example of this patriotic attitude was at the time of the Yom Kippur War, which was Israel's gravest military setback and the cause of a real national trauma. This time the "Peace Now" group demonstrated outside the Prime Minister's residence and incited the population against him.

Furthermore, the media wrongly portrayed Israel as the ag-gressor and the PLO as the blameless victim. In contrast to Britain's restrictions on the news media in its invasion of the Falklands or U.S. media policy in Granada or the Gulf War, Israel did not restrict the TV cameramen covering the military operation in Lebanon. Many Israelis severely criticized the Government for this policy, holding that it was allowing the media to turn international senti-ment against Israel.

The United States Administration was concerned by Israel's deep advance into Lebanese territory and the prolonged fighting. U.S. Administration officials appealed to Israel, urged Israel and threatened Israel with retribution if her forces did not immediately leave Lebanon. Philip Habib, a congenial U.S. official of Lebanese extraction, who grew up in a New York Jewish neighborhood and spoke some Yiddish, was dispatched to the region to shuttle between Jerusalem, Damascus and Beirut. He was endeavoring to arrange a cease-fire and to keep Syria out of the ground conflict. But as long as the PLO continued to shell the northern population, Israel continued relentlessly to attack their bases.

I was serving as Minister of Information at Israel's Embassy in Washington at the time and was acutely aware of the persis-tent demands that came from the White House for Israel to stop bombing Beirut. On 4 August 1982, President Reagan himself called Ambassador Moshe Arens demanding that these "terrible bombings" cease immediately. The Ambassador dutifully reported the conversation to the Prime Minister in Jerusalem and informed him that the U.S. President had threatened to "review U.S.–Israel relations." A few days later Israel agreed to the entry of a multinational force in West Beirut following the departure of the PLO from the area.

On 12 August, after Israel Air Force jets had carried out additional air raids on Beirut, President Reagan called Prime Minister Begin and insisted that the attacks be halted. Begin informed him that two-and-a-half hours earlier the Cabinet had decided to stop all air activity. President Reagan was pleased and ended the conversation with some warm expressions and "Thank you Menachem, Shalom."

Habib's shuttling between the capitals produced an agreement according to which the PLO withdrawal from Beirut was to begin on 21 August and to be completed by 1 September.

Some technical points remained to be clarified. For example, after some days, Israel agreed that the expelled terrorists could depart with their sidearms, but not with any other weapons.

Menachem Begin visited the United States in the first phase of the war. On 21 June he held wide-ranging talks with President Reagan and his advisors on the situation in Lebanon against a background of threatening reactions in Russia, deep concern in Western Europe and the usual unified Arab stand. Reagan called for Israeli military restraint.

At the end of their talks, Prime Minister Begin said that his discussion with the President had been "very fruitful."

"We now face a situation in the Middle East which calls for activity, great attention and understanding," he said.

"I have read in some newspapers in this great country that Israel invaded Lebanon. This is a misnomer. Israel did not invade any country. You invade when you want to conquer or annex part of another land. We don't covet even one inch of Lebanese territory and willingly we will withdraw our troops, all of our troops, and bring them back home as soon as possible – which means as soon as arrangements are made that never again will our citizens, men, women and children, be attacked, maimed and killed by armed bands operating in Lebanon and armed and supported by the Soviet Union and her satellites. There is hope that such an arrangement will be made and all foreign forces – without exception – will be withdrawn from Lebanon. Then there will be an independent, free Lebanon based on its territorial integrity, and the day is near when such a neighbor of Israel will sign a peace treaty with us and live in peace forever."

In a lengthy interview on the U.S. television program "Face the Nation," Menachem Begin expanded on these themes and outlined his hopes for the future. Those of us who were present in the studio as he faced the team of reporters were impressed by his composure and competent handling of the difficult questions. As we were leaving, I was presented with a tape-recording of the program as a personal souvenir; the transcript followed within days. Now, with the benefit of hindsight, it is most revealing to re-read his remarks. The following is a transcript of the interview:

MR. HERMAN: Prime Minister Begin, what are Israel's intentions toward the PLO forces which are surrounded and encircled in West Beirut? – forces which include Mr. Arafat and his entire infrastructure?

PRIME MINISTER BEGIN: The problem of those who are now in western Beirut is not Israel's problem. It is that of Lebanon and the Lebanese army, and they should deal with it. Israel actually brought to an end its military operation against the armed bands which used to attack us from Lebanese territory, killing men, women and children, perpetrating atrocities, for instance ordering 18 school children to lie down on the ground and then machine-gunning them, and ultimately, for years on end, shelling with long range weapons supplied to the PLO by the Soviet Union (like Katyusha rockets – range 21.6 kilometers) 23 of our villages, towns, townships in Galilee, putting our civilians into shelters.

MR. HERMAN: The men who commanded this, you do not intend to try to take them in Beirut?

P.M. BEGIN: No, no, we decided not to take Beirut, but the problem of those who are in West Beirut, as I said, is for the Lebanese Army to deal with.

MR. HERMAN: Yasser Arafat and the entire command – as far as we know – of the Palestine Liberation Organization are surrounded in western Beirut. You say that you have no intention of moving in, but are you encouraging your allies, the Lebanese Christian forces, to move against Arafat?

P.M. BEGIN: Why should I encourage anything? The Israel Defense Forces had a task to fulfill. They had to push back the so-called PLO, a terrorist organization, and that task was fulfilled. Now starts actually the political campaign, how to make sure that so-called status quo ante, which is intolerable, will not be restored.

But these are Lebanese internal questions. It is for the Lebanese government to deal with them, not for us.

MR. FAW: You say the military task has been fulfilled. Are you determined, however, to capture Mr. Arafat? Or if, in fact, he is captured, what would happen to him then?

P.M. BEGIN: We don't want to capture Mr. Arafat because we don't want to deal with him at all. I think it would be a trouble for us. Let him go wherever he wants to.

MR. PIERPONT: It is true that there are 6,000, at least, Palestinians in West Beirut and that so far the fighting seems to have quieted down. But there is no political settlement yet in Lebanon. You say it is up to the Lebanese. They haven't been able to get a political settlement among themselves for many years now. How long are you willing to have your troops stay in the area if there is no settlement?

P.M. BEGIN: This question is not being measured by days, only by criteria of security. I would like to recall our men from Lebanon as soon as possible. We don't want to keep our troops in Lebanon. We don't covet one inch of their territory. We respect their territorial integrity. I completely identify myself with full respect with the statement made by the President of the United States in his speech to the British Parliament: namely, Israel should bring home its soldiers from Lebanon – but it is not enough. I quote: "The scourge of terrorism in the Middle East must be stamped out…" I agree with both parts. We want our soldiers back home with their families, but the scourge of terrorism must be stamped out. Therefore, we said yes, we must have a distance of at least 40 kilometers – but those terrorists must not appear anymore, never again.

MR. PIERPONT: Will your soldiers stay there?

P.M. BEGIN: For this purpose we suggest the creation of a multinational force. If the United States is willing to participate, we shall accept it willingly. If the United States doesn't want to participate, let the multinational force be formed of other units. But it must be a serious force which will not permit nor make it possible for the terrorists to infiltrate its lines and again threaten our civilians with sudden death.

MR. PIERPONT: So the United Nations force that is there now, the so-called UNIFIL, is not sufficient for your purposes. You are asking for another type of peace-keeping force.

P.M. BEGIN: I agree that it is not sufficient, and I will explain why. First of all, it is a United Nations force, under the – how is it called? – the "Insecurity" Council's – control. As you could have seen the day before yesterday, I came to make a speech about disarmament and peace. Nearly two thirds of the delegations – a majority of the United Nations – were absent because they didn't want to listen to me. As Mr. Reston wrote in *The New York Times*, they didn't even have the decency to listen to the Prime Minister of Israel. And they should have the control over those troops?

We have had the experience of between 7–8,000 terrorists infiltrating within the lines of UNIFIL, and they threatened us. Therefore, we would like to have a multinational force which will sign an agreement with Israel and with the Lebanese government. Each of the participatory countries will also sign a detailed agreement with us so we shall make sure that there won't be any repetition of infiltration and terrorism. This I call stamping out terrorism from Lebanon. We don't have any territorial questions between Israel and Lebanon. I can go to Beirut and see President Sarkis the day after tomorrow, after my arrival in my country, and he may come to Jerusalem, as President Sadat did, and then we can, in Jerusalem, sign the peace treaty.

The real problem is that, for nearly seven years, the country was taken over by a Syrian occupation army and by the terrorists of the PLO whom the Soviet Union, Syria and Libya provided with ammunition and weapons. I want to tell you that we ourselves were taken by surprise. We disclose now the amounts of Russian weapons and ammunition, which will take us six weeks to take out from Lebanon if we use ten big Mack trucks working day and night.

Yesterday we discovered suddenly a store of weapons around Sidon. It will take 500 trucks to transfer that am-

munition to Israel. Lebanon became a Soviet base for the
whole of the Middle East. We undertook the operation
"Peace for Galilee" for our own self-defense. But indirectly
we did a great service to the Free World. It was a great
danger to other countries in the Middle East.

MR. HERMAN: Since you have captured this vast amount of
Soviet munitions, how do you evaluate the Soviet warning that Israel is beginning to touch on the edges of Soviet
interests in the Middle East? What do you think might
happen?

P.M. BEGIN: I can disclose to you that I got a note myself from
the Soviet Union, and I answered it very calmly because
the Soviet Union, since the days of Litvinov, has proposed
an international agreement about aggression. One of
its definitions is that armed bands operating from one
country against another country is indirect aggression.
So whatever happened between the PLO in Lebanon and
ourselves is aggression by Soviet definition. I answered
them that we don't want to hurt Soviet interests or their
embassy.

MR. PIERPONT: What did they ask you to do, or what did they
say in their note?

P.M. BEGIN: They did not ask us to do anything. They only
said that their embassy is in the vicinity of Israeli troops. I
explained to them that it never occurred to us to attack the
Soviet Embassy; that we respect their absolute immunity,
as the immunity of any other diplomatic representation
of any country.

I then used the opportunity to tell them that our
troops are in Lebanon on behalf of the great principle
of self-defense against armed bands which operate from
one country against another country – thus, committing
aggression by Soviet definition.

MR. HERMAN: You gave us your main goal – a belt at least 40 kilometers deep. How do you get from there to the outskirts of Beirut?

P.M. BEGIN: When we said 40 kilometers, we meant the line where the security arrangements are made. But they (PLO forces) were on the 50 kilometer line, 10 kilometers from our troops shooting at them. What should our troops do then? Lie down and be killed by those terrorists because they are on the 50 kilometer line?

We advanced and surrounded them. Then they stopped shooting at us. When the military action is completely over, the line will be 40 or 43 kilometers because that is beyond the range of the Soviet guns. That will be peace for the Galilee.

MR. HERMAN: So you got to Beirut not as a target in itself, but simply pursuing troops who were battling with you?

P.M. BEGIN: We didn't get into Beirut at all. We are close to Beirut and to the airfield of Beirut. Sometimes our men visit Beirut and are being received with great love by the Christian population to whom that operation is salvation.

MR. PIERPONT: What do you have as a vision for your great grandchildren, let us say in the year 2000, for Israel in its relations with its neighbors, and how do you intend to achieve that vision?

P.M. BEGIN: I believe that in my children's and certainly in my grandchildren's time, Israel will have complete peace with its neighbors. We made peace with Egypt. We gave great sacrifices for the sake of that peace treaty with Egypt – the whole Sinai Peninsula, strategic depth, oil wells from which we derived already for four years 24 percent of our annual consumption. Today, we would have derived at least 60 percent. Now we pay for that oil $1.2 billion per annum, which for a small country like ours is a huge amount of money. We gave up two airfields, considered by Europe as among the most sophisticated in the world. We had to evacuate our civilian population. We gave great sacrifices, but we have peace with Egypt. Now I believe there will soon be peace with Lebanon.

MR. PIERPONT: And the Palestinians?

P.M. BEGIN: The Palestinian Arabs are a problem for Lebanon because they are there in number. I suppose there are some 300,000. Not all of them are members of the PLO Not all of them are terrorists.

MR. PIERPONT: Palestinians in Jordan, in Syria?

P.M. BEGIN: Between 150,000 and 200,000. I believe that if there will be an independent Lebanese government without armed terrorists and without a Syrian occupation army, in a very short period of time Lebanon and Israel will sign a peace treaty and live in peace, and it will be a peaceful boundary, as it was for 19 years. Then we shall continue with our peace efforts. I believe we shall have peace with Jordan. Of course, I cannot give you the dates. You need for peace, two, at least two. To start the war, one is enough. But for peace you need two.

MR. HERMAN: Tomorrow you meet with President Reagan. One of the subjects I'm sure is going to come up is the question of negotiations for the autonomy of the Palestinians, of whom the largest part still remains within your control, in what you call Judea and Samaria, and what the rest of the world calls the West Bank.

P.M. BEGIN: What we call properly Judea and Samaria, others mistakenly call the West Bank. The West Bank is the whole territory between the Jordan River and the Mediterranean…

We produced a document about full autonomy for the Palestinian Arabs in Judea-Samaria and in the Gaza district, which is the most far-reaching autonomy proposal known in our time. I spoke with President Francois Mitterand about the autonomy given to Corsica. France didn't give statehood to the Corsican people; they gave them autonomy. I spoke with Mr. Colombo about the autonomy of Tyrol, and with Mr. Tindlmans about the autonomy given to the Walloons and the Flemish in Belgium.

Ours is much more far-reaching. For instance, in Belgium, the central government has kept under its authority education, finance, and justice. We give all these to the autonomous institution of the Palestinian Arabs.

MR. PIERPONT: Why don't they accept all this?

P.M. BEGIN: The talks are stalled because our Egyptian friends suddenly proclaimed a boycott of Jerusalem as one of the sites of the talks. We suggested that the talks should take place between the United States, Egypt and Israel – the signatories of the Camp David Accords – in the three capitals of the respective countries – Jerusalem, Cairo and Washington. The Egyptians for the time being say that Jerusalem must be out. That we cannot accept. It is our capital and the talks should take place in all the three capitals.

MR. PIERPONT: You have embarrassed President Mubarak by your invasion of Lebanon. I'm sure that that was not the intention of the Israeli Government, but I'm sure you understand you have done that. Now you are insisting that he go to Jerusalem simply to talk. Is it not possible that you could make a compromise on that?

P.M. BEGIN: Why do you use the word embarrass? We had to defend our people who were attacked. It was our duty. We didn't embarrass President Mubarak at all. I received a firm letter from President Mubarak and I answered the letter, as it should be amongst friends.

Now about Jerusalem. I don't ask for any privilege. I go to Cairo. Why shouldn't the delegate of Egypt come to Jerusalem? It's our capital. I don't decide where the Egyptian capital is. Let the Egyptians not decide where our capital is. Jerusalem is our eternal capital; it's one of the oldest capitals in history, nearly 3,000 years since King David transferred the sea of his Kingdom from Hebron to Jerusalem. Nobody should compromise. You have talks in the capitals of the countries which negotiate."

At the end of the conflict, Begin evaluated "Operation Peace for Galilee" in an address to the Knesset on 8 September 1992, in which he described three achievements of the operation.

Firstly, Peace for Galilee and in the Galilee, for all its settlements and for all its residents is a reality. I was in Nahariya a week ago. I saw the residents and the children: Laughter in their eyes, happiness in their hearts. We gave them new life, new life for 200,000 people. There are no Katyushas in Kiryat Shemona; no Katyushas in Nahariya; no Katyushas in Kfar Giladi; there are no shells. The children leave in the morning for school, return in the afternoon to their mothers and fathers. Love of life, new building, a return to Kiryat Shemona, to the whole Galilee. The Galilee will be built gloriously in our generation, in our time.

The second achievement is that we granted a large measure of peace to the citizens of Israel. I am not claiming that all incidents of sabotage have already come to an end. It is impossible. This is a time of violence. Go and see throughout the world – what goes on in London, Rome, Palermo, New York. So it is possible that it will still occur here and there but after we did away with the fighting capability of 25,000 terrorists equipped with modern weapons, we saved an unknown number of civilian lives and, to a great extent, we assured peace both for Israel and for its citizens.

Thirdly, the deterrent capability of the IDF was really demonstrated and renewed. There were times after the Yom Kippur War when it was in question. This is gone; no more. A huge deterrent capability which prevents aggression, prevents wars, before the eyes of all the Arab states and the ears of their rulers.

Begin grieved for the heavy losses suffered in an operation that was intended to be short and of minimal cost in precious human life. From his years in the Underground, as Commander of the Irgun, he was always concerned with the safety of the fighting men and pressed the planners and organizers to ensure that they "have a way back."

Recalling the subject of casualties in his Knesset statement he said: "We know the high price we paid. I wanted to say something from the heart. Woe to those people who have to take certain decisions in the day and night. But there is no choice, if the people of Israel and the Land of Israel have to be defended, they will be taken. And those appointed *will stand*, will stand with determination, strong will and patience, and will not heed slander, neither in Israel nor abroad, neither in miserable, despicable pictures or in insulting or hurtful articles. They will pay no heed to any of these and *will* do their job and fulfill their duty till victory.

"These are bitter and painful decisions; and we bow our heads before the bereaved families, national heroes no less than their sons who gave their lives, and honor them from the depths of the heart, and send wishes for speedy and full recovery to the wounded."

Israel hoped to avoid embroilment with Syria, but when the formidable Syrian army attacked Israeli forces, clashes took place. As a result, 405 Syrian tanks were destroyed, among them 9 T-72s which NATO had considered impregnable; 102 planes were shot down and 24 SAM missiles were destroyed.

There were other less obvious results, the most important of which was that, despite outspoken criticism and dissatisfaction, Egypt, which had signed a peace treaty with Israel only three years earlier, did not intervene in the conflict in any way.

In an address to the graduating class of the IDF National Defense College, Menachem Begin gave his views on "wars of choice and wars of no alternative." He maintained that the war in Lebanon was a "war of no choice." He analyzed the circumstances that led to World War II and other international conflicts and then dealt with the wars that Israel had fought from 1948 until 1982.

As for Operation Peace for Galilee, it does not really belong to the category of wars of no alternative. We could have gone on seeing our civilians injured in Metulla or Kiryat Shemona or Nahariya. We could have gone on counting those killed by explosive charges left in a Jerusalem supermarket or a Petah Tikva bus stop.

All the orders to carry out these acts of murder and sabotage came from Beirut. Should we have reconciled ourselves to the ceaseless killing of civilians? – even after the agreement ending hostilities reached last summer, which the terrorists interpreted as an agreement permitting them to strike at us from every side, besides southern Lebanon. They tried to infiltrate gangs of murderers via Syria and Jordan, and by a miracle we captured them. We might also not have captured them. There was a gang of four terrorists which infiltrated from Jordan, whose members admitted they had been about to commandeer a bus (and we remember the bus on the coastal road).

And in the Diaspora? Even Philip Habib interpreted the agreement ending acts of hostility as giving them freedom to attack targets beyond Israel's borders. We have never accepted this interpretation. Shall we permit Jewish blood to be spilled in the Diaspora? Shall we permit bombs to be planted against Jews in Paris, Rome, Athens or London? Shall we permit our ambassadors to be attacked?

There are slanderers who say that a full year of quiet has passed between us and the terrorists. Nonsense. There was not even one month of quiet. The newspapers and communications media, including *The New York Times* and *The Washington Post* did not publish even one line about our capturing the gang of murderers that crossed the Jordan in order to commandeer a bus and murder its passengers.

True, such actions were not a threat to the existence of the state. But they did threaten the lives of civilians, whose number we cannot estimate, day after day, week after week, month after month.

During the past nine weeks, we have in effect destroyed the combat potential of 20,000 terrorists. We hold 9,000 in a prison camp. Between 2,000 and 3,000 were killed and between 7,000 and 9,000 have been captured and cut off in Beirut. They have decided to leave there only because they have no possibility of remaining there. They will leave soon. We made a second condition: after the exit of most of the terrorists, an integrated multinational force will enter. But if the minority refuses to leave, the U.S., Italy and France must promise us in writing that, together with the Lebanese army, they will force them, the terrorists to leave Beirut and Lebanon. They have the possibility of forcing out the 2,000–2,500 terrorists who will remain after the majority leaves.

And one more condition: if they aren't willing to force them, then, please, leave Beirut and Lebanon, and the IDF will solve the problem.

This is what I wrote to the Secretary of State today, and I want you and all the citizens of Israel and the U.S. to know it.

The problem will be solved. We can already now look beyond the fighting. It will end, as we hope, shortly. And then, as I believe, recognize and logically assume, we will have a protracted period of peace. There is no other country around us that is capable of attacking us.

We have destroyed the best tanks and planes the Syrians had. We have destroyed 24 of their ground-to-air missile batteries. After everything that happened, Syria did not go to war against us, not in Lebanon and not on the Golan Heights.

Jordan cannot attack us. We have learned that Jordan is sending telegrams to the Americans, warning that Israel is about to invade across the Jordan and capture Amman.

For our part, we will not initiate any attack against any Arab country. We have proved that we do not want wars. We made many painful sacrifices for a peace treaty with Egypt. That treaty stood the test of the fighting in Lebanon; in other words, it *stood the test.*

The demilitarized zone of 150 kilometers in Sinai exists and no Egyptian soldier has been placed there. From the experience of the 1930s, I have to say that if ever the other side violated the agreement about the demilitarized zone, Israel would be obliged to introduce, without delay, a force stronger than that violating the international commitment; not in order to wage war, but to achieve one of two results: restoration of the previous situation, i.e., resumed demilitarization, and the removal of both armies from the demilitarized zone; or attainment of strategic depth, in case the other side has taken the first step towards a war of aggression, as happened in Europe only three years after the abrogation of the demilitarized zone in the Rhineland.

Because the other Arab countries are completely incapable of attacking the State of Israel, there is reason to expect that we are facing a historic period of peace. It is obviously impossible to set a date.

It may well be that "The land shall be still for 40 years." Perhaps less, perhaps more. But from the facts before us, it is clear that, with the end of the fighting in Lebanon, we have ahead of us many years of establishing peace treaties and peaceful relations with the various Arab countries.

The conclusion – both on the basis of the relations between states and on the basis of our national experience – is that there is no divine mandate to go to war only if there is no alternative. There is no moral imperative that a nation must, or is entitled to fight only when its back is to the sea, or to the abyss. Such a war may avert tragedy, if not a Holocaust, for any nation; but it causes it terrible loss of life.

Quite the opposite. A free, sovereign nation, which hates war and loves peace, and which is concerned about its security, must create the conditions under which war, if there is a need for it, *will not be* for lack of alternative. The conditions must be such – and their creation depends upon man's reason and his actions – that the price of victory will be few casualties, not many.

Chapter 27

SLANDER

Menachem Begin had hoped that the Christian community of Lebanon, which Israel had supported for many years, would emerge as the dominant factor in that strife-torn country.

Israel supplied the Phalange (Christian) force with arms and consulted with their leaders, who belonged mainly to two prominent Christian families, the Gemayels and the Chamouns.

In the days of the Labor Government, a safe border was established in Israel's northernmost area around Metulla which became known as the "good fence." At first, Lebanese came there for medical treatment or to acquire supplies. Some came to work or to attend studies. After some years the "good fence" became almost an open border.

Little wonder, then, that the Christian population which had suffered grievously from Syrian brutality and PLO barbarism looked southward, to Israel.

At a large Christian gathering at Jerusalem's Diplomat Hotel, we heard Major Haddad, then the commander of the Christian forces in Southern Lebanon, say: "We Christians feel utterly abandoned by the Christian world. It is our great luck that our southern neighbor, the only Jewish state in the world, understands our plight, sympathizes with us and assists us."

In a U.S. television interview, one month after the start of Israel's "Operation for Galilee," Bashir Gemayel, the charismatic young Lebanese Christian leader, expressed the hope that "we are now living in the last hours of the eight years of war" (against the Moslem community – most recently the PLO).

He explained that more than 100,000 of his people had been killed in their eight-year civil war, more than 300,000 were wounded and almost half the population was uprooted from its villages and its homes. Then he added: "And now a lot of people are coming back to the south because the Israelis are here. Today a lot of people are coming to all the villages where the Israelis are entering and the situation is improving; I'm not going to say that it has become normal, but since then, the country is being reunited every day more and more." The long-suffering Christian population in Lebanon received the Israeli troops with joy, showering the soldiers with flowers as they entered their villages. Nevertheless, Gemayel refused to join Israel's war against the PLO, saying "It is not my fight. The Israelis are not doing that for me."

Bashir Gemayel was elected President of Lebanon on 23 August 1982 and was to be inaugurated on 23 September. On 1 September he held secret talks with Israel's Prime Minister, Menachem Begin, who had ostensibly taken a "three-day vacation" at the Carlton Hotel in Nahariya, near the country's northern border. The veteran Israeli leader was disappointed when the young Gemayel rejected his call for the signing of an Israeli-Lebanese peace treaty. Gemayel wanted to defer the matter until his country's problems were resolved and the situation had stabilized. But it was not to be.

Only nine days before his scheduled inauguration, Bashir Gemayel was killed by a bomb explosion in the Phalange headquarters in Beirut. Christian-Moslem tension neared the breaking point in Lebanon.

In Israel, the campaign against the war effort continued unabated, with the anti-war forces becoming more clamorous by the day. They took their campaign to the streets, demonstrated without respite in front of the Prime Minister's home and called for immediate withdrawal from Lebanon. The argument was simply whether this war was "justified or unjustified." This stung Begin to the core, and he retorted time and again that to give safety to Israel's citizens in the north and to protect the children made this a wholly justified undertaking.

His view was supported by Labor leader, Yitzhak Rabin, who a month after the start of "Operation Peace for Galilee" said in the Knesset: "All Israel's wars, since the War of Independence to this day, are *just* wars, without any doubt, without any question." And, in a subsequent interview in the February 1983 edition of *Newsweek*, Rabin said that the incursion into Lebanon was bound to happen, sooner or later, because no government of Israel could permit a situation in which 200,000 of its residents were hostages to the PLO threat from South Lebanon. A similar view was expressed by Labor Knesset Member Chaim Herzog (later to become President of Israel), who said on 11 July 1982: "The war was unavoidable. No sovereign state can live for long with a loaded gun held to its temple."

However, the debate raged on as the number of casualties mounted, even after the formal end of hostilities. The PLO continued to attack and sabotage. Car bombs were exploded at the roadside as Israel military vehicles passed by. Unfortunate accidents also took a heavy toll. On 11 November 1992, the building housing the headquarters of the Israeli military government in Tyre collapsed due to a gas leak; 75 Israeli soldiers were killed and 27 injured. A later accident caused a dormitory to go up in flames. On 10 June 1983, three Israeli soldiers were killed near Tyre. Terrorists also attacked American and French targets in Beirut; on 23 October, 241 U.S. Marines and 60 French soldiers were killed in terrorist bombings. On 4 November, 28 Israeli soldiers were killed in a terrorist attack on an IDF camp in Tyre.

The internal controversy reached its peak after the assassination of President-elect Gemayel. Immediately following this dastardly act, the IDF was ordered to take control of key positions in West Beirut. They also surrounded the Palestine refugee camps Sabra, Shatilla and Fakahani, but did not enter them. The purpose was to flush out the remaining terrorists from Beirut.

Then, on Rosh Hashana, as Prime Minister Begin was at prayer in Jerusalem's Great Synagogue, news reached him that Phalange forces had entered the camps and – ostensibly in revenge for the killing of their beloved leader – massacred hundreds of civilians. When the news was flashed across Israel and around the world, there was an outburst of fury directed against Begin, his Government and the IDF, all of whom were accused of indirect responsibility for the massacre.

Deeply hurt by the conduct of the Opposition and their slanders, Prime Minister Begin replied to them in the Knesset on 22 September 1982:

> You are as slanderers who give a hand to the libelers. I would like to return to this expression. *A blood libel is being leveled these days at Israel and at the Israel Defense Forces.* A tragedy occurred; good people who believe in the image of man and God believed that there is humanity, and later it became apparent that the opposite was the case. Of course, it is a tragedy, of course it hurts every human being. But must it be said that the Jew is guilty? The Israeli? The Israeli officer? Read today the placard about one of the finest officers and fighters in Israel. Woe to the ears that hear this.

> I have the right to express my belief that there is no one guilty in Israel. There is no one guilty in the IDF. Just a tragedy.

> But you are walking around lately, sometimes like those who are exulting, that it is the Jews who are at fault; the Israeli

soldiers who were there, that they were given Israeli weapons. This is not the first time you cry that the Jew did what was done. Not for the first time in this generation.

So the one hand slandering, and on the other a strange and astounding rejoicing. For what? It is the Jews who are at fault!

I began by saying that Mr. Peres should be ashamed of himself. This was one chapter. Now I will relate the second reason why he should be ashamed. He visited the United States of America, and spoke with government representatives.

You go around the world and teach the President of the United States that most of the territory of Judea and Samaria has to be turned over to Jordanian control, under foreign rule. And he calls this a Jordanian option. But meanwhile – how do you mock? – The Fez Summit took place and determined that there should be a Palestinian state in Judea, Samaria and Gaza, and King Hussein accepted this decision. What does he propose? That there should be a federation between the Kingdom of Jordan and that Palestinian state. In other words: The advice you gave *there*, at the White House, leads directly to a Palestinian state, which you say *here* that you allegedly oppose.

But this is an existential threat. And *there*, across the ocean, they depend on you. And you, with huge satisfaction, say: That plan is similar to our plan. What satisfaction, that a Palestinian state will be created in federation with another Arab state, and it will directly threaten our citizens' lives, our existence and our future.

There was a television interview with Mr. Peres. The interviewer asked him about the big massacre. Then he, with an ironic air, asked: And in a small massacre, it is permissible to participate? This is libel. To whom was he referring? Who participated in a small massacre? Our people? This is the way a serious man talks – a responsible person?

And this I want to say to you, Mr. Peres: In my estimation, on the basis of my experience, there is nothing more despicable in life than to utilize a tragedy for partisan purposes.

In all periods of history when there were blood libels against the Jewish people, they stood united and together until the truth came out. This is the first time I think I can say – there has been no other phenomenon like this – there is a blood libel against our people and our army, and instead of standing together until we overcome this, without a weakening of mind, or of heart, out of a belief that the truth will out, there are images such as this; nearly every day I read in the foreign press your articles and pronouncements. Nearly every day. You are depending on America and Europe. You have become king's witnesses against Israel.

Please, gentlemen. You are demanding every day resignations and dismissals. There will be no resignations and there will be no dismissals. There will be elections. Only elections. Only motions of no confidence. If you will achieve a majority, the Government will resign. Go to the people. Go ahead, you be the party that will receive the authority to form a Government and do so. But no deceit, no slander. There will be no libels. The opposite. I tell you, gentlemen: As you failed in connection with the destruction of the atomic reactor and attacked the action which saved hundreds of thousands of Jews from the danger of death, as you failed later in connection with Operation "Peace for the Galilee," so too you will fail in this incitement. The people do not want incitement in these difficult days. The people want national unity without a differentiation between Government and Opposition.

I want to say, Mr. Speaker, that there is no one in this House, there is no one in Israel whose soul does not cry out over the tragedy that occurred. But I am prepared to stand up before everyone in Israel and before the nations with head held high and with upright stature and to tell the whole story, how our intentions were for the good, to save lives, to provide security. And this tragedy happened, and we are trying to convince entire nations that this is the truth. And there is a segment in this nation that does not want to convince them, but supplies them on a daily basis with contradictory material.

As for the blood libel, I want to explain: *There is a difference between the blood libels of the past and those which have been contrived beginning with the New Year.* Then the guilty party, the criminal was not known, and the guilt was placed upon the Jew, or on Jewish communities, or on a Jewish settlement. Today everyone knows who perpetrated this tragedy. Even you say it. And yet you charge that the Jews are guilty; Israel is guilty. The guilty party is known, the murderer is known; still there is blood libel. It is nothing, Mr. Speaker, *let them shout their shouts, make their insults, and state their libels. Nothing will avail them. The truth will win.*

The Israeli Cabinet was summoned into special session right after the Holy Days and, after studying the reports, expressed regret over the event, but rejected the libel of the clamoring opposition elements and the media.

Israel was condemned by the Security Council of the United Nations, and Egypt recalled her Ambassador from Tel Aviv "for consultations." In Israel, Opposition Knesset Members, seeing an opportunity to strike at the Government, called for an inquiry into the massacre. They were supported and encouraged by newly-elected President Yitzhak Navon, a former Labor Knesset Member, who lent the weight and prestige of his office to the call for such an inquiry.

The Opposition, together with the Peace Now camp, organized a mass demonstration in Tel Aviv's King's Square to protest the Government's actions and call for its resignation. Tens of thousands were bussed in from kibbutzim and *moshavim* and villages all over the country. The police assessed the crowd at about 75,000; the organizers claimed 400,000 were present. This led to a lengthy press controversy, with respected journalists writing to prove that it was simply not possible for 400,000 people to get into the Square – "unless they stood on top of each other in three or four tiers." Nevertheless, the claim circulated and was picked up and embellished by the world media.

After resisting for ten days appeals to set up a judicial Commission of Inquiry, the Government conceded and asked the President of the Supreme Court, Mr. Justice Yitzhak Kahan, to head such a Commission. The turnabout came at the suggestion of the Prime Minister, who wanted to end the libel, the discord and the impression that the Government had something to hide. The matter to be investigated was defined as: "All the facts and persons connected with the atrocity which was carried out by a unit of the Lebanese forces against the civilian population in the Shatilla and Sabra camps." The Commission comprised Judge Kahan, Judge Aharon Barak and Reserve General Yona Efrat.

The Commission held 60 sessions and heard 58 witnesses, including the Prime Minister. This was one of the rare occasions in Israel since 1948 that the political leadership had been subjected to investigation. When previous national tragedies were investigated – such as the Yom Kippur War – the political leaders (mainly Golda Meir and Moshe Dayan) were specifically excluded from investigation, and only military commanders were held accountable, punished and even sacrificed.

When Begin received the notification that he was to hold himself available to appear before the Commission, he was distressed and told friends that he would resign from the premiership. "Christians kill Moslems," he said "and they blame Jews." Nevertheless, accompanied by Yechiel Kadishai, the Director of his Office, and

Dan Meridor, the Cabinet Secretary, the Prime Minister appeared before the Commission and responded to all their questions.

The notice sent to the Prime Minister stated that he was liable to be harmed if the Commission were to determine "that the Prime Minister did not properly weigh the part to be played by the Lebanese Forces during and in the wake of the IDF's entry into West Beirut, and disregarded the danger of acts of revenge and bloodshed by these forces vis-à-vis the population in the refugee camps."

The Prime Minister responded that, in the conversations between him and the Defense Minister in which the decision was taken to have IDF units enter West Beirut, and in the conversations he had held with the Chief of Staff during the night between 14 and 15 September 1982, nothing at all was said about a possible operation by the Lebanese Forces.

The Commission released its findings and conclusions on 8 February 1983. They established that the massacre in Sabra and Shatilla had been carried out by a Phalangist unit, acting on its own. No Israeli was directly responsible for the events which occurred in the camps. The Commission, however, ascribed "indirect responsibilities" to Israel because the IDF was "in control of the area." Menachem Begin was found responsible for "not exercising greater involvement and awareness in the matter of allowing the Phalange unit to enter the camps."

The Commission reported that the Prime Minister had testified that

> ...only in the Cabinet session of 16.9.82 did he hear about the agreement with the Phalangists that they would operate in the camps, and that until then, in all the conversations he had held with the Defense Minister and with the Chief of Staff, nothing had been said about the role of the Phalangists or their participation in the operations in West Beirut. He added that since

this matter had not come up in the reports he received from the Defense Minister and the Chief of Staff, he had raised no questions about it. The Prime Minister's remarks in this regard were consistent with the testimony of the Defense Minister and the Chief of Staff, and with the existing documents concerning the content of the conversations with the Prime Minister.

We have described above the two conversations between the Prime Minister and the Defense Minister from the roof of the forward command post on Wednesday, 15.9.82, in the morning hours. According to the testimony and the notes of those conversations, the matter of the Phalangists was not mentioned in them at all. In a further conversation between the Defense Minister and the Prime Minister, on Wednesday at 18:00 hours, nothing was said about the participation of the Phalangists in the entry into Beirut. Similarly, on Thursday, 16.9.82, when the Defense Minister spoke by phone with the Prime Minister during the discussion in the Defense Minister's office, the Defense Minister said nothing about the Phalangists. According to the content of the conversation (see Exhibit 27), his report to the Prime Minister was in an optimist vein: that the fighting had ended, the IDF held all the key points, and it was all over. The only mention of the camps in that conversation was that they were encircled.

We may certainly wonder that the participation of the Phalangists in the entry to West Beirut and their being given the task of "mopping up" the camps seemed so unimportant that the Defense Minister did not inform the Prime Minister of it and did not get his assent for the decision; however, that question does not bear on the responsibility of the Prime Minister. What is clear is that the Prime Minister was not a party to the decision to have the Phalangists move into the camps, and that he received no report about that decision until the Cabinet session on the evening of 16.9.82.

We do not believe that we ought to be critical of the Prime Minister because he did not on his own initiative take an interest in the details of the operation of the entry into West Beirut, and did not discover, through his own questions, that the Phalangists were taking part in that operation of the entry into West Beirut. The tasks of the Prime Minister are many and diverse, and he was entitled to rely on the optimistic and calming report of the Defense Minister that the entire operation was proceeding without any hitches and in the most satisfactory manner.

We have cited above passages from remarks made at the Cabinet session of 16.9.1982, during which the Prime Minister learned that the Phalangists had that evening begun to operate in the camps. Neither in that meeting nor afterwards did the Prime Minister raise any opposition or objection to the entry of the Phalangists into the camps. Nor did he react to the remarks of Deputy Prime Minister Levy which contained a warning of the danger to be expected from the Phalangists' entry into the camps. According to the Prime Minister's testimony, "no one conceived that atrocities would be committed…simply, none of us, no Minister, none of the other participants supposed such a thing…" (p. 767). The Prime Minister attached no importance to Minister Levy's remarks because the latter did not ask for a discussion or a vote on this subject. When Minister Levy made his remarks, the Prime Minister was busy formulating the concluding resolution of the meeting, and for this reason as well, he did not pay heed to Minister Levy's remarks.

We have already said above, when we discussed the question of indirect responsibility, that in our view, because of things that were well known to all, it should have been foreseen that the danger of a massacre existed if the Phalangists were to enter the camps without measures being taken to prevent them from committing acts such as these. We are unable to accept the Prime Minister's remarks that he was absolutely unaware of such a danger. According to what he himself said, he told the Chief of Staff on the night between 14 and 15 September 1982, in explaining the decision to have the IDF occupy positions in West Beirut, that this was being done "in order to protect the Moslems from the vengeance of the Phalangists," and he could well suppose that after the assassination of Bashir, the Phalangists' beloved leader, they would take revenge on the terrorists. The Prime Minister was aware of the mutual massacres committed in Lebanon during the civil war, and of the Phalangists' feelings of hate for the Palestinians, whom the Phalangists held responsible for all the calamities that befell their land. The purpose of the IDF's entry into West Beirut – in order to prevent bloodshed – was also stressed by the Prime Minister in his meeting with Ambassador Draper on 15.9.1982. We are prepared to believe the Prime Minister that, being preoccupied at the Cabinet session with formulating the resolution, he did not pay heed to the remarks of Minister Levy, which were uttered following lengthy reviews and discussions. However, in view of what has already been noted above regarding foresight and probability of acts of slaughter, we are unable to accept the position of the Prime Minister that no one imagined that what happened was liable to happen, or what follows from his remarks: that this possibility did not have to be foreseen when the decision was taken to have the Phalangists move into the camps.

As noted, the Prime Minister first heard about the Phalangists' entry into the camps about 36 hours after the decision to that effect was taken, and did not learn of the decision until the Cabinet session. When he heard about the Phalangists' entry into the camps, it had already taken place. According to the "rosy" reports the Prime Minister received from the Defense Minister and the Chief of Staff, the Prime Minister was entitled to assume at that time that all the operations in West Beirut had been performed in the best possible manner and had nearly been concluded. We believe that in these circumstances it was not incumbent upon the Prime Minister to object to the Phalangists' entry into the camps or to order their removal. On the other hand, we find no reason to exempt the Prime Minister from responsibility for not having evinced, during or after the Cabinet session, any interest in the Phalangists' actions in the camps. It has already been noted above that no report about the Phalangists' operations reached the Prime Minister, except perhaps for the complaint regarding the Gaza Hospital, until he heard the BBC broadcast towards evening on Saturday. For two days after the Prime Minister heard about the Phalangists' entry, he showed absolutely no interest in their actions in the camps. This indifference would have been justifiable if we were to accept the Prime Minister's position that it was impossible and unnecessary to foresee the possibility that the Phalangists would commit acts of revenge; but we have already explained above that according to what the Prime Minister knew, according to what he heard in the Thursday cabinet session, and according to what he said about the purpose of the move into Beirut, such a possibility was not unknown to him. It may be assumed that a manifestation of interest by him in this matter, after he had learned of the Phalangists' entry, would have increased the alertness of the Defense Minister and the Chief of Staff to the need to take appropriate measures to meet the expected danger. The Prime Minister's lack of involvement in the entire matter casts on him a certain degree of responsibility.

However, the Commission in its closing remarks stated that, having established responsibility, "there is no need for any further recommendation." At the same time they called for the removal of Sharon from office of Defense Minister and a number of high-ranking military officers, including the head of military intelligence, and the commander of Israel forces in the north.

Chapter 28

CRUSHING BLOW

By the time the Commission concluded its work and presented its report, Menachem Begin had undergone a dramatic personal transformation. No longer the tough lion of a man he had been before the inquiry, Begin had become somber and despondent. The spark had gone out of his voice and the sparkle from his eyes.

The reason for the transformation was the death of his beloved wife, Aliza, on 14 November 1982 while he was in Los Angeles. Though her passing was a terrible tragedy to Begin, it was not as much of a shock; Aliza had been in failing health for some time, was permanently on medication, and was in and out of the hospital for treatment for her severe asthma.

Several years earlier, my wife and I were in London with Menachem and Aliza Begin, who were the guests of honor at the Annual Jerusalem Day Dinner organized by the Herut Movement of Britain. When their friends learned that the function coincided with the 40th anniversary of their distinguished guests' wedding, a special toast was proposed to their happiness and good health. In his response, Menachem Begin told a very personal story about their courtship and his proposal of marriage.

"Before I respond," she had said, "I must tell you a secret: I have asthma." And he told her: "I must tell you a secret as well: the day will come when I will be arrested and jailed." As an aside, he added: "Both were right."

Their relationship was profound. Though frail and ill, his beloved "Alinka," as he called her, was a strong influence on him. She managed his affairs – all practical matters – and he relied on her completely. He confided in her from the days of the Underground struggle until the end – excepting in the one instance of planning the attack on Iraq's atomic reactor, and afterwards he even made a special point of stressing that "no one knew – not even my wife."

In October 1982 her condition deteriorated, and she was again admitted to the Hadassah Hospital. The Prime Minister wanted to cancel an important visit to the U.S., where he was to meet President Reagan, Secretary of State Shultz, other Administration officials and members of the U.S. Congress. Prior to that, he was to address 2,000 participants at an Israel Bonds dinner in Los Angeles, following which he was to proceed to Dallas in order to appear at a rally of many thousands of Christian friends of Israel organized by Dr. W.A. Criswell, a prominent leader of the Southern Baptist Church. A few days before his departure, the doctors performed a tracheotomy and she could not speak with all the tubes connecting her to the medical equipment. When Menachem Begin told her that he had decided not to go to the U.S., she wrote a note urging him to go because his visit was important for the country. The doctors did not keep the seriousness of her condition from him, and explained that she was reasonably stable and that he could proceed.

He left on a special Israel Air Force plane accompanied by his daughter, Leah, Yechiel Kadishai, Prof. M. Gottesman (his physician), and a few other close aides.

We met Begin on his arrival in New York, where he was to rest before proceeding to Los Angeles the next day. From the moment he landed, he was on edge. "Aliza is very ill," he told me. He called home frequently to inquire about her condition. We flew with him to Los Angeles and saw his deep concern and restlessness. He arrived in Los Angeles around midday Friday and rested in his suite at the Century City.

On Saturday, 13 November, around 5:00 PM – which was early Sunday morning, 14 November, in Jerusalem – Yechiel Kadishai received a call from the Begins' son Benny with the news that his mother had died. We were all in shock, but concerned only with the question of how to break the news to the Prime Minister. We looked for his doctor who, being an observant Jew, had walked to a nearby Synagogue for the Shabbat Mincha (afternoon) services. It was some time before he could be reached, and only when he returned was Menachem Begin told that his life's companion was gone.

He broke down and uttered only three Hebrew words: *"Lama azavti ota"* ("Why did I leave her?"). And he repeated those words over and over, throughout the journey back to Israel and for weeks afterwards. He never forgave himself for having left her, and from then onwards he was enveloped in profound sadness. At the funeral and during the Shiva week we began to have real concerns whether Begin would recover from his loss.

Over the last few years, his own state of health had been deteriorating. He had suffered several heart attacks and minor strokes. He had fallen and broken his hip, and now his strong spirit simply caved in. It was painful to see him sitting in his customary seat in the Knesset, head bowed, deep in thought. His Knesset appearances became less frequent, and he spent fewer hours at the office.

The war against the PLO in Lebanon had taxed his strength and, while certain that it had been justified and that the results were satisfactory, he regretted that he could not attain peace with Lebanon.

The Government's actions in that respect continued unabated, and secret negotiations were held with the Lebanese government, which repeatedly denied that such contacts were taking place at all. They admitted, however, that negotiations – with U.S. participation – were taking place regarding, as they put it, "full Israel withdrawal and the return to the 1949 Armistice Lines." By 13 January 1983, agreement was reached on an agenda that included security arrangements, an end to the state of war between the two countries, normalization of ties and the withdrawal of all foreign troops from Lebanon.

The Republican U.S. Administration, hoping to play a no less effective role in pursuing Middle East peace than their Democratic predecessors had done, attached great importance to these negotiations. At the end of April, Secretary of State Shultz arrived in Jerusalem and shuttled for ten days between Israel and Lebanon to put the finishing touches to the agreement between the two countries. The Israeli Government submitted the text to the Knesset, which approved the agreement on 16 May. The next day the agreement was signed in Khalde and Kiryat Shemona.

The Lebanese Parliament approved the agreement a month later. By this time, however, the Syrians had succeeded with threats of military intervention to prevent Amin Gemayel, Bashir's brother and elected successor, from formally ratifying the agreement.

Nevertheless, it can be recorded that in fact Begin had finally achieved a peace agreement with a second Arab country. Article 1 of the Agreement states plainly:

> 1. The Parties agree and undertake to respect the sovereignty, political independence and territorial integrity of each other. They consider the existing international boundary between Israel and Lebanon inviolable.
> 2. The parties confirm that the state of war between Israel and Lebanon has been terminated and no longer exists.

Begin deeply regretted that the Syrians had succeeded in sabotaging this agreement, one which he believed could further contribute to the stabilization of the Middle East. Secretary Shultz, too, was disappointed that his own efforts had been undermined by the Syrians. He paid another short flying visit to the area – but to no avail. Amin Gemayel had been thoroughly demoralized and intimidated by the proximity of large Syrian forces.

Begin was to visit Washington in the latter part of July, but postponed the visit at the last moment "for personal reasons." Such a step was quite out of character, and it led to much speculation and questioning.

Chapter 29

"I CANNOT GO ON"

B<small>Y THE TIME THAT THE PEACE AGREEMENT</small> between Israel and Lebanon was finalized, my wife and I had returned to Jerusalem after our tour of duty in Washington. Menachem Begin had asked me to serve as Adviser to the Prime Minister on the Diaspora. Yehuda Avner, who had held that position since Begin was elected to the premiership, was appointed Ambassador to the Court of St. James. Begin agreed to his leaving, provided that "Harry would come back and take over." He apologized for asking us to leave Washington a year ahead of time; we assured him that we were glad to serve him in any capacity.

When I first saw the Prime Minister soon after my return, I was, frankly, shocked, but gave no hint of my reaction to his appearance. He had lost much weight, was pale and seemed despondent. "We have problems," he said to me when I inquired how he was feeling.

I spent about half an hour with him, during which he sipped fruit juice and nibbled at a few small crackers. We discussed many things, and his eyes lit up a bit when I mentioned a *Washington Post* report that Secretary of State Shultz had conceded that Jews should have the right to live everywhere, "including the West

Bank," and that the political future of the territory was a matter for negotiation.

Begin hadn't seen the report yet – and appeared pleased by what I had told him – and I handed him a cutting. "First it was 'illegal,' then an 'obstacle to peace,' and now 'the right to live,'" he said pensively. "That's progress."

As I took leave of him I looked closely at my long-time friend, and saw for the first time an exhausted, ill, aged man. He had passed his seventieth birthday a few weeks earlier, and many of us recalled that he had often expressed his intention of retiring at that age.

I was, therefore, not surprised when it happened. Saddened, but not surprised. It was Sunday morning, 28 August, and time for the regular weekly cabinet meeting. As always, the Prime Minister arrived at the office at 8:00 AM. He passed me in the anteroom and nodded slightly. He was looking paler than usual as he called out, through gritted teeth, "Yechiel!" His trusted secretary and confidant followed him into his room and emerged a few minutes later, pale as a sheet. He beckoned to me to follow him into his own adjoining office as he called Dan Meridor, the Cabinet Secretary, on the intercom. "Dan," he said, "the Prime Minister has decided to announce his resignation at this morning's meeting."

A few minutes before nine, Menachem Begin stepped out of his office and began his last walk upstairs to the Cabinet room. There, after dispensing with some formalities and preliminaries, he told the assembled ministers simply: "I cannot go on any longer." The stunned reaction gave way to a loud "No, No," and a clamor to reconsider.

A few minutes later he was back in his own office. He took my hand and said: "I'm sorry for what I'm doing to my friends but, you understand, I cannot go on."

Begin's announcement was followed by endless attempts to

dissuade him from his course – from the members of his Government, his supporters and critics alike, from the Likud faction, the Government Coalition, from rabbis, from personal friends, from delegations from all parts of the country. There was an endless stream of people going into his office.

A group of settlers from Judea and Samaria came in to appeal to the man who was primarily responsible for the remarkable fact that some 70,000 people were now living in the 200 villages in the "disputed" areas.

Rabbis urged him to withdraw the resignation in order "not to cause darkness and gloom in these days of the month of Elul before Rosh Hashana." I heard the son of the late Reb Arye Levin, whom Begin loved and revered, tell him that he had visited his father's grave that morning and "had received a message" urging Begin to reconsider. For a few brief minutes, Freda, my wife and I found ourselves alone in the room with Menachem Begin. We said: "Menachem, dear friend, you are not well and you are exhausted. Why don't you take a month's break from everything to regain your health and strength, and then decide finally."

But he could not be moved, and a few weeks later his official letter of resignation was delivered to President Herzog by Cabinet Secretary Dan Meridor.

Menachem Begin remained in the Prime Minister's residence for a short time while an apartment was being readied for him in another part of Jerusalem, overlooking the Jerusalem Forest. It was 100 meters from where his son Benny lived with his family. His daughter Leah was to stay in the new apartment with him.

The Likud Central Committee elected the Foreign Minister Yitzhak Shamir as head of the party and its nominee for the Premiership. He presented his Government to the Knesset and received a vote of confidence on 10 October 1983.

In the first months, Begin's seclusion was total. Only members of his family and Yechiel Kadishai, Cabinet Secretary Meridor, his doctor and physiotherapist and a few close friends could visit him. According to the law, the government provides round-the-clock security for every former Prime Minister. No one, other than the few on a short list, was permitted to enter.

Gradually, the atmosphere became a little more relaxed, and a few additional people visited. Freda and I were in the small group who used to gather in the Begin apartment every Saturday evening: Nathan and Lily Silver, Haim and Dvora Corfu and ourselves. (Haim Corfu was the Minister of Transport, and he and Dvora were Begin's neighbors in the same apartment building.) We spent about an hour with him, and then, as if prompted, I got up and said: "Thank you Mr. Begin" – as Presidential Press Conferences in the U.S. are ended – and we all left. The scene always brought a smile to Begin's face.

Ya'acov and Zippora Meridor came in once a week; Reuben Hecht visited every few weeks; Hart and Simona Hasten and Mark and Anna Ruth Hasten visited periodically from Indianapolis, Indiana.

On the rare occasions when Yechiel Kadishai could not travel from Tel Aviv, I visited Begin daily, bringing him the papers that were provided by the Prime Minister's Office and writing down his dictated replies to the letters that he responded to from the avalanche of mail addressed to him. It became a regular routine. "Good morning." "How do you feel today?" A few words about major news items or a birth or death in the family of friends. A cup of tea and biscuits provided by the housekeeper, who cleaned and cooked for him. (When she was not there, we prepared the tea for him.) "Now let us do some work," he would say, and start reading letters and replying either in Hebrew or English. They were brought back typed the next day or the day after for his signature. Many letters were from admirers abroad, Jews and non-Jews, some of whom also asked for an autographed picture which he willingly provided, always calling for the "special pen" with which to sign.

He paid careful attention to letters from Israeli students or school children and wrote meaningful responses.

Then, after half an hour or more, he became impatient with his "work" and turned to the newspapers on his bed.

Every day he read all the major Israeli press, as well as the *Times of London*, the *International Herald Tribune*, *Le Monde* and then the weekly *Time* magazine, *Newsweek*, and others. At one stage he devoured books – every book that we could provide. Yechiel Kadishai discussed the matter with Eri Steimatzky, head of the largest chain of bookstores in Israel, who gladly supplied copies of all suitable new books – mainly biographies, histories, and political works. We all searched our own libraries for books he might not have read. Then we began to bring new editions back with us from our overseas trips. My suitcase was always heavily laden with books I bought for him. At one time it looked as though he was sleeping in a library. There were books everywhere. Yechiel and the family periodically thinned out the "stock," transferring the books to the study or sending them to libraries.

Menachem Begin left the apartment only once a year, to attend the memorial service for his wife, Aliza, at the graveside on the Mount of Olives. Large numbers of friends and followers attended to share in the tribute, and to get a glimpse of their beloved Menachem Begin. He always arrived smartly dressed in a dark suit, tie and hat. It was usually in November and already fairly cold and raining. He was driven up to the closest spot, and walked the remaining distance holding on to the arms of his daughters Hassia and Leah. The ceremony was brief, then he stooped down and, as is customary, put a small stone on the grave and then began the walk back, shaking hands, acknowledging a greeting. The next morning he would comment on the nature of the crowd. He remembered who was there and said a word or two about some of the participants.

His only other "outings" were, unfortunately, to the hospital, either for emergency attention or scheduled treatment.

As time went on he also agreed to receive some other special guests whom the family, Yechiel Kadishai, I and others brought to him with his consent. Jedidiah Blumenthal and Percy Goldberg from South Africa visited once, as did Feige and Reuben Zimmerman, Ben and Rose Milner of Montreal, Rabbi Alexander Schindler and his wife, and Adele and George Klein and their daughters. Everyone tried to cheer him up and encourage him to return to public life – even if not to active politics.

From time to time, a few VIPs asked to visit Begin. Jeanne Kirkpatrick, who admired him greatly, was a welcome guest. Armand Hammer came several times and, on one such visit, gave Begin his autobiography. Once Hammer brought the famous Russian refusenik Ida Nudel who was moved to tears standing in the presence of Menachem Begin, the man who had fought so hard and so long for the release of the Jewish refuseniks and for the right of repatriation for all Russian Jews. Yosef Begun, who was imprisoned by the Russians because he taught Hebrew, brought Begin a handmade tin mug that he had used in prison.

Other important visitors had to be content with a brief telephone conversation which was arranged by Yechiel or, in some instances, by me.

Menachem Begin's birthday on Shabbat Nahamu was an occasion for many visitors to congregate in the apartment. In the first years of his retirement, only the members of his family and closest friends participated. He received us all warmly, pressed our hands and joined in the L'Chaim. Each year the crowd grew. No one was specially invited. He once "ruled" that "whoever remembers the date and wishes to attend will be welcome." A group of Irgun veterans came annually from Tel Aviv, bringing cake and wine. They sang the old Betar and Irgun songs, and eventually Begin joined in with hand clapping. Then the L'Chaim, and slowly the celebrants took leave of Begin and dispersed. Each year, the management of the Jerusalem Plaza Hotel sent a huge birthday cake (which was always sent on to the children's ward in one hospital or another).

The last time Menachem Begin ventured out – to everyone's surprise – was to attend the wedding of his granddaughter, Orit, daughter of Hassia and Matti Milo, at the Gan Oranim in Tel Aviv. There were rumors that he might attend and, naturally, dozens of photographers gathered around the entrance. He was brought in through a side door, seated in a wheelchair, and was wheeled into the hall to the amazement and delight of the large crowd. Then, using a walker, he proceeded to the *Chuppa* and sat under it for the ceremony. He returned to the table, relaxed and happy, and smiled at his friends. After another half hour he asked to be taken home.

Yitzhak Shamir visited him every few months to exchange ideas and reminisce a while. Occasionally, Begin touched on the current political situation, but as a rule he never discussed political matters or party affairs. On a number of occasions, however, he expressed full confidence in his successor, wished him well, and was delighted when the party he had founded won two subsequent elections (1984 and 1988) under Shamir's leadership. However, when friends visited, he sometimes did speak at considerable length about international developments, especially the historic transformation in the Soviet Union, the changes in Europe and the Middle East, and the dramatic events in South Africa (which he had visited three times).

Gradually, he also agreed to answer telephone questions from journalists and radio reporters. Yet he refused all requests for interviews from Israel TV or the major international television networks. In an Israel Radio interview on 22 July 1991, he said that he strongly objected to trading the Golan Heights in a peace deal with Syria, insisting that his decision to withdraw from Sinai in exchange for peace with Egypt was not a precedent.

In a letter to his friend, Dr. Reuben Hecht, who established the department of Zionism and Zionist Historiography at Haifa

University (which was sponsoring a symposium on the ramifications and relevance of the Balfour Declaration), Begin wrote:

> The British distorted the Balfour Declaration over the years and obstructed fulfillment of its intentions, resulting in serious consequences for the Jewish people. The Balfour Declaration was doubtless a turning point in the history of the Jewish people.
>
> The document was published for various reasons but, over the years, the British falsified its contents, especially by giving it an untrue interpretation based on the phrase "in Eretz Israel," instead of "in Eretz Israel as the national home for the Jewish people."

The present Earl of Balfour, a guest speaker at the symposium, told *The Jerusalem Post* that he concurred with Begin's view that the British government had distorted the content and intention of his uncle's famous declaration. "I can only say that governments do make decisions for economic and political reasons which can be incredibly harmful to one's friends," said Lord Balfour. Begin wrote in the same letter that:

> Ze'ev Jabotinsky demonstrated the falsification with his famous words: "If you say 'in Russia' you do not mean part of it but the country as such."
>
> Against this background, difficult relations developed regarding the declaration between the government of Britain and ourselves until...the State of Israel was established.
>
> We remember the British affectionately for the publication of the Balfour Declaration. We shall also remember...the severe results concerning the Jewish people of the falsification of its contents in the days when millions of Jews cried out for the realization of its promise. They cried in vain.

One must remember the good of the original intention
as well as the severity of the closing of the gates of our homeland.

When he took ill and was hospitalized at the Ichilov Hospital
in Tel Aviv, Begin's family decided to move him to a new apartment in Yaacov Weinshal Street, Afeka, which would also be near
his daughter Hassia, who would be better able to look after him.
His other daughter, Leah, lived in the apartment with him. Benny
traveled from Jerusalem to Tel Aviv almost daily to spend a few
hours with his father.

Begin spent the entirety of the Gulf War in the Rehabilitation
Center of the Ichilov Hospital. During the Scud attacks, he would
encourage the other patients, assuring them that "everything will be
all right." When the all-clear was sounded and everyone removed
their masks, the patients approached him to shake his hand.

Whenever my wife and I saw him in his new surroundings or at
the Ichilov Hospital, he spoke with typical parental *nachat* (pride)
of his children and grandchildren. Benny, by now a distinguished
and respected Knesset Member, gave him a great deal of satisfaction and pride. He sometimes referred to a speech of Benny's that
he heard on the radio or saw during very rare television viewings,
or to Benny's articles in this paper or that. He commented favor-
ably on his son's parliamentary work, as if he was recalling his own
days in the House. Churchill's description of himself as "a child of
the House" also rang true for Menachem Begin.

Chapter 30

LAST WORDS

Freda and i were due to visit South Africa on a speaking tour at the end of February 1992. A week before our departure, we drove down to Tel Aviv to see our friend and take leave of him as we used to do throughout the years prior to a trip abroad. We found him looking well, almost radiant. He was more talkative than usual. He wanted to know the purpose of our trip. We discussed the situation in South Africa. He inquired about mutual friends. Then we turned to family matters. He spoke about his children and grandchildren and he asked about our family and grandchildren. We enjoyed our tea and cake with him, then took our leave and returned to Jerusalem. We telephoned him on the day of our departure, and he asked if we were all ready and packed. His voice was strong and clear. "Give my love to all our friends," he said. "Have a good trip. Shalom."

We did not know that these were the last words we would hear from Menachem Begin. In the midst of our South African tour, we heard on the radio that he had taken ill and was rushed to the Ichilov Hospital in the early hours of the morning of 3 March.

His daughter Leah called an ambulance and her brother and sister. The first hospital announcement said that "Mr. Begin is being treated by a team of doctors in our intensive care unit." At first it was thought that he had suffered a stroke. Begin was unconscious and paralyzed on one side; the director of the hospital, Professor Dan Michaeli, reported that the heart attack made him lose consciousness. He remained unconscious for some time due to a "disturbance in his blood supply because of the heart attack."

A border police unit arrived at the Ichilov Hospital to take charge of all security requirements. Benny Begin firmly requested the media "not to set up a mobile broadcasting unit here while my father is in the hospital." The nation was stunned by the news. Crowds gathered around the hospital; its telephone lines were jammed. I called from South Africa and spoke to members of the family. "There is a slight improvement…he has regained consciousness…the prognosis is not good…"

Begin battled on for his life for a week, but was too frail to overcome the effects of the severe heart attack. At 3:15 AM on Monday, 9 March, an emergency team of doctors and nurses attempted to resuscitate Begin's failing heart. Begin's children who had left the hospital late the previous night were informed that his condition was rapidly deteriorating and returned to be at his side.

Menachem Begin died at 3:30 AM, but the death was not announced publicly until an hour and a half later. Shortly before 6:00 AM, the hospital's rabbi arrived at Begin's bedside to recite the Kaddish.

We heard the news at 7:00 AM in Johannesburg, South Africa. Expecting that there would be a State funeral two or three days later, we began preparations to leave by the next available plane to Europe in order to reach Israel on time. The remainder of my speaking appearances would be canceled. Just to make sure, I called Yechiel Kadishai and learned that the funeral would take place that very afternoon at 4:00 PM in Jerusalem. According to Begin's wish it was to be "a Jewish funeral" – which meant that there was to be no delay, no eulogies, no military guard of honor, and no lying in state.

I still regret that we could not return in time to pay our last respects to our friend and leader, Menachem Begin, as he was laid to rest next to his beloved wife Aliza on the Mount of Olives, overlooking the Old City of Jerusalem.

Though it was not a state funeral, it was a people's funeral. "Never Before Has Jerusalem Seen a Funeral Like This" reported *The Jerusalem Post* on its front page the next morning. Begin was buried in the presence of the nation's leaders and a vast crowd of mourners, estimated at 75,000. Thousands of mourners, many weeping, walked the four kilometers from the Sanhedria funeral parlor to the cemetery. More than 50 buses carried others through streets that had been closed off to traffic.

President Herzog, Prime Minister Shamir, all Cabinet Ministers who were in the country, Supreme Court justices, and Knesset Members of most parties headed the nation's mourners. A number of ambassadors attended, including Egyptian Ambassador Bassiouny, who attended at the request of President Hosni Mubarak. Members of the former Irgun High Command were on hand to serve as pallbearers and lower their Commander into his grave. As the grave was being filled with Jerusalem soil, many of Begin's former comrades of the Irgun and Betar spontaneously broke into the singing of the Betar anthem.

The question on many lips was: Why here on the Mount of Olives? Why not on Har Herzl, near Jabotinsky or Raziel or other leaders of the State?

Some of us knew the answer, but many learnt it for the first time on the day of the funeral, if not eight months later, on the anniversary of Aliza's death, when Begin's will was published for the first time. It is a three-line hand-written letter addressed to Yechiel Kadishai and dated 14 April 1977, one month before the Knesset election that brought Menachem Begin to power.

My dear Yechiel,

When the day comes, I request you to read to my dear ones, to my friends and comrades, this request:

I ask to be buried on the Mount of Olives next to Meir Feinstein and Moshe Barazani.

I thank you and all those who will carry out my request.

With love, Menachem

Feinstein and Barazani were two young men in their early twenties who had been sentenced to death by the British in May 1947 for their activities in Underground operations. Feinstein, an Ashkenazi, was a member of the Irgun; Barazani, of Sephardi origin, a member of Lechi. They were in the same death cell, awaiting their fate. They had requested and received in the most clandestine manner a hand grenade which they hid in their cell. When the time for their execution arrived, Rabbi Ya'acov Goldman was summoned to the Jerusalem Central Prison in order to administer the last rites to the two young men. They prayed together and asked him to leave as soon as possible. He would not do so until he had made all final arrangements and informed them that he would return in the early hours of the morning. Suddenly, they requested their last cigarettes. While he was out of the cell, he heard a loud explosion. Feinstein and Barazani had embraced each other, placed the grenade between them at their chests, and pulled the pin, thus cheating the hangman. They were buried on the Mount of Olives.

Begin always regarded them as symbols of the Jewish people's struggle for freedom, as symbols of unity – one as Ashkenazi, the other Sephardi; one of the Irgun, the other of Lechi; both of whom had reached the heights of heroism. Therefore, he chose a spot next to their graves as his – and his wife's – last resting place. And now, the multitudes who streamed to the grave of Menachem Begin also bowed their heads in homage to the two young freedom fighters.

That night thousands came to the grave. Some stayed and

prayed all night. Some fell to the ground and wept. There was an outpouring of national mourning. The newspapers appeared next morning with black borders and huge headlines. Pictures of Menachem Begin were displayed in shops and public buildings. Memorial parades were held in military camps and lessons on Begin were given in schools. And then the tributes poured in from leaders of all persuasions and from abroad. President Chaim Herzog:

> He was a man without fear. As a youth, he was not frightened by the persecutions in the Diaspora; he was not afraid and did not break in prison during those "White Nights;" he was not deterred in the difficult life of the Underground when he was hunted for days; he did not hesitate to take grave and fateful decisions in the life of the nation; he was not afraid of war nor of making peace.

Prime Minister Shamir, eulogizing Menachem Begin at a special memorial cabinet session:

> The Jewish people has lost one of its great leaders. A giant has been taken from us, a leader who was head and shoulders above all. He was one of the most outstanding leaders of the nation throughout the generations.

Yitzhak Rabin:

> The Labor Party will remember him as someone who contributed greatly to democracy in Israel, as an outstanding parliamentarian and a tough political rival with whom we had bitter ideological differences; as a statesman and Prime Minister who knew how to extend his hand in peace to the biggest of our enemies and opened a channel to a life of real peace in the Middle East.

United States President George Bush:

> His historic role in the peace process will never be forgotten. He will be remembered as the man who made a significant, courageous breakthrough.

Former U.S. President Jimmy Carter:

> I remember him as a man of intense brilliance. He was a very courageous man politically who had deep convictions that were unshakable. There is no doubt that he was one of the heroes of Israel's evolution to a sovereign nation. He was also the only Israeli leader who was successful in bringing about major steps toward peace for his people.

Prime Minister John Major:

> He was a man of great vision. His historic contribution to the cause of peace and regional understanding will never be forgotten.

Mrs. Jehan Sadat:

> I will never forget how Prime Minister Menachem Begin came to Cairo for the funeral of my husband. It was on Saturday and it was hot, and Menachem Begin insisted on walking the entire way on foot because of the holiness of the Sabbath. That won over my heart.

Equally telling were the reactions of ordinary people. The newspaper *Ma'ariv* wrote that "if you want to study the strength of the leadership of Begin you have to go to the people. And if you want to know how the people feel you have to go to the Machane Yehuda Market [in Jerusalem]. Said an old onion merchant: 'Not since the days of Moses have we had a man such as Begin. There has not been, nor will there ever be, a man like him.'"

The Chairman of the Merchants Committee in the Market said: "When they announced that he had died, I felt like my own father died. We, the merchants, the ordinary people, loved him because he was a great, straight and modest leader."

In Tel Aviv, Tamar Lam, a 22-year-old Vietnamese waitress said: "It is very sad for us that Begin has died. He was a very good man who helped us and gave us a new life here in Israel." (A reference to Begin's first act as Prime Minister – ordering the admittance of several hundred Vietnamese refugees.)

Dr. Yisrael Eldad (Sheib), a former Lechi leader who had been with Begin in his early years in Poland and in Eretz Israel, said, "David Ben Gurion was admired; Menachem Begin was beloved."

The Israeli press devoted special editions to the life and the passing of Menachem Begin, and Israel TV presented a lengthy program (that had obviously been prepared ahead of time and concluded with scenes from the funeral). In a leading article, *The Jerusalem Post* said:

No Israeli leader captured the world's imagination more dramatically than did Menachem Begin. Nor did the image of a statesman ever undergo so profound a transformation.

Viewed for years as arch-villain, incorrigible "terrorist," demagogic leader of an unregenerate "right wing," convenient target for anti-Semitic barbs and a permanent outsider, he turned into the quintessential peace-maker, a revered Nobel laureate who earned the distinguished peace prize for piercing one of the most impenetrable walls of hatred on the face of the earth.

That was the tenor of editorials in newspapers in Israel and around the world: tribute to the man who concluded the Camp David Accords and brought peace to the region. *The Washington Post*, which had been a severe critic of Menachem Begin at various stages of his career, wrote: "In an age when so many politicians changed positions in the slightest breeze, the former Israeli Prime Minister represented a rare constancy and devotion to personal principle. The odds were almost always against him, but that never diminished his ardor to do what he considered right for his people."

The New York Times said that Begin had transformed Israel in two important ways: "he led the Likud block to triumph, ending 30 years of Labor dominance and shifting the balance of Israel politics…and he secured Israel's first – and only – peace treaty with an Arab neighbor." *Time* carried a full-page article on Begin entitled "Fighter, First and Last;" *Newsweek* similarly headed its story: "The Fighting Jew."

In London, former Chief Rabbi Lord Jakobovits, who had frequently disagreed with Begin's policy, said nevertheless: "I regard him as the greatest of Israel's Prime Ministers – and certainly the most intensely Jewish."

Chapter 31
BEHIND BEGIN'S RESIGNATION

MENACHEM BEGIN DID NOT WRITE HIS MEMOIRS as he had hoped to. When he spoke about it at a Herut Convention, he said: "I will write five volumes entitled *From Destruction to Redemption*." I am certain he had all of them planned in his mind. Some friends thought – *hoped* may be the more appropriate term – that he rose in the middle of the night and, unbeknownst to anyone, wrote away for a few hours. This, unfortunately, was wishful thinking.

I tried many times to persuade and encourage him to write. Yechiel Kadishai and I offered to come to him daily with a tape-recorder and switch it on while he talked into it. He dismissed the idea.

At one point he was absorbed in reading a big volume of Churchill-Roosevelt letters. He was intrigued by the style and language, and spent much time discussing some of the episodes. His enthusiasm gave me an idea. I assembled a set of Begin-Sadat letters (not including classified material), bound them in a file and brought them to Begin. I suggested the idea of publishing these letters as a book with a suitable introduction and appropriate footnotes. He took the file from me and began paging through it. "You see here," he said, pointing to the beginning of a Sadat letter, "this is where he started addressing me as Menachem and I continued to call him Mr. President." I said that this would make an interesting footnote. He asked if he could keep the file for a while. "Of course," I responded; "it is your work." The next time I visited him, he looked very pleased. "I read all the letters. It is quite a story. But this is not enough for a book." My hopes were raised. "The material would make about 220 pages," I said, "and if we want to enlarge the book, we can add some of your and Sadat's speeches at your joint appearances."

Then came the usual disappointment. In a characteristic gesture, he raised both hands as if to suggest "Wait, not now," saying in Hebrew *"Yesh Z'man"* – "there is time."

Of course, we need not have asked his permission; this material had all appeared in the press. But so great was our respect for him that we would not proceed with the publication of such a volume without his consent. Above all, we wanted to involve him personally and actively in the project, in the hope that this would stimulate him to start writing chapters of his autobiography.

The fact that Begin did not leave such autobiographical writings has left the field open to journalists and commentators, most of whom knew little of Begin, to write his story, to speculate about the reasons for his resignation and seclusion, to attribute motives to him and even to put words into his mouth.

As one who knew Menachem Begin for 46 years, who as a newspaper editor followed his entire career, who published his speeches and statements every week and reproduced his articles regularly, who met him frequently and listened to him for many hours, who in the last years saw him regularly and frequently, I have my own assessment of the reasons for his resignation.

In my view, no one particular event brought on Begin's decision; it was due, rather, to the accumulation of a number of factors. In listing them I do not place them in any order of importance.

His own state of health had deteriorated after years of illness. He had become frail and listless and was eating little; I witnessed this when I returned from Washington to take up my new appointment as Advisor on Diaspora Affairs. When he told the Cabinet on 28 August "I can no longer go on," he meant it quite literally; he simply lacked the strength to continue the onerous duties of Prime Minister of Israel, the country in which, as he used to say, "there is never a dull moment." He explained this in his own words to the stunned Cabinet: "You asked to know the reason for my resignation and I want to tell you the reason – I can go on no longer. If I had any doubt whatever as to whether I can continue as Prime Minister, I would have chosen to continue in my duties. But I do not have even any iota of doubt. There is no possibility that I change my opinion. Please, therefore, agree and let me go to the President still today in order to hand in my resignation."

The death of his beloved wife, Aliza, was, as I have endeavored to describe, a devastating blow. I am sure that he never recovered from it and never forgave himself for having left her to go to America, nor for being apart from her when she died. He often spoke about her as the months and years went by. After her death, he discovered more about the wonderful things she had done in her quiet way for women in distress and in need, for institutions for the handicapped and for underprivileged children requiring special education. Also, as noted above, he had depended on her greatly in practical matters. After her passing, grief and sadness settled over him like a shroud, the edge of which was lifted but rarely. Hardly ever did a smile light his face anymore; his expressive, penetrating eyes lost much of their sparkle.

The events in Lebanon had taken their toll – the long days and nights of consultation, decision and waiting. Ill as he often was, he insisted on being awakened at any time of the night whenever there was a military engagement with casualties among the Israeli soldiers. He regarded each one as a personal loss. The Peace Now group, taking advantage of Begin's sensitivity and sentimentality, organized demonstrations outside his official residence, loudly chanting slogans at all hours. After his resignation, they claimed victory in their struggle against him. I saw no evidence to justify their claim and, in fact, discussed the matter with him several times; he repeatedly refused to instruct the police to disperse the demonstrators, even if only to preserve the peace of the neighborhood.

Begin's reaction was no different from that of other world leaders in similar circumstances. At the height of the Gulf War, anti-war activists took up positions across from the White House and kept up a constant drum beat. President George Bush was seriously affected and enraged by this action, and stated bluntly: "Those damned drums are keeping me up all night" (*Newsweek*, 11 February 1991).

It has also been suggested that Begin was a helpless victim in the hands of "two ruthless generals," Sharon and Eytan. From my long association with him, I would not say that he was the sort who could be misled or have the wool pulled over his eyes. In an address to the Knesset on 29 June 1982, he spoke of the sacrifices of young men in the war:

> The Jewish people can exist, with God's help, only by readiness to sacrifice on the part of our finest sons. We have paid a price – woe is me. I need not add another word. And we are unable to console the families who have lost their dear ones; only God can comfort them, and will comfort them.
>
> We pray for the quick and complete recovery and healing of all the wounded. I visited them. I came to comfort them and they comforted me. I left with feelings that have no expression in human language. A wounded, hurting man told me just one thing – be strong and of good courage!
>
> This is the stuff our sons are made of.
>
> Happy is the nation that has such an army. Happy is the army commanded by a leader such as Raful [Eytan] and happy

is the country whose Defense Minister is Ariel Sharon. I say this with all my heart and with all my power of belief. Together we will stand and together we will overcome and ensure peace for our people and country. And to our sons after us we will leave a rule, a great rule: He who comes to destroy you, disarm him in advance.

In a statement to the Knesset a year later – after his wife's death and three weeks before his resignation as Prime Minister – Begin said:

> After all the wars which have been waged in Israel, and this is the war that we had to fight in order to put an end to the ceaseless attacks on the Galilee and its inhabitants, we should not try to create the impression that there are those whose pain is greater and those whose pain is less. I will compete with no one regarding the pain felt by myself and all the Members of the Knesset at the terrible and grave losses we have suffered. I can only say that there are surely those who feel this pain as much as we do, but no one feels the pain *more* than we do.
>
> Israel does not want to stay in Lebanon. We want to bring our boys home. But when the situation becomes difficult, must there be an outcry? Was there not a war of attrition that went on for three years? Didn't boys die nearly every single day? Did any one of us [Likud] raise an outcry at the time?
>
> Yes, the situation is difficult. I don't deny it. There is at present a Syrian threat, though there has been a certain relaxation in the situation. Nevertheless, we must be on guard and if, heaven forbid, hostilities should break out, we shall all have to defend our lives, our existence and our future.

Begin flatly denied that he and the Cabinet were not aware of what the military was doing. In an interview on Israeli television on 15 June 1982, he said "The Government will keep its hand on the pulse; nothing will be done without the express decision of the Government. We did not enter Beirut because the Government had decided that we do not want to capture the city. We also did not capture the airport. We can capture both these objectives with blood losses, but we control the approach to the airport. And the same is true for the city. The Government took an explicit decision on everything."

The interviewer then observed: "You explained that the Cabinet was not confronted with accomplished facts. You might be aware that among segments of the population, there is concern or suspicion that Defense Minister Ariel Sharon dragged the Cabinet to moves which went beyond the original plan of the operation."

In reply, Menachem Begin declared:

> I say to the article writers: Stuff and nonsense. Nothing of the sort. Just idle gossip of journalists who invent things. I read all the papers every day, I simply pay them no attention. They don't know what to write.
>
> What kind of dragging? This is a functioning government. It met sometimes twice a day. All the facts were reported to it. The discussion covered every detail. A decision was taken on everything. No one dragged the Government; no one could have dragged. And why does the Defense Minister, a real veteran of combat, need to drag the Cabinet and act behind its back? Nothing of the sort. I would really like to take the opportunity to appeal to the journalists: Would you finally start writing facts? Maybe stop inventing. There was no deception, no dragging. Things were carried out in accordance with Cabinet decisions.

Both Sharon and Eytan denied that they had in any way misled the Prime Minister at the time of the war and might, therefore, have been responsible for his resignation. "I totally deny these charges and accusations," Eytan told Israel Army Radio. "Even during the planning stages, the Prime Minister and the Government knew our intentions, including the plan to close off Beirut and to advance to the Beirut-Damascus highway.

"The appropriate officers and I appeared before the Government and the security cabinet every time we were asked to give a picture of the state of the war, or for other reasons. At no point were Premier Begin and the Government asked to approve, after the fact, military operations that needed Government approval. Every stage of the war had the approval of the Government."

Eytan maintained that Begin was more involved in the course of the Lebanon War than other prime ministers were in other wars.

"Menachem Begin knew more than other prime ministers, who served during the time of other military operations. He was better informed and more involved than all of them, and he made more decisions than all of them. Both Begin and the entire Government visited the theater of battle twice."

Eytan said he was present at the cabinet meeting at which Begin remonstrated with Sharon over the bombardment of Beirut and the wounding of women and children there. "I told the premier that it was just not so – we were not bombarding Beirut and women and children were not being wounded there. It was all propaganda; it just wasn't true."

In the years of his retirement, Begin spoke with Sharon when the former Defense Minister was engaged in a widely publicized libel case against *Time* for its reporting of what happened in the Sabra and Shattila refugee camps. David Halevy, a veteran *Time* correspondent in Jerusalem who had been maligning Begin for years implied that Sharon was "indirectly responsible" for the massacre. After lengthy proceedings, the court – presided over by Judge Abraham Sofaer – found that *Time* had lied, but that it had not been proved that it had done so with malice. No damages were awarded to Sharon, but moral victory was his.

Begin followed the proceedings, which were reported extensively, with the keenest of interest. He commented on one point or another and compared U.S. law with British and Israeli law, which do not require proof of malice in libel cases.

Begin cabled Sharon in New York: "Congratulations on your great moral victory." The next morning, Sharon called Begin by telephone from New York to thank him for his cable. He promised Begin that he would shake the hand of his chief defense attorney, Milton Gould, on behalf of Begin, and would thank him for the great efforts he had made throughout the trial.

This was one of the first occasions that *Time* was found guilty of misrepresentation. The magazine's credibility was shaken.

Two other aspects of the Lebanon situation caused Begin distress and disappointment, and ultimately might have had a bearing on his resignation. The veteran Israeli journalist, Moshe Zak, wrote in a memorial tribute to Begin that Bashir Gemayel's refusal to sign a peace treaty with Israel had left Begin dumbfounded. The two had met secretly on the night of 1 September 1982, in a military camp near Nahariya. Begin looked at the President-elect of Lebanon (less than half his age) with astonishment. "Soldiers of the Israel Defense Forces had spilled their blood to help Gemayel and his Christian Community, but when he attained his goal, he violated his promise," wrote Zak.

"Begin knew how to argue with the great ones of the world. But he lacked the words to rebuke adequately the man who had led Israel astray.

"That pain," wrote Zak, "was what led, less than a year later, to his retirement." That might have been a contributory factor, but I hardly think that it was the reason for the Prime Minister's retirement. But certainly, the refusal of the Lebanese – under Syrian threat and intimidation – to ratify the Peace Treaty with Israel was a big disappointment to Begin.

By sheer chance, I was witness to a rare moment which revealed what might have been the reason for the timing of his resignation precisely that week. It was not the reason for his resignation, but could have determined why he made the announcement on Sunday, 28 August, and had not done so a week earlier, or was not prepared to wait another fortnight or a month or two. If he was going to resign, the timing was significant to him.

After many people had gone into his office to appeal to him to reconsider his resignation decision, I was left in the office alone with the Prime Minister for a few minutes. Suddenly, he looked out the window and the slightest sign of a smile appeared at the corner of his mouth: "So, now this too is resolved," he whispered. He was referring to a subject that had obviously weighed on him for some time and had reached a peak in that last week.

Germany's Chancellor Kohl was due to arrive in Israel the next day on an official visit. As Prime Minister, Begin would, obviously, have to receive him, meet with him and tender a dinner in his honor. He would be expected to welcome the guest at the airport and hear the Israel Army band play the German anthem and "Hatikvah." As is customary, the national flag of the country of the visiting head of Government was displayed in a number of places in Jerusalem which the guest would visit, including the Prime Minister's Office. Such flags, flying side by side with the flag of Israel, were visible from Menachem Begin's office.

The sight added to his pain. His attitude to Germany was well known. He had articulated it clearly in an interview on Israel Radio two years earlier:

> I have a special attitude concerning what the Germans did to our people, and this is not just a personal or a subjective

thing. I know how my mother, my father, my brother and two cousins – one four years old, one five years old – went to their deaths. My father, together with 500 Jews, walked ahead of them: He was the secretary of the community in Brest. He sang "Hatikva" with them; they sang "Ani Ma'amin," (I believe). The Germans pushed them into the river, opened fire with machine guns from both sides and the river became red with blood. The water turned to blood. That is how they died. That is how my father died. My mother was an old woman, sick in the hospital. They summoned her and all the sick women in the hospital and slaughtered them. Perhaps others have no such experiences. I don't deny it but I live with this, and will live with it until the day I die.

I have never forgiven the German people as a whole. I will never forgive them, because they bear collective responsibility. As long as Hitler brought victories, they hailed him! Later, when the decline began, they turned their backs a bit. I do not want to shake the hand of a German who participated in the war.

I am now Prime Minister and fulfill my official role. When Mr. Genscher, the Foreign Minister, came to me I received him and talked with him – of course, not in German. He spoke English and I spoke with him in English. I would not have spoken German with him. And if Mr. Schmidt had come to Israel, I would have met with him. Why? That is part of my official duties. But personally? I will tell you a story.

Once, when I was in Rome with my wife, we went to visit the Vatican Library. We both studied Latin, so we were reading the ancient Bible in Latin. Some couple approached us and asked (we were speaking Hebrew, of course) what language we were speaking. We said to them: "We are speaking Hebrew."

"Oh, you are from Israel?"

"We are from Israel."

"Oh, we like you so much. We respect you so much."

So, I asked: "Where are you from?"

"We are from Germany."

Then I asked him, "How old are you?"

"Forty-five years old."

"Forty-five years old! Then, in the Second World War you were about 20 or 25 years old."

I did not say another thing and started to back off, plain and simple. Perhaps he took part in the murder of my father or of our little children. When I speak of my father I am speaking of all the fathers; about my mother, of all the mothers. About my two little cousins, of all the Jewish children.

Such a horror has not happened since God created men, and men created Satan…among civilized people who produced Goethe and Schiller…

Kohl canceled the visit "because of the Prime Minister's resignation," and the German flags set out to welcome him were removed.

Of course, the constant strife in the Cabinet and the difficulties in the party – in which he was subjected to unprecedented criticism – was another strain that wore him down. In his last statement to the Knesset on 21 July 1983, Begin declared that in times of national stress in political, defense, economic and social spheres, the people should unite and not be frightened by threats.

"I do not want to deny that this is a difficult hour for the nation in the political and defense spheres and in the economic and social spheres. All this is true. But I think that I can say – judging by examples given by other people and compared with the reality which existed in other days in this nation – that in a difficult hour, the people become united and did not try to build up additional difficulties within," he said.

He firmly rebuked the Opposition leader, Shimon Peres, for having tried to frighten the nation, at the same time of Likud's election victory in 1977, darkly hinting that democracy would be liquidated in Israel. "Was it really liquidated?" he asked. "Democracy has never been more free in the State of Israel than it is in these days."

Admitting to difficulties with the Lebanese peace agreement, he said: "But if the enemy does not fulfill what is demanded of him, can the blame be put on our Cabinet, which manages things on behalf of the majority of our people, the majority in the Knesset?" Begin continued:

> It is true that I presented several years ago certain national objectives, not all of which have been fulfilled. This is normal. When you were in power, was there no discrepancy between your promises and the reality which was created following those promises?
>
> You have introduced motions to "Stop the Government half way." What sort of an Opposition motion is it, to stop the Government half way? You want to change the Government – introduce a no confidence motion. You want to go to the people – go to the people.
>
> We have to advance, to solve the national problems, which are difficult; to try to become united, and then I hope, Mr. Speaker, that the problems on the agenda will find the positive solution, as was the case in former days.

And then, in what was to be Menachem Begin's last sentence spoken in the Knesset in which he had served since January 1949, he said: "And we shall build the State of Israel and ensure peace and security, as we believe – this is what will be, God willing."

Chapter 32

POLITICAL TESTAMENT

On the evening of Sunday, 14 August 1983, Prime Minister Begin addressed nearly 400 leaders and representatives of the Israel Bonds Organization from all over the world assembled in the Chagall Hall of the Knesset for a festive dinner. The atmosphere was electric as Israel's leader slowly walked up to the platform. The enthusiastic audience rose to give him a standing ovation. He looked frail and pale. Guests at our table and neighboring tables commented on his appearance. When he eventually began to speak, he could be heard only with difficulty. No one in the hall suspected that they were listening to Menachem Begin's last public address, but it was, and its text may be regarded as a political statement – Begin's evaluation of the state of the nation, and his faith in the triumph of the Jewish people's cause.

Looking at the assembled guests facing him, he slowly and softly began to speak:

> This is a great gathering of dedicated people, of Jews devoted to the independence and freedom of our reborn nation in the ancient homeland of our forefathers. I know every one of you did his best in order to help us in the past, and he will do so in the future, and I want to express our deep gratitude

for all you have done and will do to develop the economy of Israel, especially at the time of real difficulties through which we live now, until we can stand on our own feet and live on our own toil.

Now, Ladies and Gentlemen, let us analyze the main problems and difficulties we face at this crucial period in the annals of Israel and of our nation. May I start with Lebanon. Ladies and Gentlemen, my dear friends, the Israel Defense Forces did not enter Lebanon in order to attack that country or because it wanted anything from it. The Israel Defense Forces used the most legitimate right for national self defense, facing for years permanent attacks, either through incursions or by long-range arms from that country by those who called themselves the PLO The Galilee was not only in permanent danger of being attacked, but Kiryat Shemonah and Nahariya and Metulla and Dafna and Misgav Am and other townships and villages faced great danger of being obliterated by the artillery with which the aggressors were armed by the Soviet Union, by Syria and by Libya. The population of the Galilee became in fact hostage in the hands of this bloodthirsty enemy. We had to defend them. It was our duty. Yes, indeed, the sacrifices we made were great, most painful. This is our greatest worry of all, but it was inevitable in order to defend the citizens, men, women and children of Israel, and especially in its northern part.

After protracted negotiations, Israel and Lebanon signed an Agreement, it being understood and on the basis of such understanding that there will be a simultaneous withdrawal from Lebanon of all foreign forces and we are prepared to do so, because we do not covet even one inch of Lebanese territory. But now everybody knows whose attitude is negative and hostile to a peaceful arrangement. The Syrian ruler declared that the Syrian forces will never recognize the Lebanese-Israel Agreement and will not withdraw from Lebanon. And meantime, there is an eternal fight between two groups of the PLO, and part of it is under the Syrian control. Therefore, we had to take a decision to redeploy our forces in order to avoid, at least to minimize any attempts to hurt our men who are still on the front in order to defend the Galilee.

Ladies and Gentlemen, now also in the United States it is clear who took the decision to prevent a peaceful agreement from coming into being, a peaceful solution being reached. Israel wants peace with Lebanon and all its neighbors. For the sake of peace with Egypt, Israel made great sacrifices. We don't have to prove our love for peace. It is in our hearts. As we hate war, we love peace and vice versa. Whenever it is necessary to defend our people we shall fulfill our duty. Therefore, we still have this problem facing us. We are prepared to do our share to reach a peaceful solution; now somebody else should be told to follow the same example given already by Israel.

As far as Judea, Samaria and the Gaza district are concerned, we have a perfect right to live and to stay there; there we were born as a nation – nobody should forget it and nobody should tell us that this belongs to past ancient history. Our people lives on its history. What would we be without our great past? But we don't want to oppress anybody. Therefore, I say that a crime perpetrated against any Arab inhabitants is a crime which we don't only regret, but if we shall find out who did this evil thing to our neighbors, no doubt he will be brought to book, whoever he is. But of course, there should be due process by law, and there is no other way to punish perpetrators of crimes against whoever they are committed. We want to live with our neighbors in mutual respect, in peace.

Concerning the question of the inhabitants of Judea, Samaria and the Gaza district, Egypt and Israel – and the United States as a witness – signed the famous Camp David Accord, which offers autonomy to the Arab inhabitants, Palestinian inhabitants of Judea, Samaria and the Gaza district. We never promised what is called a Palestinian state. We were asked to do so. We couldn't accept it; we said so. The idea of autonomy is our own original idea. Nobody forced us to bring it up. We did it because we believe in justice for all. Transitional period, and full autonomy, real autonomy. As we proved in the proposal we made during the negotiations. A self-governing authority, the administrative council, should be elected democratically, with secret ballots. We suggested to them, to take care of almost all daily affairs, reserving only security because otherwise all our civilian towns on the coastal plain would be within the range and incursions would be repeated as they have been time and again before 1967, including Tel Aviv and of course, Jerusalem and other cities and towns. We negotiated in good faith. We wanted that Agreement to come into being. The negotiations were interrupted or disrupted not by us. What we suggest – what we have suggested time and again – is to renew the negotiations on the basis of the Camp David Accord. To sign an agreement of international character – and there is a commitment to carry it out. All nations always say an international agreement requires you to be faithful to it and you should bring it to realization. This is the rule applying to all nations.

Ladies and Gentlemen, for too long has the Jew been an exception to the rules applying to other peoples. Enough of it. The rules applying to other nations will apply to the Jewish state as well. We stand by that Agreement. Again from this rostrum, as I did from another rostrum in the Knesset, we invite King Hussein to join the negotiations, because we want peace, as I said, with all our neighbors around. We need peace indeed. We didn't have one day of peace, since our independence was proclaimed 35 years ago and more. This is our approach. I think it is just. It is clear. It should be so accepted and appreciated by all.

We of course have also a very serious economic problem, and I don't have to go into details. Everybody knows about it, and you can follow now the Cabinet's deliberations about harsh measures to be taken and, therefore, we are so grateful to you for the assistance to the Israel Bonds Organization.

The Israel Bonds Organization already brought in billions of dollars in order to develop the economy on the basis of a loan. It is a great phenomenon in the life of the Jewish people and the State of Israel. So, ladies and gentlemen, I have come to you tonight in order to express our deep gratitude, and now I would like to say one sentence: Remember, my dear friends, our people suffered much, lost many, won the day; nobody gave us our freedom, we had to fight for it, to redeem it, to give for it sacrifices, to defend it. All of us without exception of party affiliation, and we won. Why? Because our cause is just.

So take note, my dear friends and when you meet your friends, tell them so. There is a rule, unchangeable. The just cause will always win the day.

Chapter 33

END OF AN ERA

THE DEATH OF MENACHEM BEGIN ended an era in the history of the Jewish people and the State of Israel. He was one of the most outstanding leaders of the Jewish people in this century. He was the last of the giants who set out to establish the Jewish State, to defend it, to protect it, and to fulfill the vision of the Ingathering of the Exiles. He was a leader of strength and determination, a man with vision and a keen sense of mission, a man of deep conviction and faith and pride as a Jew.

I was among a small group of Israeli diplomats who welcomed him to Washington in June 1982 where he was to meet President Reagan. It was a time of tension and pressure. He was still suffering the effects of a broken hip and knee injury and the subsequent operation, and descended from the plane leaning on a cane. As he stepped on the ground, American Secretary of State Alexander Haig welcomed him and asked, "How is the knee, Mr. Prime Minister?" Quick as lightning came the reply: "Painful, but unbent. Please remember that we, the Jewish people, bend our knee only to the Almighty."

The day Menachem Begin died, Israel Radio reached me in Johannesburg, South Africa (where I was on a speaking tour) for my assessment of his life and accomplishments. While I thought it too early for a considered evaluation, my comment was that Menachem Begin was a man who had done and achieved, quite frankly, the impossible. I cited a number of examples.

As Commander of the Irgun Zvai Leumi, he played a major role in freeing his country from British mandatory rule. This was a precondition for the creation of the independent State of Israel; it was also, from a logistical standpoint, flatly impossible. The idea that a few hundred young Jewish men and women, armed with pistols and other light weapons, could confront the British Empire – which had 100,000 combat-tested troops in Palestine – was clearly absurd to most, and bordered on insanity. But the psychological impact of the young Jews' heroism was out of all proportion to the numerical ratio. It aroused world sympathy and support for the Jewish cause, and made continued British presence impossible. The Irgun was not the only Jewish fighting force, and in later years Begin always paid warm tribute to the fighters of the Hagana, Palmach and Lechi. He recalled with profound satisfaction the words of the great American Zionist leader, Dr. Abba Hillel Silver: "The Irgun will go down in history as a factor without which the State of Israel would not have come into being."

Begin who had been maligned and misrepresented as a warmonger, became the first – and thus far the only – Prime Minister of Israel to conclude a peace treaty with an Arab country. Until then, peace between Israel and the Arabs had been regarded as almost impossible. Actually, he concluded a second peace treaty as well – with Lebanon – but its final ratification by Amin Gemayel was sabotaged by Syrian intimidation. Begin is the only national leader of Israel to have received the Nobel Prize for Peace in recognition of his efforts on behalf of his people.

By ordering the Israel Air Force to attack the atomic reactor at Osiraq, near Baghdad, on 7 June 1981, he restored to Israel a security that had been gravely threatened by the Iraqi reactor. Ten years later this unique action was acclaimed in Israel and around the world as a major contribution to mankind. And despite the public controversy surrounding "Operation Peace for Galilee," Begin's action in Lebanon did result in the expulsion of the PLO from that country and the removal of the terrorist threat from Israel's northern border for nearly a decade.

Menachem Begin's foresight and quick thinking initiated the moves that led to the liberation and unification of Jerusalem on 7 June 1967. Thirteen years later, on 30 July 1980, during Begin's premiership, the Knesset adopted the Jerusalem Basic Law, which declared formally that "Jerusalem united in its entirety is the capital of Israel."

Students of the period can also point to the dramatic change "on the ground" – in Judea, Samaria, the Gaza district and the Golan – in the years of Begin's Premiership. He gave impetus to the settlement movement and, as a result, the Jewish presence has become entrenched. There are now 120,000 Jews living in those territories.

In tributes paid to Begin after his death, much was made of his distinguished parliamentary career of 34 years and his role as the long-time Opposition leader who created the Israeli version of "Her Majesty's loyal Opposition" in times of war and peace.

Menachem Begin is also recognized as an Israeli leader who went out of his way to elevate the less privileged part of society – often consisting of those Jews who had come to Israel from North Africa and the Arab countries. He advocated that if the Prime Minister was an Ashkenazi Jew, the President should be of Sephardi origin; indeed, during Begin's premiership, Israel's first Sephardi president was elected. A deputy premier, ministers, chief of staff and other high officials of Sephardi origin were appointed. But his most important contribution to the uplifting of these communities was "Project Renewal," an urban renewal program which greatly improved the lives of nearly half a million Israelis through the combined efforts of the government of Israel and the Diaspora

Jewish communities of the free world. Some years after its inauguration, Project Renewal was judged by a research institute "the most successful urban renewal program in the world."

Begin believed that he was living in prophetic times in which *Shivat Zion* – the Return to Zion – was becoming a breathtaking reality. He saw the Ingathering of the Exiles as a command that demanded the marshaling of all national forces. He was one of the few world statesmen who firmly believed, even in the days when Soviet power was at its height, that the day would come when the "dark tyranny" of the Soviet threat would collapse and disintegrate.

In fact, he held out that hope in the closing chapter of his second book, *White Nights*, published in Hebrew in 1952, when Stalin was still alive and well. He believed that the prospect of change in the Soviet Union would give momentum to the *aliyah* of hundreds of thousands of Soviet Jews. But it took Israel's brilliant victory in the Six Day War of June 1967 to really awaken the masses of the Jewish community in that vast country. Suddenly, they learned of a courageous fighting nation in the sovereign Jewish land, a Jewish nation which had been victorious not only over its enemies, but also over the huge accumulation of Soviet military equipment in their hands.

Begin played an active role to arouse the free world to the "plight and fight" of Soviet Jewry. He was a key figure at the two Brussels Conferences (1971 and 1976) devoted exclusively to the struggle of Soviet Jewry. He raised the issue in the Knesset and at international gatherings. The *aliyah* from the Soviet Union started in the late 1960s, but it took on mass proportions in the late 1970s, by which time Begin had become Prime Minister of Israel. He was exhilarated by the dramatic turn of events, as I observed when I accompanied him to the airport to welcome a number of heroic refuseniks – the Leningrad group that had tried to hijack a Soviet plane and fly to Israel.

That first wave brought nearly 200,000 Soviet Jews to Israel.

Begin saw in the swelling flow confirmation of his own high expectations. Soon after becoming Prime Minister, he invited his colleague, Knesset Speaker Yitzhak Shamir, to visit him at the office. As Shamir later recounted, Begin was reviewing all aspects of national policy and then, suddenly, he rose, paced the room and said: "Yitzhak, we are going to get many hundreds of thousands of our brethren out of the Soviet Union. I am sure of it. You can write it down. Many hundreds of thousands."

And, indeed, the immigration proceeded apace.

It reached a new peak several years after Begin's resignation from office. Nearly 400,000 arrived from 1989 to 1992 – an increase of ten percent in the population of the Jewish State.

Though no longer active in political life, Begin maintained an avid interest in this mass movement of large segments of the community. He admired the heroes who had languished in Soviet camps and prisons and agreed to receive some of them in his home. Their presence vindicated his faith in the triumph of the human spirit over adversity.

And then, as if to cap a lifetime of dedication to the safety of Jews even in the remotest parts of the globe and a constant struggle to "bring them home," came the evacuation of the entire Jewish community of Ethiopia.

Because of the delicate and dangerous features of this struggle, Begin never spoke about it specifically in public. Knowing what was being done by wonderful, dedicated people in the field to organize the rescue of the Ethiopians, I felt great compassion for Begin when he appealed to Jewish organizations in the U.S., Canada and elsewhere to "give us credit."

"I will not go into any details but can assure you that everything that can be done is being done." He was upset when various busy-bodies chided him with neglecting and abandoning the Jews of Ethiopia. But in fact, it was Menachem Begin who had initiated the whole process of their *Shivat Zion*. Knowing they were Jews, Begin saw it as a national duty to bring them all to Israel.

A trickle of Ethiopian Jews found their way to Israel in the 1950s, 1960s and early 1970s. But only when Begin was elected Premier did their fate become a top priority.

The story is now being pieced together. Begin asked the Chief Rabbinate for a clear ruling on the status of these Jews and then directed Raphael Kotlowitz, the head of the Jewish Agency's Aliyah department, to set the machinery in motion for their move to Israel. He established contact with the Ethiopian ruler, Mengistu Haile Mariam, and negotiated an approval for the community's departure. By the time Begin left office, 3,000 had arrived by various means, many of them walking to Sudan, from which they were transported to Israel. The two massive organized evacuations took place after Begin's retirement, but when his Likud Party was still in office: the 1984 Operation Moses, in which some 8,000 arrived, and the spectacular Operation Solomon, when more than 14,000 were airlifted within 36 hours. On that day, Prime Minister Shamir paid high tribute to Menachem Begin for his initiative, determination and leadership in this great national undertaking.

Ethiopian Jews in Israel, now numbering some 40,000, were deeply saddened by Begin's death. Speaking for the United Ethiopian Organization, Ya'acov Babu said: "For us Menachem Begin was everything. He saved a community." And Rahamim Elazar, General Secretary of the Organization added: "It was Begin who broke down the walls. He believed that the place of the Ethiopian Jews is in Israel. He saw it as his destiny to bring the community here. He told his aides: 'I want the Ethiopian Jews here.' Before Begin, nobody wanted to hear from us. He didn't care about skin color. For him it was clear that all Jews should be in Israel. Begin was a warm Jew who loved the Jewish people."

A warm Jew who loved the Jewish people. Menachem Begin was one of the strongest and most convincing leaders that Israel has known. He was also one of the most effective, leaving to Israel a legacy of peace, strength and faith unmatched by any other modern leader of the nation. A hundred volumes could be filled with analyses of his policies and person. Yet these simple words alone – *a warm Jew who loved the Jewish people* – describe this exceptional man more completely than the most exhaustive biography could hope to. Perhaps it is with such words as these that history will remember him.

"WE NEED HIM NOW"

THIS BOOK WILL SEE THE LIGHT OF DAY in the middle of 2004 – a little more than two decades after Menachem Begin's retirement from office as Prime Minister and about twelve years after his death. In that time, mighty events have taken place within Israel and throughout the Middle East.

A substantial immigration of nearly one million Jews from the former Soviet Union and Ethiopia have helped increase Israel's population to more than six and a half million of whom close to five and a half million are Jews.

Arab hostility to Israel continues unabated and has even increased. It resulted in two *intifadas* – *intifada* is the word commonly used to describe the on-going, widespread terrorist campaign against Israel. When the first intifada began, Menachem Begin – who had already been in retirement for some time – told me and a group of friends that "whatever they are doing to our people now will extend to the rest of the world within ten to fifteen years." And so it has been.

The whole world is now caught up in a relentless and painful struggle against terrorism, which has struck the United States, Russia, Britain, Europe, South America, Africa, and the Far East.

The pattern is the same. Violence without regard for the safety of civilians, as in the case of the ruthless attacks by Al Qaida on the Twin Towers in New York, the Pentagon in Washington, and Pittsburgh. Bin Laden and his henchmen have brought the United States to a standstill more than once in recent years as airports were closed, flights cancelled and the traveling public scared off by the psychological war.

In Russia, audiences in theaters were the victims, as were passengers on the subways. And in Indonesia, more than two hundred young holidaymakers lost their lives in terrorist attacks. Large numbers were killed in attacks on the Jewish community complex in Buenos Aires. These violent actions are carried out by suicide bombers on planes and buses, or by means of roadside car bombs. Already, commentators have described this phenomenon as the "War of the 21st Century." No one can foretell which direction it will take and how it will end.

Against this backdrop we have witnessed a resurgence of virulent anti-Semitism in its worst manifestations – mainly in Europe. Strangely, that blood-soaked continent, with its culture, music, and literature, is again center-stage in this xenophobic outburst, and the Jewish leadership is making valiant, but mainly unsuccessful, efforts to stem the tide which, if uncontrolled, could have devastating effects.

In Israel, since Menachem Begin stepped down as Prime Minister, there have been three Prime Ministers from the ranks of the Likud Party – Yitzhak Shamir, Binyamin Netanyahu and Ariel Sharon – and three from Labor – Yitzhak Rabin (who was tragically assassinated in 1995), Shimon Peres and Ehud Barak. For short periods, there were unity governments that broke up in disarray and disagreement.

Each of the Likud Prime Ministers made his own specific contribution to the progress of Israel. I had the privilege of serving Yitzhak Shamir as his advisor on world Jewry. His style was somewhat different from Menachem Begin's but his dedication to the central ideal was the same.

During the term of the Labor Prime Ministers we saw the start of a new phenomenon of "independent national policy attempts" at Oslo and Geneva. This was done by a group of frustrated and desperate politicians who embarked on private activities in foreign policy, first, in Oslo and later in Geneva. They had the support of anti-Israel elements in Europe who "recognized" them politically and provided financial backing for their nefarious activities. Obviously, these activities were directed at Israeli "occupation" and sought to undermine the authority of the government. These efforts turned out to be "seven-day wonders" that fizzled out when they hit the real world. But such conduct would not be tolerated in any other Western democracy. It is unimaginable, for instance, that a number of American ex-politicians would negotiate separately with Bin Laden or Saddam Hussein in the midst of a war!

In fact, there is a law on the statute books of the United States that prohibits United States citizens without authority from interfering in relations between the United States and foreign governments. The Logan Act was introduced almost two hundred years ago. Although attempts have been made to repeal the Act, it remains law unto this day.

There has been economic and social upheaval, some of it genuine, and some of it contrived by the Histadrut and those close to it. In the period since Begin's leadership, political figures have been interrogated on suspicion of bribery and corruption, sending shudders through the population.

There have been many changes, both large and small, but remarkably one theme remains constant, and it is growing in intensity. Whenever the name of Menachem Begin is mentioned, people of all ages and persuasions react instantly: "We need him now."

What is it that "we need;" what is missing? Every Prime Minister has his own methods and abilities, whether in the field of foreign relations, economics, social affairs, or simply in his leadership. But Begin possessed something very special and that "something" is what is now missing.

A poignant example was the reaction to the announcement in February 2004 that the price of bread was to be increased. A television commentator said *en passant*:

> "When Menachem Begin was Prime Minister, he never allowed the cost of bread to increase. Bread is the staple food of the poor and they must not be burdened further. Menachem Begin had a Jewish heart and he could not bear the thought that a Jewish child should ever hunger for a piece of bread."

Perhaps Begin's consideration for the poor was a reaction to his experiences as a youth, when he himself endured poverty and distress. When I spoke at events celebrating 25 years since Begin's initiation of Project Renewal, I referred to his treatment of the poor and quoted from his statement, "We are the people of Justice. How can we countenance this situation? It is intolerable and undignified." He recalled his own youth as a law student in Warsaw, when he often slept on a bench in the park and gave private lessons in Latin to keep body and soul together.

Whenever public figures make statements that sound hollow and insincere the unavoidable comparison is immediately made with the integrity of Menachem Begin.

And throughout the period of the American wars against Iraq, commentators in Israel, the U.S., Britain, and elsewhere referred constantly and quite naturally to Israel's strike against Saddam Hussein's nuclear reactor in Osiraq in 1981, which drastically changed the military picture in the region and made the American-led coalition's task easier.

Towards the end of 2003, voices began to emerge even within the Likud calling for an end to Israel's presence in Gaza and the so-called West Bank. This is partly justified by demographic statistics that allegedly show that within ten, twenty, or fifty years the Arabs will be the majority in the country. This is not a new theme or invention. Demography has been invoked by the pro-Palestinian element for decades. And somehow the gloomy prognostications have never materialized. There has either been a growing exodus of Arabs to places where they can improve the economic status of their families, or an unexpected wave of aliyah, such as from Russia, Ethiopia and in the future perhaps from Western countries, including the United States.

There are elements in Israel urging a more vigorous reaction to the fallacious reasons for the "two-state" solution proposed by President George W. Bush in his "Road Map" plan, which requires the Palestinian Authority and Israel to take certain practical measures before reaching the final stage of discussion. So far, however, the Palestinians have done nothing to implement the minimum first requirement, which is to dismantle the terrorist infrastructure. Therefore, there is more and more talk of unilateral acts by Israel to disengage from the predominantly Arab areas and to use new security measures, such as a protective fence to prevent terrorists from infiltrating into Israel. The construction of this fence has raised an outcry among pro-Arab elements around the world and in Israel. The matter was placed before the International Court in The Hague, though there is great doubt whether the Court has jurisdiction on such a political issue. However, in preparation for the proceedings, the wonderful organization *Zaka* sent the mangled, twisted wreckage of a bus from a recent suicide bombing in Jerusalem to The Hague, where it demonstrated the gruesome results of Arab terrorism. This moved me deeply because after September 11, 2001, when discussions began on the nature of the memorial monument in New York, I thought that a monument should be established in Israel of a number of these horrible skeletons of buses piled on top of each other, reaching up to Heaven.

Over the years, various proposals were made for other Road Maps. The most interesting idea I have heard is based on a very old riddle put to a group of hikers who have walked deep into a forest, which becomes denser, until they find they have lost their way. Eventually, they come upon a clearing and there, lying on the ground, is a signpost with ten or twelve signs pointing in different directions. How do they know which way to go? They cannot answer the question until one young boy lifts the signpost and says, "We know where we have come from. Let us point the appropriate sign in that direction and then automatically all the other signs will fall into place, including the one that will tell us where we must go now."

Applying this simple lesson to the Jewish people, we know where we have come from – from Abraham, Isaac, and Jacob, who were given the prophecy to go to the Promised Land. That's it. There can be no deviation from that, although some minor adjustments or modifications are possible along the way. That was the way of Menachem Begin.

Perhaps Menachem Begin's most important and unique contribution to the Jewish People, who easily sink into despair – either politically, psychologically, or spiritually – is Supreme Patriotism, which is becoming a rare commodity. More and more frequently we hear and read accounts that show a loss of national will quite contrary to the spirit of Patriotism which, in the words of Harav Kook, the well-known Chief Rabbi of Eretz Israel in the 1920s and of Menachem Begin throughout his political career, reverberated throughout the land and the universe, "AHAVAT ISRAEL" and "AHAVAT ERETZ ISRAEL." *The love of Israel (the People) and the Land of Israel.* This type of Jewish leadership is missed and it is here that "we need him now." We miss his deep faith, his courage and his Jewish pride.

There are certain aspects of the Israel-Arab land dispute that were simply "untouchable" for Menachem Begin. The most obvious of these is the Jewish People's inalienable right to Jerusalem. As Prime Minister he placed this fact before the world as a non-negotiable subject (see page 143). His approach to other parts of our ancient land was identical.

Of course, he recognized that there were Arabs living in Eretz Israel and he offered them full autonomy as was done by many other countries for specific groups of citizens.

Yet, above all, Begin is missed because of his personal qualities of modesty, integrity, truthfulness, devotion, and adherence to principle no matter how difficult or unpopular. For all these reasons – and more – we need him now.

EPILOGUE

It has been said that leaders who were stoned in their lifetime (literally and figuratively) should have monuments built in their honor out of the stones that were hurled at them. In the case of Menachem Begin, such a monument would reach to the heavens. But such leaders usually need no monuments; the stories of their lives are their true memorials, provided that they are preserved and passed on from generation to generation. Only then they become timeless, immemorial.

Ze'ev Jabotinsky addressed this theme more than seventy years ago in his article "Kaddish," following the death of Yosef Trumpeldor in an Arab attack at Tel 'Hai, near the Lebanese border.

Upon an anniversary of a man's death, Jews say Kaddish. What kind of a connection is there between a song of praise to the Master of the Universe and sadness and graves? The significance of Kaddish probably consists in that the Sacred Name which is praised is not the name of your God, but the name of the God of the deceased, that holiness for which he lived and for which he perhaps died. Viewing it from this aspect, *"Yisgadel ve Yiskadash"* therefore means "Although you, man, are dead, the holiness which you served remains great and sacred, and we, who have survived, will continue to serve your ideals and continue to fight until the final victory."

And the Kaddish echoes: "As long as we shall remember your name, so long will your example be great and holy."

INDEX

ABOUT THE AUTHOR

Harry Hurwitz was born in Libau, Latvia, from where the family emigrated to Johannesburg, South Africa. There he became a leader in the Betar and Zionist Revisionist Organizations, and later of the South African Zionist Federation. He embarked on a career in journalism, becoming the editor of a major weekly publication, and a much sought-after broadcaster, TV commentator and public speaker.

He was a long-time staunch supporter of Menachem Begin, and when Begin was elected Prime Minister of Israel, Hurwitz and his wife, Freda, emigrated to Israel where he joined the Prime Minister's Administration as Adviser on External Information. In 1980, he was appointed Minister of Information at the Israel Embassy in Washington DC. He returned to Israel in mid-1983 to become Adviser to Prime Minister Begin on World Jewry. He continued in that position in Prime Minister Shamir's Administration until it left office in July 1992.

Following the death of Menachem Begin in March 1992, Harry Hurwitz at once proposed the establishment of a Living Memorial to Menachem Begin on the lines of an American Presidential Library. He initiated the Menachem Begin Heritage Foundation which, under his leadership, built the Menachem Begin Heritage

Center in Jerusalem on a unique site with a breath-taking view of the Old City. The building is due for completion and Official Opening in the first half of 2004.